Anonymous

Lichens From an Old Abbey

Being Historical rReminiscences of the Monastery of Paisley, its Abbots

Anonymous

Lichens From an Old Abbey
Being Historical rReminiscences of the Monastery of Paisley, its Abbots

ISBN/EAN: 9783744719988

Printed in Europe, USA, Canada, Australia, Japan

Cover: Foto ©ninafisch / pixelio.de

More available books at **www.hansebooks.com**

LICHENS

FROM

AN OLD ABBEY:

BEING

HISTORICAL REMINISCENSES

OF THE

MONASTERY OF PAISLEY,

Its Abbots, and its Royal and other Benefactors.

PAISLEY:
J. AND R. PARLANE.
MDCCCLXXVI.

CONTENTS.

	PAGE
Introductory	1
Monks of Clugni	5
The First Lord High Steward	11
The Steward's Gifts	19
Charters	25
Old Churches	33
Robert De Croc	37
The Fair Abbey	41
The Lady of Molla	51
A Shadowy Knight	57
The Gift of Dalmulin	67
Kyle	77
Alexander the Crusader	83
Scotland's Sorrow	91
Sir William Wallace	97
Walter and Marjory	105
King and Queen	117
Monks as Historians	121
Chronicus Clugniense	127
The Abbot Tarvis	137
Renovation	147

CONTENTS.

	PAGE
Lord Lyell's Gift	153
The Lord of the Isles	157
The Schawes of Sauchie	165
The Abbot's Charter	175
A Vassal of the Abbot	185
The Chapel of St. Mirrinus	195
Visions	203
A Royal Recluse	213
Queen Margaret's Pilgrimage	221
The Year of Flodden	227
The Abbot John	233
Two Harps	245
Warning	251
A Letter to Mary of Guise	257
Lord Claude, the Last Abbot	261
Demolition	269
Outside the Cloister	275
James Sixth at the "Place"	287
The Laird of Beltrees	293
The End	303
Appendix	311

INTRODUCTORY.

―――o―――

THE old Vasari wonders much, in his wise simple fashion, over the sublime indifference to renown of artists earlier than he,—how, leaving their great works nameless, they have passed away, into the twilight, voicelessly, but for the still fair life breathed into the carved stone. Vasari fondly remembers how his master, Michael Angelo—because some ascribed the glory of the altar-piece, Pieta, to another—went, alone, to the Church at midnight, and carved, by a taper's light, his name on the marble drapery of the Virgin and the dead Christ.

Well for the history of Art if all had done likewise, thought Vasari as he wrote his famous lives, and paused in those ellipses where the work survived the workman, even in tradition most dim. And all who would add, however humbly, a stone to the cairn of Art, have thought, perhaps, with this old biographer,—have wondered and desired as he.

A

A time-worn frieze suggests a story—no more. Was that strong man's agony a fact which the sculptor's own eyes attested? Did that meekness and sweetness of motherhood bless with a real presence some nook in the Abbey regality? These features frozen into stone, and that child's head long worn away into pitiful grotesque baldness and unbeauty, were they sometime happy memories or imaginings, or, it may be, sweet patient copies modelled from love's own? They stand in the white light still, but the artist's name is lost. We cannot speak of him; nor call the little daughter by name, nor the sister who was always a child gathering flowers upon the moss, or playing with the cool faint shadows of the lilies in the river near,—who, passing forth too soon, should be for ever young in stone, living in the unseen light, living on the chapel frieze, as the child set in the midst, or the infant Timothy, or St. John. Yet, not to be for ever beautiful these, for the features moulder on the stone, moulder on the time-eaten walls of churches scattered far and wide,—meagre outlines of the ancient cherished forms, surviving both their beauty and their story—an old, old dream.

One architect's name indeed is preserved to us in some rude lines carved in Melrose Abbey,—a name, and that is all, seven hundred years old.

Obscure in the depths of obscurity, the Abbey of Paisley has stood; consigned—its partial completeness and constant use notwithstanding—to a fate of even deeper oblivion than has befallen most Scottish monasteries. Its rise with the royal Stewards, its first prestige and power;

the still earlier memories which storied the hill and meadow, gifted to the Church, not to speak of its own chaste beauty in the homely-featured town, long had scarcely availed to secure for it any niche of distinction in the land. Its fortune was that of a forlorn genius, or some singer forgotten with his song. And there was no Sainte Beuve to rescue its story for posterity.

One of those social eccentricities, which at certain dates—without premonition, without apparent motive or cause—revives old facts, old fictions, old lives, old relics, old shrines, hid from all but curious eyes by the dust of gathered ages and neglect, has given at length an interest to this old and beautiful foundation, and discovered that here Scottish royalty had both cradles and graves.

The work of Sainte Beuve has been done, and yet without a Sainte Beuve. And through the Benedictine cloister another small vista has been opened into Scottish mediæval stillness, and Scottish mediæval strife.

To gather some scanty lichens—antique, yellow or grey—encrusted through seven centuries, in the Gothic mouldings of the Abbey; to preserve some fragmentary leaves, too obscure for the general historian, yet precious, because history is a mosaic, and composed, in its finest pictures, of infinitesimal details which are apt to be overlooked; to diverge where divergence is useful; to linger where delay is sweet;—this, and no more, do these pages propose; no more do they offer to the reader.

MONKS OF CLUGNI.

―――o―――

THE visions all are fled—the car is fled
Into the light of heaven, and in their stead
A sense of real things comes doubly strong,
And, like a muddy stream, would bear along
My soul to nothingness; but I will strive
Against all doubtings, and will keep alive
The thought of that same chariot, and the strange
Journey it went. *Keats.*

THE land was low and sweet. They had called it *Pasgel-laith*. And they meant what the name meant—a moist bit of pasture-ground. Is it a conceit that thoughts grow best where flowers grow? Or, was it a benign chance that the monks always set their feet where a painter might stand and sketch—where a little song might be sung?

Not that any vivid picture is made by these low distant lines; nor is any romantic combination formed in the quiet strath. 'Tis a mild diffusion of beauty, which the painter would express not *once*, but in many shifting scenes imbued by his own thought,—a sunset mist from the mountains of Argyle, flung across the long level fields,—a play of slow brown water, with a scant grouping of rugged trees. The Abbey has survived the oaks; but some tall, ghostly Lombardy poplars cut the vision here and there,—solitary, trembling. And one cannot tell whence should wake the singing of that little song, nor why one should know surely that this was once the haunt of flowers.

Here, in the twelfth century, came that colony of the Monks of Clugni, whose cloisters were to learn so much of Scottish chivalry and sorrow,—thirteen monks from Wenlock in Shropshire, invited by Walter the Steward to settle in his green Strath, and build a house of devotion. So they came from the mother-priory among the Shropshire woods,—came across the stormy border while Henry the Second was on the throne. The records of the monastery tell us nothing more of this,—if they were grave men, or gentle,—how they laboured, and how they taught.

In the heart of a great oak-forest their history began. Under the ripening acorns, the fallow-deer browsed at will. The summer-whisper in the branches had no prophetic sound.

From among the thirteen strangers, Walter chose one as prior. His name has not come down to us, nor his lineage, nor his history. The Steward chose him as a grave man,—discreet, virtuous;—chose him because in his eyes, on his lips, was serene command,—that kingship innate to a few certain souls. Yet, lest his judgment had deceived him, lest the eyes had been false to the soul, Walter makes provision in his charter that he may depose and choose again. The prior alone excepted, he may choose whom he will from Wenlock to govern his new convent on the banks of the White Cart.

And so they begin their history. The Romans had been there before them. Already the memory of the legions of the Cæsars was several centuries old. But in the green forest-land, and among the braes and the mosses, they had left the ungrateful memories of victory and power and disdain. Fosses and dykes of earth protected the high Prætorium which had looked its conquest on the low land,— its despair on the purple north. And from this same Prætorium might be seen two little green hills (any wayfarer may see them still), one lying soft to the south against the further braes; and one in the lap of the west, where these glorious Hebridean sunsets sent their long flashes of splendour through the lingering summer night. And these little green hills had a story; for, hither and thither, once paced the Roman sentinal,—once spread the hated stranger's camp. And where is the grace of the toga, or the music of the Latin tongue? Hard are the southern arts for northern people to learn. So round the little green hills, where pleasant grass now waves, grew the bitter olden tragedy, with no patience in its grief.

But these black-robed Benedictines come with the cross in their hands, and raise their beautiful house of God at the end of the Roman hill. And the White Cart, wandering through a rich and pleasant land, will lave the edge of their orchards, and be as a sweet thought to those lives which have left out love and kinship.

The old Prætorium of the Romans has left scarcely its name behind it; while the Abbey, built so silently among the shadows of the oaks, is still a centre and a stronghold in the heart of restless human life.

One returns with a grateful sense of peace to that early purity and strength. Disorder and disgrace shall come. There will be passionate questions, and light disbelief, and scornful laughter. In those constant evolutions of thought recurring since the world was young; in that misunderstanding and reproach, through utter self-absorption and disability to enter the heart of a system alien to habit and temperament,—there will come to be accepted an image unbeautiful and untrue, or at least true only to a time much later than this, when prosperity and worldly fame shall have sown throughout the church the seeds of decay.

The Clugniacs, when they crossed the border, were worthy of the reputation they bore. The Burgundian Abbot, Odo, who founded the order at Clugny, had been at rest two hundred years and more ; but the order was still pure. It must rise and decline, like the many other orders springing from the order of St. Benedict; like many other orders, not religious, in that perpetual rhythm of history which enchains the fancy, as do the numbers in a sonnet or an ode; while it challenges science, perplexes reason, and suggests or dispels theories, like that old one of the earth's motion, or the true tale of Job's patience and sorrow.

Some steps in the decadence of the Clugniensian purity there might already be, and were. Yet, such a monastery was still a rest and a benison in the land; and the sanctity and charity of the monks made them everywhere welcome neighbours.

Two masses they said daily. There was no idle talk. Their psalms rose high from the convent garden while they worked among their healing herbs, and the ring of their axes was heard among the forest trees. The convent gate was open, and to it, all in want might come and take sweetly, as from God's hand, the fervently offered and ungrudged aid. Of meal alone, one hundred and twelve bolls was the yearly dole from Paisley Abbey. The Church was a tender mother, and cared for her poor children,—their bodies as well as their souls.

As for the sanctity of these early monks, so reverent and careful was it, that wheat was selected grain by grain for their Eucharistic bread. Like pearls the grains were handled, washed, and ground between curtained stones, that no impure particle might enter the sacred symbol.

The early monastery of Paisley was worthy the prestige it won. It was not alone a sense of safety, but the intuitive homage which the human heart offered to pure goodness, that gathered its subjects round its feet. And so it rose serene among the oaks of the forest,—the best boon which the Steward could have gifted to fair Strathgryfe.

For the convent was the gift of Walter the Steward of Scotland. By his invitation, in the year 1160, the Clugniensians settled on the banks of the White Cart.

THE FIRST LORD HIGH STEWARD.

Banquo.—   My noble partner,
You greet with present grace, and great prediction
Of noble having and of royal hope
That he seems rapt withal; to me you speak not.
If you can look into the seeds of time,
And say which grain will grow and which will not,
Speak then to me, who neither beg, nor fear
Your favours nor your hate.

*First Witch.—*Hail!
*Second Witch.—*Hail!
*Third Witch.—*Hail!
*First Witch.—*Lesser than Macbeth and greater!
Second Witch.—Not so happy, yet much happier!
Third Witch.—Thou shalt get kings, though thou be none;
  So all hail, Macbeth and Banquo!
                    Shakespeare.

WALTER merits a chapter. His antecedents and posterity bring him out in high relief among the rude war-loving barons of Malcolm the Maiden's time. The poetical account of his family, long undoubtingly received, may be read with interest, at least as a story, if now as nothing more.*

* See Appendix.

His ancestor was the Thane of Lochaber, of Shakespearian renown,—a dim enough figure but for the luminous poetry shed by the wonderful dramatist on that old time.

Banquo was the son of Ferquard, younger son of Kenneth Third; and therefore himself, by birth, not far removed from the throne, when the witches on the Forres heath hailed him "Father of Kings!" Shakespeare has in this particular only followed the tradition of the time. So grave an historian as Buchanan relates the prophecy of the witches with all its circumstance and sequence.

Banquo was a man of renown. He had put the Norsemen to flight, and saved the little Scottish kingdom in more straits than one. Therefore when Macbeth usurped the throne, Banquo was safe no more. Shakespeare has told the world the rest of the tragic story.

Fleance, the son of Banquo, fled to Wales, to escape the jealousy of Macbeth; and married Nesta, a Welsh princess; and died in his place of exile. But Walter, the son of Fleance, returned to the court of Malcolm Canmore, and gained amends for his adversity in honour and trust from the king. "Being a valiant man, he was employed as his Majesty's general against a formidable rebellion, where he did great service." And Malcolm, who was wise and grateful, created him *Seneschalus Domus Regis*,—Steward of his household, and Lord of Kyle and Strathgryfe.

From these brief sentences, nearly the whole that history leaves us, we may weave a romance, if we will, but that is all.

Nesta is much more shadowy than Hecuba of Troy; and

Fleance, having had no Homer to preserve his valour and misfortune—nor continue the stern old story, which drops abruptly from the Elizabethan page—subsides, with Griffith Apleven the prince, into impenetrable shadow, and becomes a link, and no more, in the long, illustrious, chequered story of Banquo's race of kings.

Walter's son and successor was Alan, "a man of great action in his day, especially in martial affairs. . . . He accompanied diverse other Christian princes in that famous expedition to the Holy Land, in the year of our Lord 1099." Such is the record of his life, briefly closing, like the old Hebrew genealogies, of the sons of Noah and their sons, with "he died."

But Walter, the son of Alan, advances boldly into history. The first Lord High Steward of Scotland, he, as founder of Paisley Abbey, is the hero of this brief chapter.

Walter was a good man, and favoured of David First, who, himself devout and wise, enriched the old Culdee seats, filled the land with new Abbeys, nurtured the Church so tenderly, and gave so beneficently to her, that the aureole was lit around his memory, and he is Saint David to this day. He wears, too, his saint-hood on his king-hood as few have worn it besides. Even old George Buchanan, who loved neither king nor saint, pauses in his stately Latin to record the virtues of David; to tell of the *dool* of that May-day when the hawthorn whitened by the burn sides; but the wisest of the land had passed away,—beyond the scent òf hawthorn, beyond the clamour of council, beyond the ring of war,—"so dear to all, that his loss appeared to be rather that of the best of fathers than that of a king. . . . As he equalled the most excellent of the former kings in his warlike achievements, and excelled them in his cultivation of the arts of peace, at last, as if he had ceased to contend with others for pre-eminence in virtue, he endeavoured to rival himself. And, in this, he so succeeded, that the utmost ingenuity of the most learned, who should attempt to delineate a good king, would not be able to conceive one so excellent as David."

And that quiet, most sweet death, was granted him, which suited the end of such a life. Says Aldred, the old chronicler: " His death was so tranquil, that you would not have believed that he was dead. He was found with his hands clasped devoutly upon his breast, in the very posture in which he seems to have been raising them to heaven."

No excuse is offered for transcribing sentences familiar to so many readers. A beautiful life and death may be long lingered over, and again and again recurred to with the same sense of gladness.

It was this King David who changed the *Seneschallus Domus Regis* into *Seneschallus Scotiæ*,—the first High Steward of Scotland. The office which his grandfather had bestowed, was ratified by Malcolm "the Maiden" to Walter and his heirs.

Malcolm was a king of eighteen when he granted this charter to the Steward,—a peaceful, mild young king, with a girlish fair face;—a boy to whom the hopes of a people, always prepared to love their sovereign, had turned, as one who would repeat the virtues of their venerable old King David. And they found him peaceful to slothfulness,—

wary, yet not wise; following Henry of England to France, and pleading constraint for so doing; swearing some sort of fealty to the king, whom his grandfather had knighted at Carlisle; obeying the behests of a foreign monarch, who was pledged to make none. Malcolm was very young, yet younger men than he had been brave and wise. From the lords of Galloway to the meanest of his serfs, bravery was the virtue most highly prized. But peace was no virtue,— no grace on the mountains and moors. "From that time, the king began to be despised by his people." *

This oppression of scorn was over him, when he granted Walter's charter, which refers to some gladder days— "before I took up arms." The inevitable taking up of arms was on him against his will. He could not be a king of Scotland and refuse the king's sword.

The "Charter in Sir James Balfour of Kinnaird, Lord Lion King-at-Arms, his collection," is given by Crawford, the historian of the Stewards; translated thus:—

" Malcolm, king of Scots, to the Bishops, Abbots, Barons,
" Justices, Sheriffs, Provosts, Officers, and all other good
" men, Clergy and laity, French and English, Scots and
" inhabitants of Galloway, through all his dominion, both
" present and to come, greeting: Be it known to all men,
" that before I took up arms, I granted, and have, by this my
" charter, confirmed in hereditary succession to Walter, the
" son of Alan, my High Steward, and to his heirs, in fee-farm
" and inheritance, my High Stewardship, to be held of him
" and his heirs, of me and my heirs, as well and fully as King

* Buchanan's History.

"David gave and granted him his High Stewardship. I
"farther confirm that grant which King David, my
"grandfather, gave him, namely, of the lands of Renfrew,
"Paisley, Polloc, Tulloch, Cathcart, Le Drip, Egilshim,
"Lochwinioch and Innerwick, Inchinnan, Hastenden,
"Legerwood and Brickbenside, with all the pertinents of
"those lands; and in every burgh and regality to me
"belonging, one full toft, and with every toft, twenty acres
"of land for his entertainment therein: Wherefore my will
"is, that the same Walter and his heirs hold, in full, all the
"premises, as well those which he had by the grant of
"King David, as those which he hath had by my grant,
"for giving me and my heirs, for that fee-farm, the service
"of five soldiers. At the Castle of Roxburgh, on the feast
"of St. John the Baptist, in the year of God 1158, and fifth
"of our reign. Before these witnesses :—

"EARNEST, Bishop of St. Andrews.
"HERBERT, Bishop of Glasgow.
"JOHN, Abbot of Kelso.
"WILLIAM, Abbot of Melrose.
"WALTER, Cancellor.
"WILLIAM AND DAVID, brothers of the King.
"EARL COSPATRICK.
"EARL DUNCAN.
"RICHARD MORVIL.
"GILBERT UMPHRAVIL.

"ROBERT BRUCE.
"RANDOLPH SOULS.
"PHILIP COLVIL.
"WILLIAM SOMERVILLE.
"HUGH RIDDEL.
"DAVID CLIFARD.
"WALDEN, son of Earl Cospatrick.
"WILLIAM MORVIL.
"BALDWIN of Mar.
"LIOLPH, son of Maco."

A quite suggestive leaf from the old obscure annals of
the land,—the royal greeting from the maiden king to all
the good men of his realm, to the French and English,

Scots and the men of Galloway; the tofts and the twenty acres of land, and for that fee-farm the service of five soldiers; the twenty-one great men of Scotland who witnessed the young king's hand, on that summer day in the border castle, when Walter's estates were confirmed.

Walter built a castle on the new land gifted by the king—Dunenald, or Dundonald—very near the sea.

On a little rising ground, near the village which has taken its name, roofless and dateless it stands now in a setting of dark trees. The curious might long distinguish—perhaps may still—carved upon the dismantled wall, the arms of the house of Steward. But its history is meagre enough. Chalmers briefly relates all he knows regarding it:—

"The manour and parish of Dundonald belonged to Walter, the son of Alan, the first Steward, who held the whole of the northern half of Kyle in the beginning of the reign of William the Lion, and it might have been granted to him by David I., or Malcolm IV. Perhaps the castle of Dundonald was built by the first Walter, who had no appropriate castle or house when he settled in Scotland. It seems to have been the only castle which the Stewards had, in their extensive barony of Kyle-Steward, but many of their vassals had small castles in that district."

THE STEWARD'S GIFTS.

SWEET are the thoughts that savour of content,—
 The quiet mind is richer than a crown!
Sweet are the nights in careless slumber spent,—
 The poor estate scorns fortune's angry frown:
Such sweet content, such minds, such sleep, such bliss,
Beggars enjoy, when princes oft do miss.

The homely house that harbours quiet rest,
 The cottage that affords no pride nor care;
The mean that 'grees with country music best,
 The sweet consort of mirth's and music's fare:
Obscured life sets down a type of bliss,—
A mind content, both crown and kingdom is!
Old Sonnet.

WALTER'S great gift to the church and to his own vassals, was made after ruling for two years the country of Kyle and Strathgryfe.

His charter, granted to English monks, and dated at an English castle held in feudal tenure by the Scottish king, opens many a picturesque suggestion. They are mere suggestions, however,—no more. Earl Henry, the young Sir Kenneth,[*] who discoursed to the Saracen beneath the

[*] The Talisman.

palm, and could fight as well as he discoursed, and who was Edith's lover, and the king of England's friend, has no larger space, in the charter, than Grimketel the rude serf, who owned that one carncat of land—as much as a plough could till—which Walter, his liege lord, took from him to bestow upon the monks. Walter surely made amends. Walter, who was gracious and just, gave to poor Grimketel some moist, sunny toft beside the river, where he might raise his little hovel of twigs or turf from the moors.

And who is this Radolph of Kent, who looks out a moment from the dark, with no ancestry, no surroundings to give him *pose*, or group with his mates? Is he a skilled workman, and though not of the monastic band, come to aid in rearing into stately beauty the church's floral sculptures and shrines? And this "chest of silver in the mill," does the knight, Walter, give in payment for good work done beside the river Cart?

Yet Innerwick is far away, in the wild, lovely Highland Glenlyon. It gives its name now to a little Parish Church, and that is all. There is no tradition of the mill which held the silver chest, and was turned by the joyful torrent, which, so deep in the gorge of the mountains, still breaks in whiteness through the tremulous dark of the "birks," and keeps its old-world stories of the Macgregors and Stewarts of Garth.

They tell how, at set of day, swords have been washed in the Lyon till the stream ran red among the rocks, and dyed the very moss and the lady-ferns that were wet on their ledge by its spray. But of the peaceful mill, which ground the oats for the Glen, and where old Radolph of

Kent kept his said silver chest, nothing at all may be gleaned. It was but of small account. The name of Stewart of Garth, however, is one explanatory note; and another side light is thrown on the gift of the mill and the chest in the chartulary of Kelso Abbey, which records "a lease of certain wood and lands to the men of Innerwick, approved of by Alan, the son of Walter, to whom the men of Innerwick belonged."

This "belonging of the men of Innerwick" opens a curious page. "The lands and the men;" "the men, the lands, and the waters," are frequent grants, to the different Abbeys, by the barons and kings of Scotland. In the chartulary of the Abbey of Dunfermline is found bestowed by King David: "Ragewin, Gillpatrick, and Ulchill, his own serfs, for the glory of God, and the use of the holy brotherhood."

Ragewin, Gillpatrick, and Ulchill, under the shadow of the Abbey—the calmest shadow of the land—with horses and oxen yoked together, will guide the heavy plough, and watch the springing of the young wheat, and bind the autumn sheaves in those rich, fertile fields, which the skill and wealth of the monks have made as gardens in Scotland. Patient and obedient souls, with few fears and no distrusts; with their rude psalms to sing, as their heavy feet go backward before the team; and on the rough land, at the verge where it meets the oaks, their trysts to keep, undisturbed by any thought for the morrow. Even serfdom, to certain moods, suggests its own beguilement. The oats, the flax, and the barley; the wheat and the meadow hay; the river and the fair church,—

these were inalienable possessions; God-gifts to the men of toil.

As for the matter of the mill, it recurs again and again; runs through every monastic charter, like the sound of its own ceaseless wheel. Through and beneath the convent psalms, we hear the busy water plash—for the corn must be ground, and the people must be fed—as none knew better than these Benedictine monks. And the great mill, beside the river, ranked but second in importance to the monastery,—a joyous, strong, careless thing, with rights given and guarded by the king's own hand.

A distant memory there was, how each house-wife, in her own stone *quern*, ground the corn, like Eastern Sarah, for her guests, and kneaded her cakes in haste. And the big, round, smooth stones, in many a farm house, stood useless and forbidden, with grandmother stories clinging round them.

But now those royal, fatherly laws, which ruled the very households of the people, commanded that all the grain should be carried to the water mills.* And every farm in the country was *thirled* to its own mill, to which, without fail, the farmer must send his corn. The miller—with *multure* of all he ground, sometimes as much as a tenth—became traditionally happy and songful, as his own merry water wheel. He was the primitive ideal of the prosperous, privileged man; and his daughter, the *well-tochered* beauty of all old-fashioned songs. Mill and miller were both of great account in the land.

* Ancient Farming Customs of Scotland—Transactions of the Highland and Agricultural Society, 1872.

But when less and less of his oats and his barley were returned; when the wheel · went merrily round in the stream, but the corn was both badly ground and scant,—the farmer complained, as he might, to his lord abbot or baron; and hence those constant *Mulcture Courts* which the baron-bailies held.

It was a valuable privilege, granted the monks of the Abbey, that of grinding, without *mulcture*, their corn in the Paisley mill.

1

CHARTERS.

"RECORDS that eke out, scantily, to late
Posterity the measure of old days,—
Which speak through silences, yet scarcely speak,
But mutter words of meaning only guessed;
And tell from out the dry, blenched lips of eld,
Passions that erst were young and green and gay,—
Passions—O grave!—they are not passions now;
How doth the parchment crumble in the hand?"

THE reader may himself peruse, if he will, a translation of Walter's charter. Sufficiently exact and defined it is, yet the definitions grow shadowy, with these long centuries of action and thought between. We follow them mistily, uncertainly, as the mind sometimes is conscious of following a thought which eludes it.

The charter will explain the relation subsisting between the monasteries of Paisley and Wenlock,*—a relationship

* Milburgh, daughter to Meroaldus, Prince of Mercia, had the fair manor of Wenlock . . . given to her by her father for her portion. She, quitting all worldly wealth, bestowed her inheritance on the poor; and answered her name of Milburgh, which, as an antiquary interpreteth, is good or gracious to town or city. Living a virgin, she built a monastery in the same place; and departed this life about the year 664.
Fuller's Worthies of England.

afterwards dissolved when Paisley was erected into an Abbey.

The following is a translation of the original charter relating to the foundation of Paisley Abbey:—

"Know all present and to come, that I, Walter, son of
"Alan, steward of the king of Scotland, for the soul of
"King David, of King Henry, and of Earl Henry, and for
"the souls of all my parents and benefactors, and for the
"salvation of the body and soul of King Malcolm and of
"myself, to the honour of God, and by the power of his
"grace, shall establish a certain house of devotion, below
"my lands of Paisley, according to the order of the brethren
"of Wenlock, that is, according to the order of the monks
"of Clugny, with the universal consent and assent of the
"Prior and convent of Wenlock. And for forming that
"house, I have received thirteen brethren from the house
"of Wenlock; and the prior who shall be preferred among
"these thirteen, to the rule of the aforesaid house, shall be
"chosen through me, and by my appointment. And if it
"shall happen that the prior is deposed from his priorate,
"either by death, or by criminally betraying his trust, he
"shall be deposed by me, and by my appointment. And
"he who shall succeed him in the priorate, shall be chosen
"through me, and through my appointment, and that from
"among the brethren of the house which I shall found, if
"there can be got therein a person of prudence, and suitable
"for receiving such a dignity. But if not, I shall chuse, for
"governing the house which I shall establish, whoever I
"will from among the brethren of the said house of

"Wenlock,—the prior himself excepted; and so as that
"house shall not be dependent in any way upon the house
"of Wenlock, except only as to recognition of the order.
"Which privileges for the use of the house that I shall
"found, the prior and convent of Wenlock shall obtain for
"me, from the abbot of the monks of Clugny, and from the
"prior of La Charite, who shall confirm these privileges to
"religion in Paisley by their charters. And for obtaining
"these privileges, I shall give to the aforesaid house of
"Wenlock, in perpetual alms, one full measure of land in
"my Burgh of Renfrew, and one fishing-net for taking
"salom in my waters, and six nets for catching herrings, and
"one boat. And these privileges shall be preserved
"uninjured, between me and the brethren of Wenlock, and'
"others of the Clugniac order; and after my decease,
"between my heirs and the brethren aforesaid, present and
"to come. Before these witnesses :—

   "INGELRAM, Chancellor of the King of Scotland.
   "The Abbot of Rievall, by name AIELRED.
   "SIMON, Cellarer of Wardun.
   "RICHARD, Chaplain of the King of Scotland.
   "SIMON, brother of Ingelram the Chancellor.
   "ROBERT of Costentin.
   "SIMON, brother of Walter, the son of Alan.

"At Fotheringhay."

Fotheringhay was held by Malcom, along with the earldom of Buckingham, as their ancestral Normandy was held by the English kings. And there was yet no forecasting of the storms that would rise for poor Scotland, when this unhappy vassalage was over-reached and misconstrued.

As for the witnesses named, they briefly emerge from the dark, take shape among the shadows, and as briefly pass away. There is no story round them, of wisdom, love, or war, to leave an after-glow on the cold records of the time. One becomes Bishop of Glasgow, and one Bishop of St. Andrews; of much account, each in his day, but the day is passed. And only the Lord High Steward comes down in the glitter of his mail; his iron-gloved hand always protecting the interests of church and priest.

His charter quaintly suggests many customs and privileges to be treasured, because such are only found in these quiet bye-ways of history. It will only be fully valued by those who can think through others' thoughts; who love the shady annals, where the din of war never comes, nor the perplexities of treaties, nor the glare of a royal court; to whom the sound of a mill wheel is resonant of happy life, the moors are glorious with purple, and the forests o'er-arch primrose beds; to whom—"for light of the church"—suggests a shadowy beauty of starlight, blent with the glimmer of tapers, and the whisper of tranquil or passionate prayers going up through lonely oaks; to whom the salt sea-odours blown along the Inch, and the milky fragrance of kine in the forest, where the acorns lie,—have all a joy and sweetness as real then, when Malcolm the Maiden reigned, as if between themselves and this document there lay no dim centuries of musty parchment.

A further charter runs thus :—

"I will also give the monks of Paisley, in perpetual alms, "and exempt from every temporal service, the church of "Innerwick, with the mill thereof, with its pertinents, "except one chest of silver in it, which I have given "Radolph of Kent; and the church of Legerwood, with all "its pertinents, and one carncat of land which Grimketel "possessed; and the church of Cathcart, with its pertinents, "and all the churches in Strathgryfe, except the church of "Inchinnan; and the church of Paisley, with its pertinents, "carncats of land, measured and meithed upon the water of "Cart, hard by the church; and that land, lying beyond the "Cart, which I and Alan, my son, meithed to them; and "that portion of the land which is below the dormitory of "the monks; and the whole Inch, near my town of Renfrew, "with the fishing between that Inch and Partick; and one "full toft in said burgh, and half a merk of silver of the "revenue of that burgh, for the light of the church; and the "miln of Renfrew, with the land where the monks formerly "lived; and that carncat of land which is between Cart and "Gryfe: I have also given and confirmed to them the "church of Prestwick, and that whole land which Dunenald, "the son of Ewen, meithed to them, between the land of "Simon Lockhart and Prestwick, as far as Pulprestwick, "and by Pulprestwick as far as the sea; and from the sea, "along the river, between the land of Arnold and Prestwick, "as far as the marches of Simon Lockhart, and the church "of my Burgh of Prestwick; and the whole salt pit in "Callandar, which belonged to Herbert Cameron. I have "further given them four shillings out of the miln of Paisley, "for the light of the church, and the privilege of grinding

"there without mulcture; and the tenth of that miln, and of
"all the milns which I have, or may have. I have,
"moreover, granted them the tenth of all my muirs, and of
"all my lands below my forest of Paisley, which have been
"improved, or may be improved, and pasture thereon for
"their cattle. And to this foresaid charity of mine, I,
"moreover, grant, with its privileges and liberties, *sac*
"and *soc*, *thol* and *them* (all malt, tholing, fire, and
"water)."*

After sixty years, the convent of Paisley was freed from its dependence on Wenlock. It owed its elevation, primarily, to a quarrel between pope and king. For Alexander Second had joined Louis of France in league against John of England. And over his unfaithful son, restored, the pope had a special care. The pope excommunicated the two princes who made war against the penitent John; them and their whole kingdoms,—a sentence then of dreadful meaning.

Another history describes the gloom and terror which such an interdict involved :—

"The nation was of a sudden deprived of all external exercise of its religion; the altars were despoiled of their ornaments; the crosses, the relics, the images, the statues of the saints, were laid on the ground; and—as if the air itself were profaned, and might polute them by its contact—the priests carefully covered them up, even from their own approach and veneration. The uses of bells entirely ceased in all the churches; the bells themselves were removed

* Crawford's Translation.

from the steeples, and laid on the ground with the other sacred utensils. Mass was celebrated with shut doors, and none but the priests were admitted to that institution. The laity partook of no religious rite, except baptism to new-born infants, and the communion to the dying. The dead were not interred in consecrated ground; they were thrown into ditches, or buried in common fields; and their obsequies were not attended with prayers, or any hallowed ceremony. Marriage was celebrated in the church-yards. And that every action in life might bear the marks of this dreadful situation, the people were prohibited the use of meat, as in Lent, or in times of the highest penance; were debarred from all pleasures and entertainments, and even to salute each other. . . ."*

In the last days of the year 1217, the interdict was removed from Scotland,—the king and pope were reconciled. Alexander Second received absolution at Tweedmouth, from the Archbishop of York and the Bishop of Durham, who were delegates of Gaulo, the pope's legate.

And once more the glad solemn music of church bells rang through Strathgryfe—down the oak-glades, and over the mosses—and comforted the hearts of the people. And they crowded down the long nave, and knelt before the saints' shrines; and were married at the altars joyfully; and laid their dead, with peaceful prayers, in the shadow of Walter's Priory.

And the pope, Honorius Fourth, took back the Scottish king to his heart; and blamed his legate, Gaulo; and showered favours on the little kingdom. And one of these

* Hume's History of England.

favours was the erection, into an independent Abbey, of the Clugniensian Monastery, founded by the first Steward.

Crozier, mitre, and ring, the abbot, William, assumed. Who was this first Abbot William, the history has not told us. Only, that, with full consent of Walter the son of the founder, and command of the pope Honorius, he ascended the conventual throne. The abbot in the little French town, whence the Clugniacs had taken their name, was abbot of abbots in his order, and such he had always been. This nominal supremacy was guarded with jealous care from the first. No other monastic superior, William of Paisley now owned.

OLD CHURCHES.

YE who sometimes in your rambles
Through the green lanes of the country,—
Where the tangled barberry bushes
Hang their tufts of crimson berries
Over stone walls grey with mosses,—
Pause by some neglected grave-yard,
For a while to muse and ponder
On a half-effaced inscription,
Written with little skill of song-craft;
Homely phrases, but each letter
Full of hope, and yet of heart-break;
Full of all the tender pathos
Of the Here and the Hereafter;
Stay and read. . . . . .
Longfellow.

THERE is a religious sympathy—in some minds amounting to a passion—which finds in every old church a sort of spiritual poem. Wherever men have worshipped God; wherever the human heart, in its wants and aspirings, in its deep contritions and unwhispered struggles, has risen up to the light,—there gathers a Living Presence which departs no more; like, yet unlike, that symbolical fire before the wandering Hebrews' tent.

The old Norman, or Scottish castle, is haunted by intense humanity; but divinity broods above the little church where the humblest people have prayed.

Prestwick, Legerwood, Innerwick, and Cathcart—four churches not included in the general gift of the churches of Strathgryfe—are named in the charter granted to the monastery of Paisley by the Steward.

Prestwick was dedicated to St. Nicolas. It stood in that little parish which is now Monkton and Prestwick, and skirts the open Ayrshire coast. Long and low and flat it lies, with loose yellow, sandy knolls, and only the fair Frith to redeem it from dreariness. Some traditions of Wallace, which blind Harry has kept, float here and there among the bent grass and the broom, and gather round the old kirk of monastic memories. Till the year 1837, the Scottish psalms were sung in this kirk of Monkton. It was then united with Prestwick, and both sister-roofs were forsaken for one new church, which stood mid-way between them. Old Monkton was also the gift of the Steward to the monks of Paisley.

The church of Legerwood lay in the Lady of Molla's land, on the edge of Berwickshire, among the border peel-towers, and soft low-wooded slopes. The Blythe water meets the Leader, and the Leader meets the sea. And both rivers water the near little glens, which scarcely make shadows in the landscape. The "kirk town" yet lies near the centre of the parish. A very little parish it is,—dreamy and sweet, with its old-world memories round it, mossed with border-story; and still preserving traditions, that Walter, the first Steward, held the lands from Malcolm

Fourth; and that, as the charter says, the little kirk, with its pertinents, was gifted by this Lord Walter to the monks of Paisley.

Cathcart modernised, is too much changed to favour tradition of any sort; and the memory of Queen Mary there, has eclipsed that of her early ancestor.

Of Innerwick—the little kirk beside the mill in the glen—there is scarcely anything more to tell.

But in the gift of the churches of Strathgryfe, exception is made to Inchinnan; which, as well for its history as the beauty of its site, merits more than a sentence.

It was gifted, by King David, to the Order of the Knights of the Temple, in the days when the order was but young. And none foresaw what a terrible thing Hugh de Payens did for Christendom, in sending forth those armed priests, with their two-edged swords in hand. The white cloak and red cross might protect the pilgrims in Palestine, and be, among the heathen Saracens and the shadeless wastes of sand, but a secondary evil, or perhaps no evil at all. And they could not overlook the present—Hugh de Payens, nor the wise King David—and foresee how the quiet villages, which lay among the oaks at home, would tremble when the useless swords came back; and the sacred name of *priest*, which once brought security with it, was borne by the fiercest soldiers.

In the year 1312, while Bruce still wore the crown, the Order of the Templars was suppressed in Scotland; and Inchinnan, with all its pertinents, was transferred to the Knights of St. John.

Perhaps they used their power more gently, these

Hospitallers, whose chosen vocation was to aid the poor sick pilgrims, and extend hospitality to them. But soon they too were made soldiers, and fought alongside the other Christian knights. And from the fords of the Jordan, and the guarded Holy Sepulchre, and the "mount that is called Olivet," they came back, to this sweet retirement by the waters of the Cart, with a fame that was scarcely less warlike than that which the Templars had previously brought.

Yet, neither they nor the Templars have left many legends round the place.

"In the churchyard, all the old tombstones, of which many remain, have crosses of different forms sculptured upon them. The parishioners point out what tradition has taught them to call the Templars' graves. The stones covering them—now reduced to four in number—are not flat but ridged; and on their sloping sides, figures of swords may be distinctly traced."

There is no more than this. The waters of three quiet rivers flow under the willows to the sea,—meeting so close, you may almost hear their ripple round these soldier-monks' graves. And in a summer twilight—with a crescent moon above the tower, and that shimmer of cold white light which a summer twilight lays across streams, within the solemn mass of shade, gathered nightly by these ancient trees, and with that trinity of waters flowing near, on, for ever on—you may echo poor Shelley's thought of another last resting-place;—" it might make one in love with death, to think that one should be buried in so sweet a place."

ROBERT DE CROC.

CERTAIN it is, that as nothing can better do it, so there is nothing greater, for which God made our tongues, next to reciting His praises, than to minister comfort to a weary soul. And what greater measure can we have, than that we should bring joy to our brother, who with his dreary eyes looks to Heaven and round about, and cannot find so much rest as to lay his eyelids close together,—than that thy tongue should be tuned with heavenly accents, and make the weary soul to listen for light and ease.
Jeremy Taylor.

A BIT of wall, with a Gothic window, a tower with a loop-hole or two,—this is nearly all that remains of the castle of Robert de Croc, an old Norman gentleman who left some footprints behind him.

The family settled in Scotland at an unknown date, and held their lands in vassalage to the first Lord Stewards. Pleasant lands they were, which the Cart and the Leveran watered,—meeting, picturesquely, not far from the castle walls. De Croc was a witness to the charter which the Steward granted to the monks. His name comes down on the parchment attesting Walter's gift. But a much more tender memory invests the old Norman's name. An unlooked for gleam of tenderness and charity, which, whether rightly or wrongly, we scarcely expect to find in any Norman story.

What moved this rude old vassal to such a gentle thought? He built not far from his castle gates, close beside the pleasant stream—no cell for monks, but a house and a little chapel, where poor and frail old men might be nourished, and rest in peace; might wait and pray serenely after long fevered lives.

Two centuries later, a similar house was founded in Glasgow by the bishop. And, in the same city, at nearly the same date, the good, devout Lady Lochow built, on St. Ninian's Croft, a leper's hospital, which she anxiously cared for and endowed. Works of mercy were not neglected by the mediæval church. Yet, none the less, we wonder over, and ask the story of De Croc,—that beneficent old story with the Steward's strongest vassal for its centre, instead of bishop or lady, whose life could only be made complete by such charities.

And we cannot fill it in. No shadow of detail has come down. Only, in meagre brevity, the fact that, at such a date, Robert De Croc built a house and a chapel for infirm old men; that he prayed the monks of Paisley to take them under their care, and send a priest, who should daily say mass at the altar he had raised; that he promised in return to the monks, all the offerings on the chapel altar; thus owning that monastic feudalism which extended over all Strathgryfe.

And then no more is told us. How many prayerful years the old men spent upon the green burnside, going to and from the chapel, and drawing nearer God perhaps in these last quiet hours; how loving Robert De Croc went out and in among them, and protected them like a feudal chief, and cared for them like a son; or how with the natural ties of kin, broken in some untold way, they gathered them up, as best they might, round this generous Norman soldier; we must make out for ourselves, for the simple reason that it is not told us.

On the banks of the little Leveran—the haunt of greenness and flowers, still fresh and sweet with violets and primrose clusters, and shady with hazel and birch— there is not now standing one stone upon another of the old men's house and chapel.

But the castle of Robert De Croc has gathered history round it. A son of the second Steward married the daughter of De Croc, and became lord of Crockstone and Darnley, and the ancestor of Mary's husband. And the love and sorrow of the queen has wrapped Croc's town, or "Crookston," in such romance, as makes the poetry of its Norman founding, in King Malcolm's reign, comparatively a forgotten thing.

But honourable distinctions attend the family name in successive generations: Honours won for wisdom in diplomacy, for gallantry in war—won at home and abroad— in France and Italy and Spain. One, Sir John, in reward for military services rendered to Charles Sixth, some time soon after 1424, is created a Marechal of France, and Count d'Evreux and Seignior de Concorsant. Another makes himself famous in the early Neapolitan wars, and receives still larger acknowledgments from the gratitude of Louis Twelfth. Duke of Terra Nova, Marquis de Gyralle and Squilaggo, Count of Acri, Grand Constable of Sicily and Jerusalem, Viceroy of Naples, Governor of Calabria, Captain of the *Gard de Corps*, Lieutenant-General of the French army in Italy,—are some few of the crowd of titles bestowed on this scion of De Croc. One at a later date is Governor of Milan; another is Governor of Avignon; repeatedly they are commanders of the Scottish *Gens d'Armes* in France. The family, French and Scottish from the days of its Norman founder, made good, over Europe, its motto, "Avant Darnley."

In the culmination of its glory, when Lord Henry married Mary queen of Scots, another motto was adopted by the queen and the new-made king. The legend, *Dat gloria vires* (glory gives strength), inscribed on a coin, with the names, *Marie et Henricus Dei gratia R. et R. Scotorum*, was subsequently proved too strongly and significantly false to call for any comment.

The pleasant little stream, which began its story in the bounty of Robert De Croc, gathers round it other interests, but had no sweeter memories than these its earliest.

THE FAIR ABBEY.

LET my due feet never fail
To walk the studious cloisters pale;
And love the high embowed roof,-
With antique pillars massy proof;
And storied windows, richly dight,
Casting a dim religious light;—
There let the pealing organ blow
To the full-voiced choir below,
In service high, and anthems clear,
As may with sweetness, through mine ear,
Dissolve me into ecstacies,
And bring all heaven before mine eyes.
                            Il Penseroso.

HERE is in the spring woods a moment of ecstatic beauty;—catkins white on the birches; tender, pale seedlings of beech, newly cleft through their shiny heart; the chestnuts, in great rosy knobs, enfolding their fan-shaped leaves, their embryo stately flowers; through the forest, a faint purple glow,—a premonition of summer. All who love the spring-time know it,—that flush, of waiting, on the landscape, that hour not of fulfilment, but desire.

Then bursts forth a sunshiny day; and, suddenly, in the

night, comes, in exuberance of strength, and with queenly gait, the longed-for summer, bringing that gladness and peace which, hitherto, had only been heralded.

Some such joyous floresence awoke late in the twelfth century; only, as it happened here, the blossoming was not of brown boughs into leaf. The quarried stone had its summer; and in a strange fusion of loveliness, rose those religious thoughts, high aspirations, offerings of faith, and all that beauty, till now but forecast, as the spring-time prophesies of summer.

Paisley was happy that in this space her ecclesiastical life began. The Clugniensian monks crossed the border to build on the White Cart, in the busiest, and perhaps the sweetest period of English architectural history.

It was in the rich transition time, from late Norman to early Gothic, when the Orientalism, brought back by the Crusaders, and grafted on the Romanesque, stirred conceptions of the graceful, solemn loveliness which developed into Gothic architecture. At Carcassone, one hundred and fifty years earlier, the symbolical palm leaves had been wreathed with all reverence in the consecrated stone. And slowly but surely would the builders learn how the leaves of their own woodland (twice tender, because they grew round castle bowers and lowlier homes, and made the green gladsome twilight of their English forest chase) might wreath their churches as devoutly as the Crusader's palm.

Besides, about this period, was discovered the use of the chisel, and with it great possibilities in effects of shadow and light. The rich, rude, shallow Norman mouldings, the axe had fairly rendered. But all those delicate darknesses of rolls and leaves and flowers; those exquisite undershadowings; those veins of paleness; those local twilights, which showed the joyfulness of light,—these the axe was impotent to render. The chisel brought other attainment near.

It is said, a great delight filled the builders of the time, a certain devout emulation, which spread like a passion through the land. St. Hugh of Burgundy, a few years later, was appointed to an English bishoprick, and immediately began to rebuild his cathedral, aiding with his own hands. " His church of Lincoln he caused to be new built from the foundation,—a great and memorable worke, and not possible to be performed by him without infinite helpe." In 1174, the architect, William of Sens, was appointed by the monks of Canterbury to restore their "glorious choir of Conrad." And step by step of the transition time may be seen, as, year by year, the beautiful stone work advanced to its completion in 1184. Christ Church Cathedral, Oxford, begun about 1160—the same year as Paisley—is an example of the same transition work.

The late Norman lingered still, and for years after this, side by side with the beautiful Gothic, which was to supplant it at last. One may see it still, in many a ruined Abbey and old English Parish Church,—the gorgeous yet formal moulding, the deeply recessed doorway, the heavy rounded arch. And the same ivy, clambering round it, clasps, with its facile fingers, drip-stones of the early Gothic.

The Norman window has been displaced much oftener than the Norman doorway; as seen in Paisley, and in many other monastic buildings of the time. The one single relic of Norman architecture in the Clugniac houses founded by the Steward, is a low round doorway in the south-east end of the nave. A plain old doorway it is—dark and much obscured, in the deep angle formed by the chapel and the long nave—yet distinctly Norman in its character, and therefore of historical significance, notwithstanding its poverty of sculpture and adornment.

This doorway opens on the cloister court, which has the peculiar interest of being the only remaining specimen of this feature of monasticism in Scotland. It has little now to recall the monastic seclusion of the middle ages. The green grass and daisy, "whose home is everywhere," grow indeed in the shady stillness; and, for a brief hour, some shadow of dwarfed trees plays across the ancient nave. The small common houses of the town closely invade the cloister, deepening the shadows on the green grass, and looking nearly as grey and ancient as the Abbey, with its seven centuries. The sombre and chaste stone, gathering, with gathering years, a certain grace of antiquity, always redeems an old Scottish town from that air of utter meanness and *unbeauty*, which oppresses a northern eye among similar surroundings in the south.

But this impression is not vivified by any of its wonted aids. The common height of the buildings; the steep, ridgy, hilly outline which these environ, or in which they are oftener set; the castellated effects of distance in mellow sun, or tender mist; the appeal to the imagination; and the sudden investiture, with picturesque attributes, of many a small Scottish town, whose details are miserable enough,—these are all familiar to those who have ever, with artistic eye, watched the sun rise, or set, behind the chimnies of some crooked old northern High Street.

No such charm is here. Steep ridgy streets, Paisley has; but these do not rise up from the Abbey, which, as the reader knows, lies in a rich *champaign*, with hills for landmarks and boundaries, but not once encroaching upon its skirt. And while the river stole softly among its lilies and its reeds, and the outer land waved with corn fields, and the near land was white and red with orchard blooms, nothing could have been fairer or more sweet to see, than this rich and low land set in its upland frame. But it is a picture of the past. Orchard and corn field are historical. In the black, slow, winding water, a cress, or a lily, or a reed, would now be as great an anachronism as if the Crusading Steward, who gave gifts to the Abbey long ago, were to appear with cross upon his armour in the dull modern streets.

In lack of the champaign beauty; in lack of close, ridgy heights, the obtrusion of modern masonry is distasteful to eye and thought. And the Abbey gains nothing from what must once have been its joy,—the near restful river, and the wealth of level land. Nothing but its name, with the cloister court, recalls the peace, seclusion, and prayerfulness of the Benedictine life.

And again, through the noisy streets, this old round Norman doorway takes us back to the Clugniensians, and the transitions of the twelfth century,

If England was rich in religious foundations, Scotland, at this period, almost excelled her in wealth. On the throne of the northern kingdom was a king who loved the church, and spared nothing to advance its prosperity. The monasteries, which rose in Scotland in the middle of the twelfth century, crowd the pages of its history; and gratefully suggest how that deep religious sentiment, which would often, in the future ages, find manifestations rudely and strangely adverse to itself, was yet one and the same,— inherent in the heart of a nation, which, with all fixity, looked God-ward through its sorrows and triumphs and strifes. The "ane sair sanct for the crown," as James First styled his ancestor David, through the church, blessed his kingdom with beauty as no other monarch had done.

Already, in 1113, while his brother was still on the throne, David brought, to the Selkirk forest, Benedictine monks from France. These, when he had been four years king, he translated to Kelso. For the same French monks, in 1140, David founded an Abbey at Lesmahago, a very lovely and secluded village on the banks of the Nethan water. In this ancient, most sweet parish, not a stone of the monastery now remains; only a tradition, and the name of Abbey Green. In the same year, was founded the monastery of Kilwinning, also for French Benedictines; and before the close of the century, more religious houses, for other orders, were erected than can be named.

Trefontane in Lammermuir, Gulane in East Lothian, Rossedal in Dumfriesshire, Pittenween and Lindores in Fife, Holyrood, Melrose, Jedburgh, Cambuskenneth, Tongland, Withern, Saulseat, Dundrennan, Eccles, Lincluden, Blantyre, Saddel, Glenluce, Coldstream, Restennot, Newbattle, Kinloss and Mauchline, are but some of the names in Scotland which have gathered round them religious and picturesque memories, by virtue of monastic charters granted in the twelfth century.

The spread of the Tyronensian order, composed of monks from Tyrone in France, must have had a perceptible influence on the civilization of the country. That the architect of the fairest structures was frequently Norman or French, we should have divined even without the aid of the record of the monk Gervase, or the entablature on Melrose Abbey.

This last, inserted in the south side of the transept door of Melrose, is nearly all the information we have of the Parisian architect; to whom, as the inscription tells us, we are indebted for the beautiful mason work of St. Andrews, Glasgow, Paisley, Melrose, Niddesdale, and Galloway. Time, and also, it is said, the zeal of the reforming clergy, have obliterated many of the letters on the old Abbey wall. But what these have destroyed, old chroniclers fortunately have preserved; so that we may still read this curious masonic epigraph, with its quaint sympathetic blending of assertion and self-abnegation.

The builder offers no prayer for his own salvation and peace, while he fondly commits his kirk to divine and saintly protection. It is as if his best part had breathed itself into the blossoming stone. His life has passed into his labour. His thought, his faith, his desiring, have escaped into the arches he has raised. He no longer divides between *me* and *mine.* He is careful to assert his personality, and identify it with his work. But his own personality is secondary to the kirk, for which only it was valued—yet, therefore, valued much—as a tool of the fair kirk's rearing. It is an appeal to futurity; an appeal as for a child by a parent, whose guardian hand death must loosen, and who feels, with the tremour of love, that on this, the offspring of his genius, eyes much less fond and careful and appreciative than his own must look.

The appeal has been in vain. Among the ruins of Melrose, the inscription may be seen as follows :—

>John ; Morrow ; Sum ; Tym ; Callit ;
>W. S ; . . . D ; Born ; In ; Parysse ;
>Certainly ; And ; Had ; In ; Keping ;
>Al ; Mason ; Werk ; Of ; Santan
>Drays ; Ye ; Hye ; Kirk ; Of ; Glas
>Gu ; Melros ; And ; Pasley ; Of ;
>Nyddysdall ; . . . D ; Of ; Galway ;
>I ; Pray ; To ; God ; . . . D ; . . . Y ; Baith.

. . . .

As found in the old chronicles, it has been read thus :—

> "John Morrow sum tym callit was I,
> And born in Parysse certainly ;
> And had in keping al mason werk,
> Of Santandrays ye hie kirk,
> Of Glasgu, Melrose and Pasley,
> Of Nyddesdall and of Galway ;
> I pray to God and Mary baith,
> And sweet St. John, keep this haly kirk fra scaith."*

Paisley cannot indeed compare with Melrose, the favourite child of the architect. Yet, it is worthy of the same parentage, and a beautiful specimen of its style. In the deep, receding, pointed doorway, the shadows brood all day long. O, the pure cloistral beauty of these suites of

* See Appendix.

Early Gothic mouldings! the coolness, the quiet, the simplicity of line within line! Deep and deeper grow the lines, as our thoughts grow deep and deeper, till the tranquility of the carved work is on us; yet not the tranquility of stone, but the ineffable repose of faith which art can only symbolize. And we know why these Early English mouldings have, for many eyes, a charm which is wanting in the elaborate ornament of Norman and Tudor times.

For the windows above the string-course, over this old shadowy doorway, one cannot claim the same beauty, and yet they are fair enough. Each window has three lights; the mullions diverging into tracery, which seems of a later date. As in all old religious structures, the slow, long progress of the building is marked with sure precision, by these changes in windows and doorways. The two most westerly windows of the nave, with plain mullions crossing at the top, point to late in the thirteenth century, when troubles were gathering for Scotland; but which time was, notwithstanding, still a busy period in her architectural history.

Probably this is all that remained of the original foundation of the Abbey, which was burned by the English about the year 1300, in that *diram guerram*, as it is pathetically called in the charter of the old monks.

There was no thought of such near sorrow, in the glorious summer time, when the first stone of the monastery was laid among the forest oaks.

The trees were felled near the river, and little vistas were made; and the scared deer fled away from their invaded solitudes. And the stone was brought from Walter's quarries, and hewn and carved into beauty; and the Abbey rose in that pleasant open glade, which the axes had made among the oaks.

The prior and his twelve monks, with all the perfectness of patience, wrought;* not grudging labour, but giving it as love and prayer. And "John Morrow," still in the beginning of his art, was with them. John Morrow had come from Paris when Louis Le Jeune was reigning, when the church of St. Germain des Prés was building in Louis' capital. St. Germain des Prés was building,—not finished then; and stately old Notre Dame was as yet but a thought,—a projection. And Le Jenne—a Capet, a Crusader—had his quarrels with Henry Second, and with young Malcolm of Scotland, who fought in Henry's train. And Eleanor, divorced from Louis, was the wife of Henry Plantagenet, and weaving her own quarrels with the silken thread and fair Rosamond.

These were the names which made history—outside the cloister, beyond the border, and across the seas—while the Clugniensian monastery was rising on Walter's land.

* See Appendix.

THE LADY OF MOLLA.

Round her she made an atmosphere of life;
The very air seemed lighter from her eyes!
They were so soft and beautiful and rife,
With all we can imagine of the skies.

. . . . To look upon her sweet face, bred
New thoughts of life, for it seemed full of soul;
She had so much—earth could not claim the whole.

Byron.

WALTER the Steward has still a brief page of biography. We are apt to forget this fact. The Abbey absorbs his personality, and his gifts overshadow his life.

Modestly stands the devout knight on the threshold of a whole history. His donations occupy many pages of the obscure annals of his time.

"Twenty acres and one toft of land in Dunfermline, with a toft in his burgh of Renfrew;" this to the Abbey of Dunfermline.

"The land which he possessed in Roxburgh, and one

acre of land in the village of Molla; that one, viz., which was in controversy with him and the church of that ilk; and, in his village of Renfrew, that land which lies near the toft which King David gave to the foresaid monks, as far as the river which descends from the mill of Clyde;" this to the Abbey of Kelso.

The donation is made "for the safety of the souls of David and Malcolm, kings of Scotland; and for the good estate of his sovereign lord, King William; and for the safety of his own soul, and of the souls of his ancestors and successors."

But the Steward, only thus known, gloved and mailed, rests—a silent presence—in the deep repose of the shadows. He, himself, is not once brought forward into the history of his time. The father of kings now reigning (the son of kings if we admit the poetical legend stretching back into traditionary dark); he, himself, is no king—has only an obscure identity. Strictly historical he is. His existence, in a certain manner for Scotland, is the key-stone of two decades of centuries. On the one side is that fabulous dynasty, reaching back its tenacious hand to establish its starting time at the beginning of the Christian era; on the other side that long, unborn race—chivalrous, weak, strong—who were to suffer and be loved, as has been the lot of few kings; to rise and fall, and find renovation in a dynasty which is at once both the strongest and the purest that has ever blessed the world.

And Walter, in the silence of the centuries, stands unconsciously between, singing his Te Deum for the yet ungathered greatness of his race; in the lofty, fair Abbey, raising his instinctive thanks to God through the psalms of the Benedictine monks. A clear, distinct figure, standing out in high relief; silent, too, as a sculptured form, but full of brave beauty and repose.

"Eschine de Londonia, lady of Molla," becomes the wife of the Steward. That she was beautiful and worthy of her lord, we are entitled to believe. One of the privileges of fiction, which history has a right to claim, is this faith in the beauty, grace, and virtue, of all those who have come down to us from remote traditionary times, without contrary imputations. Particulars having been denied us, we philosophically generalise, and accept the individual for the type.

The woman, veiled in the obscurity of eight centuries, becomes the ideal lady. Norman, by no means, she;— Scoto-Saxon, with eyes softly blue; some Celtic fervour and devotion spiritualising her face; her aspect generous, and features pearly fair, with the rosy flush of Northern breezes, like a soft dawn, lighting them into the purest human sweetness; reasonable and benign; no fickle impulses, no exacting egotism, no self-worship; a woman of household pleasures—to be loved by her husband with a constant love, to be tenderly revered by his vassals. Her brown lashes droop not coyly, they are lifted with modest, serene trust in herself and in her world. Her thoughts keep company with her.

Such must Eschine de Londonia be. Her name has come down to us Latinised through the charters of the monks. Of her family we know little.

"Robert of Londonia, son of Richard, son of Maurice, son of Thomas," confirms the church of Lasswade to the canons of Dryburgh. The heiress of this family married Robert, a son of King William the Lion, and gives her own name to her children,—that of her husband, for some unexplained reason, seemingly was set aside. A grant by the prince is extant "to Robert of Londoun his son, of one full toft in his burgh of Melrose." And there is also a grant by "Robert of Londonia, brother of the king of Scotland, to the monastery of St. Mary of Dryburgh, of the yearly revenue of three shillings of silver, and one measure of pepper from Lasswade."

Eschine must be daughter of this Robert, and niece of Alexander Second. She has neither father nor brother when she weds Walter, the Steward. Thus much we assume from the lofty solitude of her name. "Eschine de Londonia, lady of Molla," she comes down in the monkish annals.

Moll was a very old parish on the eastern edge of Roxburghshire, now included in Morebattle; its former name is scarcely known. The village and the ancient kirk stood on the Bowmont water,—that beautiful little stream, a favourite haunt of the angler, which flows through the wavy, pastoral land that was once held by Eschine.

In one of these towers, or peel-houses, which dotted that border country, Walter, the Steward of Scotland, had wooed the lady of Molla. Supreme and lonely in her youth, till the mailed, silent figure of the knight crosses the holms and the howes; and the Bowmont water sings musically as it never sang before, and the turret of her father's peel becomes a most happy watch-tower, and

Eschine weds Walter, the Steward, and also becomes historical.

That she was like-minded with her husband, both devout and beneficent, may be inferred from those old chartularies, which sometimes afford unwitting glimpses into lives that would otherwise have passed irrecoverably away.

These record, "to the monks of Kelso, a gift of the patronage of the church of Molla, for the salvation of her soul, and of Walter, the son of Alan, her husband."

"And to Paisley she gave in pure alms, one carucat of land, with pasturage for fifty oxen, for the soul of King William, and of David, Earl of Huntingdon, his brother."

This Earl David, for the safety of whose soul the monks of Paisley received Eschine's gift, is already familiar to all readers of Scott's "Talisman." His adventures, and picturesque history, scarcely need the touch of the novelist to make them read like romance. How he fought in the Holy Land, was shipwrecked in the Mediterranean, made a slave by the Saracens, sold to a Venetian, recognised and ransomed by some English merchants, and landed at last on the Fife shore, is told by the soberest of historians. In gratitude for his deliverance, David founded a religious house in Fife. And Eschine, his kinswoman, remembers his soul, when she gives to the Abbot of Paisley the pasturage for fifty oxen, and the one carucat of land.

After this last donation, Eschine passes away. She has one son, Alan by name, as later history discloses. And tradition has assigned the castle of Dundonald, in Kyle, as her husband's chief residence.

Motherhood is always the same; so also are the daises in the meadow, and the crowfoot submerged in the loch; and the molten gold behind the Arran mountains; and the gleam and shade and evanescence of light and colour on the Frith.

Eschine's life, undefined, becomes, if we will, a picture, filled in by easy fancy, with truthfullest lines and lights. When or how she died, no record has told; nor whether she was laid among the green holms of Moll, or within the new Abbey of Paisley. But Walter, left alone, became a monk of Melrose, laying aside his mail for the scapulary and white Cistertian garb. He died in 1177, and was carried by his brother monks to the Abbey he had founded on the White Cart seventeen years before.

His are the first remains recorded to have been laid in the Abbey of Paisley.

A SHADOWY KNIGHT.

>'Tis like the wondrous strain
>That round a lovely ruin swells,
>Which, wandering on the echoing shore,
>   The enthusiast hears at evening :
>'Tis softer than the west wind's sigh ;
>'Tis wilder than the unmeasured notes
>Of that strange lyre, whose strings
>   The genii of the breezes sweep :
>   Those lines of rainbow light
>   Are like the moon-beams when they fall
>Through some cathedral window, but the tints
>   Are such as may not find
>   Companion on earth.
>   *Shelley.*

THE son of Walter and Eschine has left no story to tell. Yet human life always possesses fascination enough to make us linger around it. Its humanity does not altogether recede from us with the years that make it dim.

Perhaps in the exact proportion to our secret knowledge of ourselves, to the analysis of the springs of our own thought and feeling, have our sympathies become the touchstone for other souls, and the human bond a bond strong enough to knit us for all time.

The eagerness with which we ask for all the details and surroundings of a dim, shadowy life, partakes of the nature of *gossip*. Where history refuses us facts, we construct them for ourselves, more truthfully than we know, through that guiding human instinct we possess.

Alan's memory dimly descends as a court-favourite, and a friend of the church. In long hose and laced sandals, silken tunic and jewelled gloves, not a mailed figure like his father, he peacefully moves among warlike men. That his tastes were peaceful, we gather from indirect inference, yet, that inference, perhaps, not less true for its being indirect. By the greenness of the moss we know where the hidden runnel flows. But between us and the runnel of that old, old life, there lie whole voiceless centuries; we only know it is there. We see the church lands grow richer; of the lives which made them so, we catch a sudden sheen through the grasses—that is all. All, and enough. Having served their generation, it is sweetest that they pass away into the kindly darkness which wraps the faces of their kin.

The Lion-King has wedded Ermingarde, the cousin of English Henry—wedded her at Woodstock on a September day. She has left the softer south before Eschine goes to rest; and the red autumn sun sheds its glow on the purple heather of William's land, when Ermingarde comes across the border. O, that chivalrous debateable land, and its marches, and its wardens, and its peels, and its long, tragic history unforecast in the gleam of the silver Solway!

The king favours Alan, the Steward. Queen Ermingarde favours him also. He inherits the ancestral piety. William has no time for that. What with those defiant Highland lords, and with Galloway but half at rest, and rumours of Harold of Orkney, the king's foot is always in the stirrup.

Ermingarde may say her prayers, and give forest or fishing to the monks, for masses to be performed for the soul of her rude, stern-featured Lion William. Ermingarde may do this. We do not read that she does. She is a Norman Princess; perhaps not devout like Eschine. But the king does it not. None the less the gracious Lord Steward, with his delicate sense of right—his faithful, reverential soul, charms the Lion King, as gentle things charm the strong.

The king will rest upon his sword when the Gallovidians are quelled.

(It is before that great household tragedy, when the Tay, irreverent as King Canute's sea, broke through the palace walls, and swept away in its flood the baby-prince, still held in his nurse's arms, down among the green links, and under the birks and the hazels,—till the dank hair clung round a dead little cold face. O poor Queen Ermingarde! But Lord Alan, ere that time, shall lie beneath the Abbey altar.)

The king, in his moments of rest, will talk—in his palace on the Tay—with this devout, trusty Steward, of many and weighty things; of the brave Earl Gilchrist, outlawed now and a wanderer, yet so ill spared to disgrace,—he, who had put to flight the rebel men of Galloway; of the Earl David—bless him—not yet come home from the wars— true brother and knight who fights for the Holy Sepulchre;

perhaps of the cruel Earl Harold of Caithness, and his own most cruel revenge, meditated over and planned as might befit that fierce king who has left nought but ungentle memories for even the fondest historian.

And Alan, the Lord High Steward, an Isaac in that old time—an anachronism outside the cloister—will listen, will modify, will suggest. It was his voice, perhaps, which pled wisely and well, when the king came back from the Moray shore with the glare of Donald's burning fleet reddening the pine-woods behind him,—some few scattered banditti all that remained of his foes; his voice, too, which pled for the three poor beggar-men—whose strange nobleness under their rags was marked by the king and all his soldiers; and his the quick sympathetic eye that was first to recognize Earl Gilchrist and his sons, thus forlorn, upon the highway.

The page is a sealed page. Shadowy, even as his forbears, Alan, Lord High Steward, flits, a ghostly knight, across story.

And in still more shadowy guise flits his wife, the daughter of Swene. Even her name is lost. She leaves no grants behind her for the monks to write and con;—perhaps so truly womanly was she that her distaff and spindle were enough, and the little Walter at her feet, and Alan her Lord, the Steward. And that lapsed personality may have a sweet significance of its own—the daughter of Swene, son of Thous—wife of Alan, the Lord High Steward.

For biography of Swene we may search the old records in vain; only by a process of induction we know him to have been a person of account.

The chartulary of Scone contains a confirmation by

"Walter, High Steward of Scotland, to the Abbey of Scone, of the lands in Tippermuir, which Swene, son of Thoraldus, grandfather of the same Walter, gave to the said monks."

There is also a ratification by this "Swene, son of Thoraldus, to the Abbey of Holyroodhouse of his claim in the church of Travernent."

So he had lands, broad and fair; and this nameless wife of Alan was of no unequal birth, though so utterly obscure in history.

But Alan's life is the record of his giving; all that is distinctive, individual, and pronounced therein, lies in the attitude he maintains towards the monks and the church. The chartulary of Paisley records his gift of "the patronage of the church of Kingaff, in the isle of Bute, to the monks of Paisley, with the tithes of all the churches and chapels within that isle."

And the goodliness of such a gift will find its full appreciation. A suggestion of almost ideal loveliness, does the brief unadorned record bear. How the opal on the crest of the little waves will flash with a pure splendour—making possible all the glories of nimbus and saintly palm. How the pale receptive dimness—of hills faint in a film of light—gives aerial distance to the thought, as it does to the actual vision. Those "positive reds and blues" which Fuseli, with a reservation, admits to invigorate the eye in painting, the Scottish typical landscape can by no possibility express. Sweetness, distance, uncertainty, the vagaries of sudden mists that gather on the skirt of a sunbeam, the cloistral sense of seclusion, stillness, mystery, repose;—these make a Northern Frith in nature, like a picture of

Caracci in art—a glimpse into infinite solemn tenderness, a dream, a note of rest. And this dimness, this neutral-toned paleness, this mystery of land and sea, with its daily and hourly changes, its folding in ineffable shadow, its endless revelations of form, its gleams of tenderest light,—is it possible whole generations of clear-sighted human eyes, should close, and open and close on such influences with no reciprocity of life ? Do they not half explain that curious fact somewhere noted, that—Presbyterianism notwithstanding, and Knox's great revolution—Scotland clings to her primitive saints with a reverence and a tenderness of which ritualistic England but feebly conceives ? For the light on those silver Firths was scarcely less inexplicable, than the Divine humanity, learned through the holy words and lives of St. Serf, and St. Ninian, and St. Blane. The paleness of the Northern landscape is spiritualistic in the last degree—any bright bit of colour would dissolve the phantasy—a constant gospel of wonder is in the water and the sky. And the mediæval fancy was quick to acknowledge such.

Bute is ecclesiastically rich. St. Blane had come from Rome two hundred years before the Steward, near the end of the tenth century, when Kenneth Third was king. The chapel, which he had built on the little hill above the bay, was then in the prime of its celebrity. Penitents came from all the neighbouring shores, from Galloway, Kyle and Argyle, and crept with uncovered feet round the stony edge of the cauldron which had such demoniacal fame, in the rude superstitions of the time;—and Arran, with its superb mountain-range, purple and dim before them, then as now, with grandly serrated outline, relieved against the pale sky.

The sons of the thane Somerled make war in its glens; but that will not disturb the sister isle. Large red and white roses blow around old St. Blane's—and the bright, cool iris flags flaunt—and the coc-koo flowers spring under the hedge. And the penitents who moor their open boats in the shallows of the sunny bay, will catch the sweet gleam of the wood-sorrel, there then, as now;—and learn from the glowing greenness of the moist, triple leaf, that lesson of trinity in unity which so many things in nature teach.

For the mediæval symbolism has reached its splendid development;—it has seen the sacred form of the cross in all attitudes of nature and humanity—and even found its aureole, in the misty exhalations from the warmth and ripeness of the summer noon.

The poem of Rhaban Maur of Mayence is already an antique. But the thoughts and devout conceits of this old ingenious Archbishop have permeated the whole church. A curious and interesting chapter is the symbolism of this mediæval period—tempting divergence, larger than permissible, yet by no means irrelevant to the subject of these chapters. For much of our knowledge of Scottish Abbeys must come from such extraneous sources. Sometimes these invaluable side-lights of history are the only lights to be had.

The constant flux and reflux, to and from Rome, would, of necessity, unite those conservative religious separatists, even had there not existed an already prepared bond, in the one earthly headship which all owned as supreme. The poverty and wars of Scotland, as well as the isolation which sea and distance gave it, to a certain extent raised a barrier against imitation and rivalry. Yet the pilgrim, returning from Rome, still came over the Alps, bearing some delicate ivory of the beautiful benign Christ, bearing some precious mosaic, with typical fish or scroll, or slender Resurrection Cross, shining blue amidst the bloom of vines. And the fame of Gulielmus Durandus travelled northward and westward; and with it the elaborate symbolism which his pen had fixed. Wise and good men, in the seclusion of these northern cells—probably all the purer, because they were far from the southern source of their faith—still preserved and perpetuated the history and legends of their time, transfused with those subtle influences imparted by their local setting. Emulation of Jacques de Voraigne, who then compiled the Légende Dorée, would brighten under the Gothic arches newly reared in Strathgryfe and Kyle.

And that old church of Kingaff (modernized Kingarth), over which, henceforth, the Abbey of Paisley shall stretch maternal hands—it too shall hear, in the tidal waves upon the sand, blending with its sweet constant psalms, with its vaes and its credos,—the Eternal music of love, the voice of the Infinite Fatherhood, the voice of the Lord Christ who vitalized every legend and all hymns.

But to return to the charter, from which we scantily glean. "Further, to the Abbey of Paisley, this Alan grants the lands of Monobroe in Strathgryfe, with an annuity of five merks, payable to him out of Machlin by the monks of Melrose, . . . which grant he makes for the soul of Walter, the son of Alan, his father; and for the soul of

Eschine de Mollo, his mother, for which they covenanted to celebrate his *obit*, as solemnly as for any monk of their own convent."

And a few years later this covenant was kept, when the Steward lay in his shroud, and the convent *obit* was performed with great funeral pomp.

Mass for the dead was chanted in the monastery among the oaks, and the solemn lauds and matins, which the church ordained, were sung. And Alan, the peaceful Steward, was gathered to the dust of his fathers, under the high altar of the new Abbey of the Clugniacs.

> "Lord, redeem us from the grave,
> And ransom us from death for ever;
> Redeem us, Lord, for ever:
> Our trust is in Thine out-stretched arm.
> Give us peace, and bring us
> Unto Life Eternal."

THE GIFT OF DALMULIN.

FRESH to that soil thou turn'st, where every vale
   Shall prompt the poet, and his song demand;
To thee thy copious subjects ne'er shall fail;
Thou need'st but take thy pencil to thy hand
And paint, what all believe, who own thy genial land.
There must thou wake perforce thy Doric quill:
   'Tis Fancy's land to which thou sett'st thy feet;
   Where still, 'tis said, the fairy people meet,
Beneath each birken shade by mead or hill.

  .   .   .   .

E'en yet preserved, how often may'st thou hear!
   When to the pole the Boreal mountains run;
   Taught by the father to his listening son,
Strange lays, whose power had charmed a Spenser's ear:
At every pause, before thy mind possest,
Old Runic bards shall seem to rise around,
With uncouth lyres in many-coloured vest,
Their matted hair with boughs fantastic crowned.
                                         Collins.

IN the year 1204, the second "Walter, son of Alan," in his castle in Kyle by the sea, began his Scottish Stewardry.

His surroundings are clear enough. William is still on the throne—an old man, but not detached from his times.

Struggling with his stormy Border country, the old king's life wears away. Berwick and Tweedmouth are each defiantly looking upon the other; and faithless John of England is at Norham; and in king William's own heart is a certain taunting remembrance of homage done long ago for the fair little kingdom which had owned no lord but himself. Excommunication comes; then reconciliation and favour, even the golden rose from pope Lucius Third; and then death for the wearied king. In the year 1214, in the dark days of December, William the Lion died in the castle on Stirling rock.

Walter the Steward has held his office for ten chequered years, when Alexander Second takes his father's sceptre in his hand.

Then one pauses. One is only recounting history; only, the great setting, which is very large in the past, yet at best is merely a setting to the humblest biography. To each life, it is a much smaller thing than the daily being and thinking, the deeds of every hour, the passions, hopes, and the fine emotions, of which no record is made. One realises and accepts the truth, that a stack of chimnies at Dundonald, threatened by a fierce storm, while the little Alexander and Walter slept in a turret below; or some tempestuous night, while a faithful old retainer, out fishing on the Frith, in sight of the castle walls, fought for life with a west wind on the crest of a greedy wave; or a day breaking goldenly along the Argyle shore, reflecting strange portentous light in the sombre sea between, while the priest held the crucifix before the dying eyes of the tender, nameless mother—that these make biography, and not the Border raids, court favour, or papal bulls, which stand out so boldly in history.

Walter the Steward, nevertheless, had court favour. He was already aged—nor was Alexander young—when he crossed the sea to France, for a second bride to the king. And he brought back Mary de Concy, the daughter of Ingelram Le Grand; reasonably called *Le Grand*, for three royal ladies he had successively wedded. And he bore upon his flag a motto of sufficient arrogance :—

"Je ne suis Roy, ni prince Aussi,
Je suis le Seigneur de Conci."

Yet this episode in the Steward's life is passed briefly by. It is not dilated upon, as, with pardonable curiosity, the reader is apt to desire. A man both upright and gentle, with ways as courtly as the Scottish palaces could furnish, would be selected, doubtless, for a mission so delicate and honourable. And Mary de Concy takes her place notably in Scottish history as the mother of Alexander Third, whose death began Scotland's long sorrow.

A much longer page is devoted to the Steward's benefactions to the church, and rightly; for Walter, in this, keeps true to the traditions of his family.

Besides, the time was rich in such good deeds. The genius of the age was religious. The fervent impulse to devote and sacrifice had spread like a passion through Europe. Nicola Pisani was labouring on the tomb of San Domenico, drawing Christian inspiration from antique pagan marbles, whose perfection of grace and beauty had filled artists with despair. The Pisan fleets had brought spoils from all parts of the old world for their great cathedral. That, indeed, was a by-gone tale. But Buschetto, the Greek, lying between the doors of the great marble façade, was distanced by two centuries, but not by the spirit of his labour, from Nicola, who wrought the frieze for San Martino, with its masterly perforations, and the wondrous half relief of its figures, grouped round the central cross; and who told the story of the life of Christ, in nearly detached marble, round the pulpit of the cathedral of Siena, in the days of the fourth Steward.

The mosaics, the enamels on silver, the marble pulpits richly carved, the sculptured arabesques, the storied doors and fonts and friezes, constitute a dazzling page in the ecclesiastical history of mediæval Italy.

And this outlying province of the church—this mountain land wasted by war—poor, except in courage, faith, and loyalty, and that deep, human poetry, with which a Divine compensation seems to bless all mountain lands—gave, at least, its mede of sacrifice, and reared, in chaste beauty, abbey and cathedral and chapel, from the Border country to the sea.

Of the painters, sculptors, and musicians, whose names have made all time their debtors, Scotland has few to claim. Yet, to her, Italy is indebted for its school of flowing melody. One late distinguished, but solitary name in painting, shows her poverty in art, as a taper may show the darkness of a moonless, starless; night. "Necessity created genius,"* the kind as well as the degree. The poetry which was elaborated in sunnier lands into plastic

* Schiller.

art and flowing melody, helped in this elaboration by all the circumstances of authority, emulation, and wealth, could but become intensified in Scotland into one pure sentiment, for which all expression was denied, except in that quickened life of patriotism and natural religion, which are both true poetical developments. These were, for a small nationality, with a brave and powerful foe upon its borders, the only conditions of existence through the mediæval centuries. And these were not denied, but granted in bountiful measure, to that little, and almost sea-locked land, whose history is a tragedy.

The deep religious instincts of both the Celtic and Saxon race accepted, with reverend and vivid faith, the forms of traditional authority. The best lands of the nobles were cast into the lap of the church. Twenty-eight Augustinian convents were already founded in Scotland—besides Bernardine, Carmelite, Dominican, and numberless other orders less renowned.

Earl Gilbert of Strathern founds the Abbey of Inchaffray. The Earl of Fife builds, at North Berwick, a convent for Cistertian nuns. Queen Ermingarde, in her late widowhood, founds a convent of Dominicans. Red Friars are at Houston in Renfrewshire. Carmelites are settled on the Tay, somewhere near old Perth. The black-robed Dominicans have a convent in Glasgow, founded by the soldier Bishop Wishart, who, it is said, helped old John of Fordun to compile his Scotichronicon.

Of Walter, the Lord High Steward, it is recorded: "In his acts of charity and liberality towards the church, . . . he in a manner strove to outdo his ancestors." Then follows a relation of his gifts to the fair, favoured Clugniac monastery, where his fathers are at rest—of his ample confirmation of all that was granted by Alan and the first Walter; of the fisheries and the forests and the moors—and the salt pit in Calender, and the land by Simon Lockhart's marches; the grinding without mulcture in the mill of Paisley, and the mills on all the pleasant waters; and the rural, shady churches; and the low, rich pasture for the kine. Walter also adds a gift of the "patronage of the churches of Senischar, Dundonald, and Auchinleck, with the tithes thereof. And an annuity of six chalders of meal for the support of a priest to celebrate mass for the soul of Robert Bruce, lord of Annandale."

The last sentence arrests imagination. There must be a sacred story, which the monks have not told, which, perhaps, Walter himself never told till the end, under this brief grant for a priest to say mass for the soul of the lord of Annandale. Was it some passionate friendship, like that of Theseus and Pirithous, cemented by companionship in arms through many a Northumberland raid? or, possibly, some love like that of David and Jonathan? Does the passion, projecting itself—as love always will and must—beyond the darkness of the grave, still hold fast the friend that is lost?

That name, subsequently to grow so dear to Scotland, is as yet unrenowned. And history offers no explanation of this bond which first unites the Bruce and the Stewart. That it may, however, have been no such bond, but only a token of some wrong afterwards repented of, many contemporary episodes may lead us to surmise.

Nicola Pisani, in these same years, is busy at Tagliacozzi, rearing a church and Abbey, by command of Charles of Anjon. Its beauty shall exceed all beauty, by the prince's own injunction; no cost of gold or labour shall be spared. And what the prince enjoined was fulfilled. Vasari speaks of the wonderful patience of the sculptor, and how his genius was spent in giving loveliness to souls restored to their bodies in paradise. When the Abbey is reared, night and day the monks shall say mass for those slain in battle.

The battle slain! It is no Morgarten; no suffering, even to death, for God and hearth, or for those fair traditions which are as a people's life; but it is a page as darkly stained and sorrowful as any we meet in history. On the site of the lovely Abbey, fell the last of the Hohensteins, when the chivalrous boy, Prince Konradin, was made prisoner by Duke Charles. Konradin's gage, flung down, on that October morning, from the scaffold where he died, among the crowd of Naples—the dreadful Sicilian vespers—shall be taken up and fixed in the world's memory.

This is the story enlinked with the Abbey of Tagliacozza. We cannot ask how many fair foundations were reared and endowed on such. The story suggests that wrong done is often as powerful a motive as love; that remorse is of kin to affection, and often will manifest the same outcome.

But, perhaps, the most notable event in the life of this Walter the Steward, is his foundation of a convent for monks and nuns near Ayr; curious, chiefly, on account of the extreme brevity of its existence.

The convent was established in 1229, for the order of Gilbertines. This was a monastic sect some eighty years old, named from its founder, in Lincolnshire, St. Gilbert of Simpringham. It included monks and nuns, who, with but a high wall between, inhabited adjoining houses, although following separate rules. For the monks were Augustinian, while the nuns were Benedictine. Nine such convents St. Gilbert himself had established south of the Tweed.

But there were none in Scotland in the days of Walter's Stewardry. And the devout baron thought to plant them in his own land of Kyle. He invited monks and nuns from Sixhill, in the county of Lincoln, to people the fair, new cloister, among the sandy knolls of Ayr.

Very soon the last trace of this Gilbertine *cell* had disappeared. But the charter granted to it by the Lord High Steward is still preserved.

"Walter, High Steward of Scotland, greeting in the
" Lord: Be it known to you that I, from a regard to the
" Divine love, to the honour of God, and of the blessed
" Mary, have founded a house of canons and monks, of the
" order of Simpringham, in the place which is called
" Dalmulin, above Ayr: And to the said monks, I grant
" and confirm, for ever, the whole land of Mearns, with all
" the contents below those divisions as the river descends
" into Ayr, between the new village and the foundation of
" the chapel of the blessed Mary; and so in ascending by
" the same river, as far as the divisions of Hauchincrew,
" even to the land of Richard Wallace of Hauchincrew, and
" so by the divisions of the same Richard as far as Ayr.
" And besides, the free and full common in the turf moors
" of Prestwick, and the half of all my fisheries which are

"between the castle of Ayr and the village of Irvine: In witness whereof I have affixed my seal. Before these witnesses :—

"WALTER, Bishop of Glasgow.
"REGINALD of Crawford, Sheriff of Ayr.
"WALTER OLIPHARD, Justice of London.
"MALCOLM LOCKHART, and
"MALCOLM LOCKHART, his son.

"HUGH, son of Reginald.
"RICHARD WALLACE.
"JOHN of Montgomery.
"HECTOR of Curry."

In the light of one more decade, the grant, *for ever*, of the whole land of Mearns, of the turf moors, and of the fisheries, and the land by the river side, reads pathetically. For only ten years later, Dalmulin was a solitude. The canons and monks of Simpringham had all passed away from Kyle.

The monks and nuns, from the fen country, had no love for the turf moors, nor the broad yellow sands that were lit by the Arran sunsets. There was a sting in the moist salt sea-wind that came from the wide west. It brought health to the rosy Scottish children, but disease to the English recluses. The health of the Gilbertine monks and nuns suffered here on the edge of the sea. Probably it was from this, if not from some other unknown cause, that they went back to Lincolnshire.

And so Walter's gift became, in some way, an unaccepted sacrifice. And the Steward, like all Eve's best sons, must learn to look through and beyond disappointment, to a never-failing sure and certain hope.

But all the Steward's gifts to Dalmulin reverted to the Abbey of Paisley, which, it seems, held a sort of superiority over the Gilbertine house.

The old Parish Church of St. Quivox marks the site of the convent of Dalmulin.

There is no more to record of Walter, the fourth Steward. He died, and was buried, with his fathers, in the Abbey Church in Strathgryfe. Walter, his second son, became Earl of Monteith; and confirms to the monks the church of St. Colmanel in Kintyre, for "the safety of the souls of his ancestors, buried in the monastery of Paisley."

KYLE.

O WILD, traditioned Scotland!
Thy briery burns and braes
Abound with pleasant memories,
And tales of other days.

Thy story-haunted waters
In music rush along,
Thy mountain glens are tragedies,
Thy heathy hills are song!
Mary Howitt.

A BRIEF page may be spared to this the patrimony of the first Stewards, with its storied name now disused, and to many readers unfamiliar.

Kyle, the famous district so often alluded to in the chartularlies of the monks, must not be confounded with the same familiar and sweet word, to which are attached so many memories of islet and green sea. It is by a mere accident that the green sea Kyles of Bute, and that strip of contiguous sandy mainland, marching with Lanarkshire and Cunningham, should bear similar names. Here, however, the resemblance begins and ends.

For Kyle is a Celtic word, and means simply a little strip of sea. Kyle Aiken and Kyle Castle, Kyle Rhea, Kyle Mure and Kyle Scow, and other Kyles innumerable, stretch among the lonely hills. For beauty, the Kyles of Bute are unique.

But the origin of the mainland name, at least as the old histories tell it, lies quite apart from these, in wonderfully remote antiquity; so remote it must have come down through many generations of Sennachies, and long before the pen of the first Culdee wrote the story on monastic vellum. Buchanan fixes the date as "about the taking of Babylon, nearly three hundred and thirty years before Christ!"

He gives the date with frank gravity, and with no hesitation; making no comment on its remoteness; nor does he cast any suspicion on the deeds which the Sennachies sang.

This word Kyle, we are told, is a corruption of the name Coilus or Coila, which was borne by a British king—Macedonian, Alexander's contemporary. But how a British king's name was affixed to the soil of the Scots, is a somewhat long story, abbreviate it as we may.

In the beginning of history, while the Scots dwelt in the west, scattered in clanships among the stormy Ebudean isles, there came a fleet of shipwrecked men—Picts from Germany—driven by the wind upon their shores, and craved leave to settle in their midst. But the isles were rocky and small, with scarce corn enough for those who held them. And the Scots made a courteous suggestion, that the Picts should try the more hospitable mainland.

Which the Picts did, and there settled,—neighbours to the Scots, and as friends.

Many generations passed with much intermarrying of sons and daughters, and with various social interchanges. By degrees the Scots, also, fixed their habitation on the mainland, and became both numerous and powerful, so that the Picts began to be afraid; for it had been foretold, by an oracle, that the Picts should be subdued by the Scots. This rumour had reached the realm of Britain, and was told to Coilus, the king.

So crafty Coilus, like the politic Russian of later days, will try the use of art. Northward he sends his ambassadors to treat with the king of the Picts. Coilus with his Britons will falsify the adverse oracle, and make the Picts not only not the subdued, but subjugators; always, however, with the Briton's aid. And the Pictish king listens to promises so fair, and gathers his own armies to join those of his ally in the field.

Meanwhile, rumour is again busy at court. But this time its evil sound reaches the Pictish ear. Ambassadors of King Coilus have been secretly with the king of the Scots, promising victory to him also, and against the arms of the Picts. And the treachery is understood. Coilus, in the heat of the battle, will turn his arms against both, and claim the North for his own.

So hate does the duty of love, and unites in a solemn bond the arms of the Scots and Picts against their common foe. Into the land of the Briton march the barbarian soldiery, wasting his fields far and wide, lading themselves with plunder—beginning that border warfare which their sons, in later generations, were to carry to such tragic issues, ere all the history was told.

Coilus was righteously resentful. And when Scots and Picts had got home, safe among their Lowlands on the Frith, they found a Southern army behind them. Then Fergus First, king of the Scots, issued a hasty command. "The womankind to the mountains with the children and the flocks and the herds." Did they go over the Frith, and up among the Argyle fastnesses, or back to the sheltering hollows of the burns among the low Largs hills? The king was strictly obeyed, and none but armed men waited the approach of the British Coilus and his host. Every pass was guarded. The friendly Picts would come anon.

And the Picts, from their farther east, came speedily. Between the two kings a meeting was held on the yet un-named shore. For the army of Coilus had crept to the banks of the river Doon—the gentle, shady, "bonnie Doon," which has since been set to so many songs.

Before daybreak, while the Britons slept, falsely secure, came the Scots and Picts, front and rear, and a dreadful battle was fought. The Britons were overcome, and Coilus, the king, was slain. Coilus was buried, says tradition, where the parish church of Coilton now stands. Till lately—perhaps still—a great stone might be seen, which was said to be the monument of "Auld King Coil." The district where the battle was fought also took the name of this king, and, by an easy transition, became at length *Kyle*.

"Kyle," says George Buchanan, "was more productive of brave men than of corn or cattle."

With which honourable note from that learned old historian, who was sparing of his compliments, we close this brief paranthetical chapter on the old land of Kyle.

ALEXANDER THE CRUSADER.

---o---

> Ah then, St. Hubert, who so pleased as me,
> Wandering at will beneath thy forest tree;
> Or where the antlered herds at early dawn,
> Graze the green wealth of many a flowery lawn;
> Or listening, in thy chapel, legends old,
> Of the brave knight, and of the spurs of gold,
> By the grey Sacristan in mystery told!
>
> *Parnell.*

THE history of the Abbey of Paisley is so completely identified in its first centuries with that of the early Stewards, that we shall most truly follow the story of the old religious house through the fortunes of the family to whom it owed its foundation.

In 1246 there succeeded to the Stewartry, "Alexander the son of Walter." Alexander was then thirty-two years of age, being one year older than St. Louis of France, with whose adventures the future of the Steward's life is closely linked.

Of this saintly Louis of France, whom not only the decree of the pope Boniface Eighth, but the voice of

Christian Europe, canonized, with one accord, De Joinville and Matthew Paris have left us admiring records. And Guizot, for many more readers than the ancient chronicles can reach, has outlined a happy picture of this same good heroic king.

His refined and delicate features, his brilliant complexion, his long fair hair, the personal beauty, the graceful presence of the king, perfectly typify that ideal character which gained wondering, admiring reverence even from the sons of the desert.

> "Where gat he such rich sweetness for his brow?—
> King, yet the crown upon his golden hair
> Dimmed and outshone by some exceeding light—
> An aureole shedding its Diviner gift
> Upon Heaven's favourite son, Louis of France;
> Prince among princes, yet a very dew
> Of graciousness and pity on his lips!"

And in the chaste prose of Guizot, his latest biographer, a still fonder tribute is paid to this mediæval king.

"Born to a throne, a powerful monarch, a valiant soldier, and a noble knight, the object of devoted attachment to those about his person, and of admiring respect to those further removed from him, whether friends or enemies, these honours and pleasures failed either to dazzle or intoxicate him. They held the first place neither in his thoughts nor his actions. Before all things, and above all things, he desired to be, and was, a Christian,—a true Christian, guided and governed by the determination to keep the faith, and fulfil the law of Christianity. If he had been born in the lowest worldly estate; or if he had occupied a position in which the claims of religion would have been most imperative; if he had been poor, obscure, a priest, a monk, or a hermit, he could not have been more constantly and passionately pre-occupied with the desire to live as Christ's faithful servant."

Louis had been very ill; so ill, that those around him thought he had breathed his last. "One of the ladies watching him," says Joinville, "wished to cover his face, saying he was dead; but another lady on the opposite side of the bed would not allow it, for she said that the soul had not yet left the body. The king heard these ladies speaking, and by the grace of our Lord, he began to breathe again; he stretched out his arms and legs, and said, in a voice as hollow as the grave, 'The Dayspring from on high hath visited me; and, by the grace of God, recalled me from the dead.'"

And he sent that same hour for the bishops of Paris and Meaux, to affix to his weak shoulder the Cross, the sign of the Crusade. Blanche and Margaret, queen-mother and queen-consort, kneeling, implored him to wait, to take no such vow upon him in the midst of his feebleness and pain. They were devout queens, both; but the king was their dearest. "I will touch no food," said the king, "until I have received the Cross." And deeply moved he received it, kissed it, and laid it down very gently on his breast.

Three years elapsed before he could fulfil this vow. At length (his kingdom set in order, and Blanche, the queen-mother, appointed Regent of France), on a June day, 1248, Louis went to St. Dennis, to take the oriflamme, and the pilgrim's wallet and staff. And in August of the same year, he set sail for Cyprus, the appointed rendezvous of

Crusaders, who hastened from all parts to join his standard. Among this crowd of crusaders, Alexander the Steward of Scotland emerges for the first time into a shadowy light.

The date is but two years later than that of his father's death, in which same year Alexander Second had concluded the truce of York.

King Alexander was wise and gentle and brave, no unworthy centemporary of the good monarch of France. "A devout, upright, and courteous person," says the oft-quoted Matthew Paris, "justly beloved by all the English nation not less than by his own subjects." And there was peace in this year. No unsheathing of swords, north or south of the Tweed; no border forays to urge on, or to suppress; no flutter of lawless Highland tartan to call for a muster of Lowland lieges on the marches of Stirling or Argyle.

To the barons who loved war, and could find none at home, this Crusade proclaimed by St. Louis had a perfectly native charm. St. Louis himself recognised this, the *worldly* side of the Crusade, when his vassal Counts of Champagne and Brittany set earlier sail for Palestine.

And the Steward, having no monastic vocation, yet the family traditions to maintain, not only for lack of nearer battle-fields, but because of the weird laid upon him, set his face, with military Europe, towards the Jerusalem tomb. In this compromise (altogether not of the nature of a compromise, for that is frequently a double despoiler, while this act of the Steward, on the contrary, unites all the prestige, glory, and enthusiasm of a great passion, and the strange, incongruous, intertwisted laurels to be gathered from religion and war) he shall bear his own name truthfully and bravely, as the Alnas and Walters of his race had done before him.

Alexander, possibly, with a certain bitterness and pride, may remember the life-disappointment of the good knight Walter, his father. That "for ever" in the new charter to the Gilbertine monks and nuns, may taunt him, as it did not taunt the devout founder who gave of his best to God, and perhaps took back, as from God's hand, meekly and patiently the rejected gift; and so possessed his soul more quietly, and received upon his spirit all the benign dews, without the pride of sacrifice.

But these dews are not for the son. The fair new-built cloisters of Dalmulin are deserted on the sea-shore. Already no psalm is chanted there, nor any mass said; the sea mews from Ailsa Craig flap their white wings; and the owlets cry at night, securely; and the thistle-down, wafted from the near sandy knolls, has blossomed into thorn and purple in the gardens of the monks and nuns. The Steward cannot ride south, of a morning, from his castle of Dundonald, but this deserted Dalmulin taunts him through his father's memory. No such gift of land shall he give; but the strength of his gauntleted hand, which cannot be flung back unregardfully by cowled monk or veiled nun.

So when Louis Ninth of France proclaims his first Crusade, and knights from all Christendom flock to join his standard, Alexander, the Lord High Steward, assumes the cross with the rest, and sets his house in order, as King Louis did his kingdom of France. His Castle of Dundonald claims his care; his sandy lordship of Kyle;

but most of all the Monastery of Paisley, to which yet he gives no new gifts.

He ratifies and confirms to the monks all the donations of his ancestors; all the forests and the fisheries; the pastures and the rivers and the mills; all the churches scattered hither and thither in the fair shady straths and glens; the lands once given to Dalmulin; the lands which once were Eschine's. And by special charter he provides that in case he shall fall by the Saracen's hand, by sickness, or by any disaster among the Christian armies of the east, his successors shall be obliged, "at the peril of their souls," to ratify to the monks of Paisley this his last deed.

And having thus piously provided for all contingencies of his enterprise, the Steward, a pilgrim soldier, left the Scottish shore.

The story of this crusade centres in the person of St. Louis. Alexander, the Scottish Steward, is lost in the crowd of warriors. He would winter gaily at Cyprus, with his train of vassals from Kyle; and weather that fierce storm which drove one hundred and fifty ships astrand on the Syrian shore; was perhaps one of those Crusaders who met on board the king's ship "Montjoie," and heard the voice of St. Louis ringing clear and courageous and kind: "My friends, good and true! if we are inseparable in our love, we shall be invincible. . . . Let us fight for Christ, and Christ will triumph in us, not for us, but for the honour and glory of His blessed name;"—saw, perhaps, the great tears of the king when the Count of Artois fell, and he answered nothing to his knights, but only: "Let us praise God for all His good gifts;"—or was one of that faithful remnant of Crusaders who avenged the Christian workmen of Sidon, and saw the delicate jewelled hands which the two queens, Blanche and Margaret—tender mother and wife—had kissed and fondled and called fair—tending with reverent piety the ghastly pile of slain; doing (in that human pity which shrinks not for love's sake) what his knights and nobles recoiled from; and chiding, though compassionately, their idle or reluctant hands. "Do not loathe these poor bodies, for these men are martyrs, and in Paradise!" Did he see the brave king in chains, pale and ill and weak, so that he could not stand? or float a prisoner in the Sultan's galleys down among the lilies of the Nile, with the young, knightly, free-spoken Dejoinville, who was bold enough to council St. Louis against all his soldiers—tried in arms—and his courtiers old in policy? After the death of the Earl of Dunbar, the Steward became commander of the Scottish Crusaders; and whatever adventures may have befallen him in the east, we know that he at last returned safely from the Holy Land; and, in grateful thanksgiving to God, he still more richly endowed the monastic house of Paisley.

In was in the year that Louis proclaimed, in Europe, his second Crusade, while Christendom again was arming against the Tartars and Mamelukes of the east; while pope Urban's earnest appeal to the "Most Christian King of France," had made gay Paris prayerful, had banished feast and tournament;—that on the pleasant breezy shore of Largs, the Norsemen fought their last disastrous battle with the Scots, and Scotland was henceforth freed from the incursions of the old sea-kings.

Alexander the Steward commanded, along with the young King Alexander Third. And the sea also fought for the little, brave, rock-bound land. And when the Norsemen were driven back to their battered ships in the Frith, and, in the stormy sunrise, their slain lay forsaken on the shore, Alexander, the bold Crusader, who had fought in Egypt and Syria, who came back unscathed to his Scottish Castle from the perils of Damietta and Mansourah and the Nile, lay dead on the sands among his vassals in his own barony of Kyle.

> "He was ane valiant knecht,
>   Most terrible in fecht':
>   Here the letters failed outright, but I knew
>   That some stout Crusading lord
>   Who had crossed the Jordan's ford,
>   Lay here beneath the sward
>   Wet with dew."

But it seems that no letters were ever carved to mark the Steward's grave. He was not carried to Paisley to be laid among his fathers' dust. In the old churchyard of Rothesay there may be still seen, in a roofless, ruined chapel, hard by the parish church, the effigy of a knight recumbent in his armour, to which uncertain tradition has assigned the name of this Crusader.

SCOTLAND'S SORROW.

When Alexander our king was dead,
Whom Scotland led in love and le,
Away was wealth of ale and bread,
Of wine and wax, of game and glee.

Our gold was changéd into lede;
Christ, born unto virginity,
Succour Scotland and remede,
That stad is in perplexity!

Earliest Scottish Ballad.

THERE comes a significant pause in this early history of the Abbey. Was there silence among the oaks? Did the Benedictine psalms cease when that stately English army, in the pride and flush of its power, with its gay captains and its dauntless king, came into the kingless land? Or, did the sound of English axes ring among the great trees, in these long glades, this tangle of wood, which made ambush for their Scottish foes?

The story lingers still,—how, when John of Gaunt crossed the Tweed, the ring of eighty thousand axes was heard through the long summer day.

> "He gathered folk about him then
> Till he had near ten thousand men;
> And wood-axes gart with them take,
> For he thought he his men would make
> To hew Jedwort forest sa clene,
> That na tree suld therein be seen."

And why should the long oak-vistas of the Steward's fair Strathgryfe have any better fate when the English invade its borders? "My forest of Paisley" had been specially gifted to the monks by the munificent Walter, a century and a half agone. Its green glades were sweet; its masses of light and cool shade. Here the Clugniensian brothers, in their black garb, had walked and mused; being, we are prone to suppose, in the heat of this late era, all meditative men; to whom the oak-shadows were silences, and the lights serene gladnesses, like the glories round the brows of their saints.

Here the brothers of muscular vocation had come in the late autumn, when the acorns grew brown overhead, and the October storms had torn some scarred old branches from the big, red, half-stripped trees;—gathering wood joyously for the fires in the great locutorium; wood that must burn and crackle for many a guest—noble and pilgrim and hind—before Yule, and after.

Here the lord abbot had come to hunt the fallow deer, mounted as a prince should be, on some such fiery Spanish jennet as the cardinal rode with Matthew Dandolo—chasing for skin of deer to bind the books written in his Abbey; a chase which Charlemagne's decree had made always seemly for an abbot.

Half a century later, the Princess Marjory hunted in

SCOTLAND'S SORROW. 93

Walter's forest. So there was not an utter destruction, and fallow deer still browsed among the oaks. But the green shade was fainter than of old, and spread not so far nor so fair. Oaks from the royal Scottish forests were the frequent rewards of Edward First, to those who served him well in his wasteful journey through the land.

Twenty oaks to repair his church of Duffus were granted, from the forest of Longmorgan, to the canon of Elgin, who was Edward's host upon a time; fifty oaks to the Earl of Buchan, from the forests of Buchan and Kintore; two hundred oaks to Raufe le Chene, from the forests of Tarnaway and Longmorgan; fifty oaks from Selkirk, to the favoured abbot of Melrose; and twenty oaks to the abbot of Jedburgh, from a forest further north.* Such grants make it scarcely likely that Paisley would be exempted from tribute, in one of those proud progresses which the English king made through the land.

There were "upon his banner three leopards courant, of fine gold set on red; fierce, haughty, and cruel;—thus placed to signify that the king is dreadful, fierce, and proud to his enemies; for his bite is slight to none who inflame his anger; not but his kindness is soon rekindled towards such as seek his friendship, or submit to his power."

So wrote Walter of Exeter, a friar of the Order of St. Francis, whose story has been recently translated from its old Norman-French.

Walter went north with Edward and his army, in the summer of 1300; and saw, with a pleased fancy, "the good king and his household set forward against the Scots; not

* Pictorial History of Scotland.

in coats and surcoats, but on powerful and costly chargers; and that they might not be taken by surprise, well and securely armed. There were many rich caparisons embroidered in silks and satins, many a beautiful pennon fixed to a lance, and many a banner displayed; and afar off was heard the neighing of horses; mountains and valleys were everywhere covered with sumpter horses, and waggons with provisions and sacks and tents and pavilions; and the days were long and fine."

So, like a summer pleasure party, Friar Walter describes the enterprise.

And this is the *diram guerram*, of which the monks of Paisley write, crowding penitent, mournful, desolate, in some fragment of the ruined cloister, on which relentless Edward has done his worst now. Some blackened bit of lovely arch is left, some heap of shapeless stones, the old Norman doorway, and the fair southern transept window, and the deep shadowy mouldings above the west entrance to the nave. But the poor defenceless monks have scarce a shelter for their heads, nor their vassals any sanctuary left in the last hour of despair.

And there is a long vacancy in the list of abbots who ruled, which has a forlorn significance set in the history of the time.

The Abbot William, in the year 1225, "makes an agreement with Sir Hugh, the son of Reginald, about the lands of Auchincloss." Who this Sir Hugh might be, and what he agreed with Abbot William, is of no consequence now. But the date acquires a certain importance in the chequered annals of the monastery.

Immediately afterwards, there comes that long interregnum, when, for nearly a hundred years, no mention is made of any abbot of Paisley. Probably the Abbot William reigned for many years, and donations are still made to this Clugniensian house.

About this date, there is recorded a confirmation " by the Steward to Hugh the son of Reginald, of the land which Hugh his grandfather held of Baldwin de Bigres, the king's sheriff, and afterwards of Walden his son, and afterwards of Robert the son of Waldun, viz., the lands of Kilpeter."

Henricus de Irskin is witness to a grant which Ameleck, brother of Malduun, lord of Lennox, made to the church of Paisley, of the patronage of the church of Roseneath, in the year 1226.

In 1262, "the kirk of Colmanal, in Kintyre, was gifted to the monks of Paisley, by Walter, Earl of Monteath."

A donation, out of his lands of Mearns, is made by "John Maxwell, Lord of Nether-Pollock, in the year 1273."

"Sir Geoffrey Ross, son and heir to the late Geoffrey Ross, confirms that land in the village of Stewarton, from the grant of Sir James Ross, of happy memory, to the monastery of Paisley, in the year 1281."

These last grants are made in that palmy time when Alexander Third was king,—brighter, calmer days for Scotland than many future centuries would see. They are but a few gifts extracted from the wealth which was showered upon the Abbey. But no abbot is named from the year 1225, till, in the reign of Bruce, Andrew de Kelcow wears the impoverished mitre of Paisley.

We know in the ruined scriptoruim there was then no

parchment traced, no fishing by the monks in the river, no pearl-oysters gathered in the sand. And if the autumn woods grow thinner, so that every brown leaf is seen with separate distinctness against the Clydesdale sky, it was not the monks who thinned them; each old noble tree which fell, as so many have fallen, met its fate by an enemy's hand.

A gift in the reign of Bruce, by a certain master of Tarbart, who held forestry in the old Templar lands of Inchinnan, seems an unwitting comment on the English devastation of the fair monastic lands. The notice is of " Donaldus M'Gilchrist, dominus de Tarbart, who was a benefactor to the monastery of Paisley, by giving, to the monks and their successors, the privilege of cutting wood for supporting of the fabric of their monastery, in any part of his woods that lay most convenient to them; which deed he expresses to be made for the health of the souls of his ancestors, and for the welfare of his own soul."

SIR WILLIAM WALLACE.

O MELANCHOLY, linger here awhile!
O Music, Music, breathe despondingly!
O Echo, Echo, from some sombre isle!
Unknown, Lethean, sigh to us, O sigh!
Spirits in grief, lift up your heads and smile—
Lift up your heads, sweet spirits, heavily,
And make a pale light in your cypress glooms,
Tinting, with silver wan, your marble tombs.
Keats.

WITH a face of wonderful beauty; a frame of miraculous strength; a soul most devout and gentle; a will most resolute and bold—Wallace is the typical hero; and heroes, it must be owned, are *human*, and not *national*, and in all lands and ages, differ less than do the forest trees, or the little pale flowers about their roots.

The Greek Theseus, as he is limned by fancy, might sit nearly for the Scottish Wallace, with but the difference which the Christian light makes always round her sons—that nimbus of sunlit softness, of which Pagan art, and above all, Pagan biographical art, had a supreme unconsciousness. The strong self-abnegating spirit, seized in the nation's heart, becomes its own by right; and receives, from its broad humanity, whatever of grace or virtue is fair in this nation's thought.

And this lavishness of beauty is with perfect justice so assigned. It is but the law of compensation, which, as it cannot preserve those delicate individualities (idiosyncracies of strange preciousness, which must be always large in men who, in any way, stand out among their peers), has, by silent consent, agreed to give what it can, for what it cannot, and wrap these old heroes in a garment nearly universal, as the sculptors clothe them in the Roman toga, when they carve, in stone or marble, the symbolical outer man.

The passion of unselfish devotion, which, uncrowned, fought for a people of whom her own king despaired; which gave all, and won nothing but the deep, shrinking, fearful love of a nation in her last sorrow; which dared the high thought of evoking what latent, lingering hope or energy might still slumber in that down-trodden nation's heart,— this could have no reward; this transcends poetry.

No land so poor as to be without its heroes; yet scarcely to any other did Heaven send such as this. And many a silent century acknowledged the heroic altitude, by raising no memorial stone to this patriotism and tragedy.

It agrees with the unique devotion of Wallace, that brief success came to him, that final triumph never vulgarised the pure passion of his love, that to the end there was *giving* of that sublime temper which a few noble lives and deaths have proved to the world's need. It was not simply more dramatic that the hero should be a sacrifice, that the land's great extremity should culminate in this. Every great life, cut short, has an outcome of infinity; *escape* is the soul's refuge in its troubled thoughts of such. And *escape* is an upward thing, a bird's flight, with not the ether, but Eternity for its region and home.

So, perhaps, there came to the people, through its great sorrow and loss, some meed of higher elevation, some note of softer sound, which would linger through all the centuries—because of this dead hero. And hence the sweet pathos in their songs of every birk and burn and brae.

A pitiful poetical justice—obscuring and falsifying the purest pages in life—it is, which assigns happiness to the unselfish, and good to the good, and success to the brave. Those solitary examples, rising here and there in history, of human capability of devotion, which is its own necessity, are the true Divine poetry, and themselves the arraigners of justice so uncomprehending as would judge and assign their reward.

And among such lives we must place this old hero, who will have no monument but his own idealized life, kept, not commemorated, among other fair antiques.

Wallace, himself, was not a benefactor to the monks of Paisley. Yet memories of him naturally cluster round the Abbey walls. Elderslie, his birthplace and ancestral domain, lay on the very skirt of the monastic lands. The castle of Elderslie, neither strong nor notable, yet remembered in old records, was a near neighbour to the Abbey.

Perhaps the traditional reverence of Wallace for all

priests, rose from gentle recollections of some Clugniac brother on the Cart, who fulfilled his vocation so earnestly, with such devout purity and love, as made him the typical priest, who rose up in the fiercest battle between the soldier and his foe, and caused the surplice to be safer shield than any coat of ringed mail.

Robert Wallace, an ancestor of Sir William, witnessed the charter of foundation, granted to the monks of Paisley by the Steward in the reign of Malcolm Fourth. And, as might be expected, there linger, on these ancestral estates, tales, wonderful enough, of the old Scottish defender.

A stone near the top of a green hill, some few miles from the Abbey, was long marked as Wallace's chair, and invested in story nearly as miraculous as that of an early saint.

For it is said deep water circled the low green hill—waters where the shadows lay, and with reedy margins for lapwings, and shady, wet places for forget-me-not, and crowfoot, and maiden-hair. And when the little army of Scotland was dispersed before the great English host, and the bravest barons mustered their vassals no more, and Wallace was a lonely outlaw, in some wonderful way he covered the loch with turf, green turf from the moors, and retired to this little Barbrae.

They would make no conditions with him—the command was peremptory, "surrender at the king's pleasure," and the patriot had yielded at last. Messengers came to the governor that Wallace waited unarmed. And so they came and saw him seated alone on a stone, among the green grasses of that little Barbrae,—only between him and

the army, the faded turf from the moors. But when the soldiers at last went forward to take their prize, the turf sank down in the loch with the heavily armed men.

And so an English army was lost, and Wallace sought another retreat. The loch is a strange tradition. No trace of it now remains. But its meaning is the love of a people who, in no common way, could attribute to their chosen hero enough of wonder and romance. And so they must add to his prowess, wisdom and stratagem; and nature must pay tribute to him, and the turf moors and the loch do homage to the cherished memory of this uncrowned king.

But a little way from this, and still on the skirt of the Abbey, stood a more authentic memorial of Wallace.

It was a great oak, which bore his name to the last; said once to have sheltered the knight of Elderslie with three hundred of his men. The oak, a sylvan giant, with scant green clusters of leaves, and great arms twisted and torn—picturesque even without its story—survived, for nearly six centuries, the hero it had sheltered in extremity. It was uprooted in the storm of 1856, on such a night as lives long in men's memories.

And in a poetical light, the history of the tree ended well. Symbolists we all are;—symbolists through unconscious acknowledgment of restraint; of the meeting of the finite with the infinite; of the dim perception of truths, which humanity cannot articulate; of the setting of material things and processes for immeasurable spiritual realities.

And that inherent love of symbolism which penetrates the human heart, was satisfied with the tragedy of nature, which, a second time, seemed to link the fate of the oak of Elderslie with the thirteenth century hero.*

An oak which stood in Torwood forest, and perished through old age some seventy or eighty years ago, was storied, as indeed so many oaks have been, with the same legend. For on the July night which preceded the battle of Falkirk, Wallace slept his watchful soldier-sleep among the green leaves of the tree. And among the same branches, after that disastrous fight, it is said he found a safe concealment from the search of the victorious English,—a suggestion of the human interests which abide in old oaks.

But perhaps the closest link of connection between Wallace and the Abbey of Paisley lies in a mere tradition, which is yet very fair to hold. It has no semblance of authority,—an appropiation all the same, discarding even the minstrel's own protest—

> "I can nocht speak of sic divinity;
> To clerks I will let all sic matters be."

This couplet seems to mean that he was no monk at all, only a simple and unlettered man, who sang from his full heart what the old men and woman round their ingle-neuks had told for nearly two centuries. But later writers have taken pains to rescue the blind minstrel from the imputation of ignorance, which his own modesty has brought upon his fame. They have discovered as a certainty that Blind Harry knew the Latin language—which discovery is almost

* A scion of this old oak was tenderly preserved, and flourishes now, in hopeful youth, in the "Fountain Gardens" of Paisley.

equivalent to that of his belonging to a religious order. And it is not strange that the Abbey, which lay on the edge of Elderslie, should, failing all certain knowledge, claim the singer with the hero he sang.

Besides, Blind Harry himself confesses much of what he relates to be taken from an old book which was written by Master Blair. Master Blair was Wallace's faithful chaplain through the years of battle and hiding; and, after the tragical end, became a monk of Dunfermline. Here he spent the cloistered hours in writing all he knew of the patriot; of his childhood and his manhood; of his thoughts and his deeds and his daring, as none could know better than the chosen confessor and friend. The book has long ago perished; but it was known to Blind Harry, as it was only probable to be known if he himself were a monk.

> "Master Johne Blair was oft in that message
> A worthy clerk, baith wise and rich sawage;
> Levyt before he was in Paris town.
> He was the man that principal undertuk,
> That first compylit in dyte the Latin buk
> Of Wallace's life,—most worthy of renown."

From this sprang the long, rude song, which has come down four centuries, bearing its portentous title: "The Acts and Deeds of the most Famous and Valiant Champion, Sir William Wallace, Knight of Ellerslie, and Governor of Scotland." And hero and singer both, though linked but slenderly with Paisley, yet claim a treasured place among the memories which cluster round its old Abbey walls.

For the deep religious sentiment of Wallace has been preserved through all the troubled times,—his tender care of the church, his devout submission to her, and how he prayed to die with the psalter before his eyes, in that last tragic hour—the saddest in Scottish story.

Had this religious sentiment been nursed and tended in the school of the Paisley monks? The vocation of the true Benedictine was no less to teach than to pray. It was more than likely that Wallace had learnt, in his boyish days, among the Clugniensian cloisters, all the lore which became a Scottish knight.

There is nothing said of this. The hero is not once named. The memory of his family is kept in the monks' page. But Sir William, in song and story, is kept yet more steadfastly.

WALTER AND MARJORY.

> THY worth, sweet friend, is far above my gifts:
> Therefore to equal it, receive my heart.
> If for these dignities thou be envied,
> I'll give thee more; for, but to honour thee:
> Is the king pleased with kingly regiment?
> Fear'st thou thy person? thou shalt have a guard:
> Want'st thou gold? go to my treasury:
> Would'st thou be lov'd and feared? receive my seal.
> Save or condemn, and in our name command
> Whatso thy mind affects and fancy likes.
> Christopher Marlowe.
>
> The shadowy kings of Banquo's fated line,
> Through the dark cave in gleamy pageant pass'd.
> Collins.

HERE is no finer picture in the chivalrous annals of Scotland, than that of a June daybreak in the year 1314, when the king's army was gathered on the banks of the Bannock burn.

There are always elements in victory, which lessen our pleasure in contemplating it. There blends a vulgar pride with any great triumph, even where the cause is good, which sensibly lessens our sympathy, or the satisfaction which such sympathy yields. It will not be more frequently chosen by the painter for his canvas, or by the poet for his song, than will the still hour of noon, when the sun is in the zenith, and the shadows are shortest, and the light unsubdued. For purposes purely artistic, defeat is more precious than victory. Possibly because, under defeat, there lurk possibilities of rarer virtue; and that, in our heart of hearts, we hold in profoundest admiration those strong passivities, that endurance, that sublimity of patience, which only sorrow or disappointment can evoke from the human soul.

Flodden, and not Bannockburn, has filled the land with song.

This moment in the June morning is not that of victory—but of the hush which precedes it—the tension of uncertainty and hope. There is no elation, no assurance, here. The Abbot of Inchaffray, bare-footed, in the grey dawn, holds the cross before the kneeling soldiers who thus prepare for death.

The priest confesses the penitent; and in that devotion and stillness, which the gayer, more versatile enemy misinterprets, cannot understand, there is the presage of success; the unconscious, unaccepted presage.

And when their prayers are said, and their banners are unfurled, and their ranks are close, and the morning sun is reddening over the strath, a ceremony, not religious, is performed in Bruce's camp; and Walter, the young Lord Steward, is knighted with others of his peers. It was something to receive the acolade from a knight so famous as the king.

Walter was scarcely eighteen, but commanded the left wing with Douglas, and bore himself so nobly that he won the praise of Bruce. Many honours which are oftener reserved for age, were bestowed on the young Steward. He was appointed "to keep Berwick-upon-Tweed;" when, in the year after Bannockburn, that border town, so hard to take or hold, was recovered from the English soldiers. And "to keep Berwick-upon-Tweed," was a feat which the bravest old noble, on either side of the marches, was proud enough to perform.

Bruce could do him no greater honour, but by giving him the hand of Marjory,—Marjory his only daughter, and, at that time, the heiress to his crown. Buchanan makes his curt comment on king and princess both:—" It was right they should choose for her a husband worthy of their princess and the crown; for it was deemed more equitable that a girl should have a husband chosen for her by the nation, than that the nation should have a king chosen for them by a girl."

From which, we infer that young Walter was the people's choice, as well as the king's; whether he was the choice of Marjory, who was but a girl, it mattered not.

The dowery of the princess will appear from a royal charter, dated at Berwick, and granted to the Steward in the year 1318.

"Robert, by the grace of God, king of Scots: Be it "known to you that I have given to our dear and trusty "Walter, High Steward of Scotland, with our daughter "Marjory in free marriage, the barony of Bathgate, the

"barony of Rathœ, with the land of Riccarton, and the
"lands of Barns, near Linlithgow; and the lands which are
"called Le Brome, near the loch thereof; and the lands
"of Bonnington, Kingalach, and Gallowhill, near Linlithgow;
"and the annual revenue out of the carse of Stirling, which
"the abbot and canons of the monastery of the Holy Cross
"of Edinburgh hold of us; and an annual revenue, to be
"raised from the lands of Kingpont and Edina, in the
"sheriffdom of Roxburgh; to be held by the same Walter
"and his heirs, to be begotten between him and the said
"Marjory, our daughter."

Of the castle of Renfrew, whither Walter carried his bride, there is no trace now, nor any memory of Walter. Crawford finds it necessary to quote from the monastic charters, even to prove the existence of this old castle and barony.

"Walter the son of Alan, Steward of the king of
"Scotland, for the love of God and the salvation of his own
"body and soul, gives the church of the Holy Trinity of
"Dunfermline, in perpetual alms, one full toft in his burgh
"of Renfrew."

The grant of James, High Steward, "to Stephen the son of
"Nicolas, for his homage and service, that whole land which
"was given to Patrick of Selvinland; which lands lie near
"the town of Renfrew, where the water of Gryfe runs into
"the water of Clyde: for the said Stephen and his heirs,
'giving us and our successors, every year, twelve pennies

"of silver, in name of fee-farm. At our manor of Renfrew, "before these witnesses :—

"THOMAS RANDOLPH.   "ROBERT BOYD.
"WILLIAM FLEMING of Baruqhan.   "FINLAY of Houston, baronets.
"ROBERT of Conningsburgh.   "GILES of Eastwood."
"ROBERT SEMPLE, Steward of the barony of Renfrew.

This manor of Renfrew, as tradition says, stood high, and was near the river's edge. It had round it "a large and deep fosse," and a pleasant prospect of land.

Here Marjory came a royal bride, in her silken or velvet kirtle, in her wimple garnished with its gold and pearls, in her brilliant and glad youth.

Marjory was a gay spirit. The fervour of her father's nature found scope in battles and sieges. But Marjory could not gird on a sword, and ride with her young Steward, or with the Lords Randolph and Douglas, on forays through Tynedale and Cumberland. There is, indeed, the "Fair Maiden Lilliard," the border heroine, who went out to battle with her clan, and lies buried on Ancram Moor. But Marjory was a king's daughter, yet not a queen to rule her own destiny, as a crowned queen might.

And, perhaps, this border Lilliard—her sweet name notwithstanding—had a sterner heart within her than the Princess Marjory. Marjory's spirit, it seems, found its full content in the forest. The love of hunting is the one passion of this mother and daughter of kings, the memory of which descends to posterity. Marjory is the Scottish Diana, dim enough among the sylvan shades, with her tall handsome beauty, and the bow and arrow in her hand.

Standing, as this princess does, at the cradle of a long dynasty, one reasonably asks concerning her, many questions which are not answered. Scottish annalists, at this period, were busy over graver matters. With constant peril on the borders, a wasted kingdom to restore, and excommunication and famine threatening them on either hand, those delicate household touches which might show the bride Marjory's heart, and the king's, and the young Steward's, are not to be hoped for, nor sought. Yet, notwithstanding, one does seek, and from little takes much; and, in her strong, simple youth, makes a queen of Marjory.

The people will have her so—the people in Walter's old barony. A century ago they pointed to an ancient cross, and called it "Queen Blearie's Stane," and told the story of its having been so named.

Marjory, on an autumn day, was following the sport she loved, chasing the fallow deer in her husband's oak-forest of Paisley, when she was thrown from her horse, not far from her own castle, and lifted, with dead young face, from among the drifted leaves.

They raised the cross of stone on the spot when the princess fell. Long after every vestige of the oak forest was gone, among the low tufts of broom and wild roses, stood this old solitary cross. If ever inscription were carved upon it, it was long worn away; but the fond tradition of its naming lingered tenaciously round it, not to be dispelled by any reasoning that Marjory was not a queen.

After having been preserved for four centuries, the cross was demolished. A hundred years ago, when Pennant wrote, part of it formed the lintel of a neighbouring barn door; a vandalism not to be wondered at, when the Abbey itself was despoiled, and its images, even then, lay broken in the open cloister among the rank, neglected grass. Nor does it equal the sacrilege perpetrated in a nook in England, where the stone coffin of a daughter of Edward First lay, for two hundred years, in the bed of a little brook, and was used as a watering trough for the horses of the farmers round.

Marjory was buried in Paisley. She had been scarcely a year married.

A few months later, Walter gifted the church of Largs, for the salvation of the soul of Marjory, to the monastery where she lay.

"In the chartulary of Paisley, in the reign of Robert Bruce, Robert Semple is witness to the donation of the church of Largs, which Walter, High Steward of Scotland, father of Robert Second, gave to the monks of Paisley, for the health of his soul, and for the soul of Marjory Bruce, his deceased wife—1318." *

Walter did not cherish his sorrow, as the husband of Eschine had done. He did not retire to the cloister, but went back to the busy world, and married a second wife, whose name, however, remains unrecorded.

Two years after the death of Marjory, Walter is commanding Berwick; and it is St. Mary's Eve, and the English are round the walls. And history tells us how his young, dauntless bravery (for he was not twenty-five), his generous kindness, and his cheerful heart, inspirited all his men; for in the deadliest danger, his presence was always

* Crawford's History.

seen, bringing victory, and making despair an impossibility. So that, at length, the English were fain to go back to their own country, and leave to the young Steward the castle which he held for the king.

A few months later than this, the Steward is at Aberbrothock, gathered with eight earls and thirty-one barons, to sign that loyal protest against the displeasure of the church, which reads so earnestly trustful, so passionately and pathetically true.

The letter reminds pope John the Twenty-Second, of how a long line of one hundred and thirteen kings had ruled in Scotland, none disputing their sway; of how St. Andrew himself had converted this mountain land; and how the former popes had ever been tender of it, as being under the patronage of the brother of St. Peter.

"Under such free protection did we live," continue the Scottish lords, who defer to pope John, although they could defy the Plantaganet, "until Edward, king of England, and father of the present monarch, covering hostile designs under guise of friendship and alliance, made an invasion of our country at the moment when it was without a king, and attacked an honest and unsuspicious people, then little experienced in the arts of war.

"The insults which the prince has heaped upon us, the slaughters and devastations which he has committed, his imprisonment of prelates, his burning of monasteries, his spoliations and murder of priests, and the other enormities of which he has been guilty, can be rightly judged, or even conceived, by none but an eye witness. From these innumerable evils have we been freed, under the help of that God who woundeth and maketh whole, by our most valiant prince and king, Lord Robert, who, like a second Maccabeus or Joshua, hath cheerfully endured all labour and weariness, and exposed himself to every species of danger and privation, that he might rescue from the hands of the enemy his ancient people and rightful inheritance; him, Divine Providence, and the right of succession, according to those laws and customs which we will maintain to the death, as well as the common consent of us all, have made our prince and king. To him are we bound, both by his own merit and by the law of the land, and to him as the saviour of our people, and the guardian of our liberty, are we determined to adhere.

"But if he should desist from what he has begun, and should show an inclination to subject us, or our kingdom, to the king of England, or to his people, then we declare that we will use our utmost effort to expel him from the throne as our enemy, and the subverter of his own and of our right, and we will chuse another king to reign over us, who will be able to defend us. For as long as a hundred Scotsmen are left alive, we will never be subject to the dominion of England. It is not for glory, riches, or honour, that we fight, but for that liberty, which no good man will consent to lose but with his life.

"Wherefore, most reverend father, we humbly pray, and from our hearts beseech your Holiness to consider that you are the vicegerent of Him, with whom there is no respect of persons, Jews or Greeks, Scots or English; and, turning your paternal regard upon the tribulations brought upon us and upon the Church of God by the English, to admonish the king of England that he should be content with what he possesses, seeing that England of old was enough for seven, or more, kings, and not to disturb our peace in this small country, lying on the utmost boundaries of the habitable earth, and whose inhabitants desire nothing but what is their own . . .

"If your Holiness do not sincerely believe these things, giving too implicit faith to the tales of the English, and, on this ground, shall not cease to favour them in their design for our destruction, be well assured that the Almighty will impute to you that loss of life, that destruction of human souls, and all those various calamities, which our inextinguishable hatred against the English, and their warfare against us, must necessarily produce.

"Confident that we now are, and shall ever, as in duty bound, remain obedient sons to you as God's vicegerent, we commit the defence of our cause to that God, as the great King and Judge, placing our confidence in Him, and in the firm hope that He will endow us with strength, and confound our enemies; and may the Almighty long preserve your Holiness in health."

And so in this Abbey near the sea, with no thought of infallible judgment, but solemnly reminding the pope of the sin which may lie at his door, the little land casts its sorrows with all humility before him,—"this small country, lying on the utmost boundaries of the habitable earth."

Pope John Twenty-Second was a poor umpire to go to in such extremity. Pope John, busied and concerned with the rivalries of two emperors, himself inflicting such sorrows as the Scottish barons prayed him to avert. In the Rhineland and the Papal states they offer no such prayers. Tauler, filled with a passionate piety, retires into himself, making no revolt nor protest, but silently drawing round him a few pure, fervent souls. Tauler and Eckhart, and Ruysbroeck and Nicolas of Suso, are the group of charmed mystic names, contemporaneous with the eight earls and thirty-one barons who sign, in the Scottish Abbey, this appeal to the power of the pope.

This grave remonstrance, this solemn appeal to right, rising, from a little land, in the midst of her great perplexities, was not much to the subtle pope John, with imperial Frederick at Aix-la-Chapelle to support against imperial Louis; and a battle imminent, and an issue uncertain; clergy to instruct; an interdict to proclaim; and a secret antagonistic brotherhood rising up, an unspoken rebuke, before all Christendom.

But the remonstrance is valuable indeed, as proving the temper of those strong old barons who gathered with so bold a front round Bruce's throne.

One of this resolute group of Lords, is Walter the High Steward. He appears at later intervals in raids with Randolph and Douglas across the Cumberland border, and then is seen no more.

Walter died at Bathgate, in the year 1328,—one year earlier than Bruce, and eleven years after Marjory. His remains were carried to the Abbey on the banks of the Cart,—a desolate and stricken place,—and laid, among its ruined splendours, by the side of his royal wife.

Barbour, in his rhythmical Life of Bruce, records the sorrow of the land, when Walter, the High Steward, was laid in his early grave.

> "When long time they their dule had made,
> The corpse to Paisley have they had,
> And there with great solemnity,
> And with great dule eirded was he."

And, when many years later, the son of Walter and Marjory ascended the throne of Scotland as Robert Second, the first Steward King, the prophecy to Banquo, uttered by the witches on Forres heath, found its fulfilment.

KING AND QUEEN.

———o———

"HERE rest her well—the knotted grass,
    It gleameth not above the queen;
Nor any peasant feet may pass
    And leave a track where they have been.

The daisies, that once grew so fine,
    Are gathered sharply into stone;—
The mother of a royal line,
    She lieth tranquil—not alone.

The cowl'd head, bent above its book,
    And passing ever to and fro,
May sometime spare a thought—a look,
    For this pale queen that sleepeth so."

A QUEEN'S grave! The first is made in the Abbey when Robert had been three years on the throne. The endless Border warfare was then at its wildest. Percy was lord warden of the English Eastern Marches: The Gordens forayed Northumberland; and the men of Northumberland took swift revenge, and encamped on the starlit summer nights among the Lammermuirs.

"Henry Percy, Earl of Northumberland, a high spirited gentleman, who was then lord warden of the Eastern Marches, indignant at the devastation of his estates, collected above seven thousand men, and encamped near Dunse, a village only remarkable as being the birthplace of John Scotus, surnamed the subtile. The countrymen and shepherds, armed only with rattles, such as they use to frighten the deer and cattle, which wander everywhere wild in that district, assembled in the Lammermuir hills, in the neighbourhood of the village, during the night. . . . With this species of rattle, having raised a tremendous noise on the hills which overhang Dunse, the horses of the English, terrified at the sound, broke loose from their bindings, and running about disorderly, became the prey of the countrymen. In the army, all was confusion and calling to arms; and believing the enemy to be close upon them, they passed a sleepless night. Discovering the mistake in the morning, and many of their draught horses missing, like fugitives, they retreated six miles,—for the village is that distance from the English borders,—leaving their baggage behind. . . . In the western borders, John Johnstone, likewise, acquired both plunder and glory; he so harassed his neighbours, by short but frequent incursions, that he did them not less damage than greater armies are accustomed to do."

Should we expect, among such crowded paragraphs, any more than the brief notice, "Euphemia, the queen, daughter of the Earl of Ross, died?" The monastic chronicles supply what wider historians omit, and tell us how Queen Euphemia was carried to Paisley Abbey, and there laid beneath the high altar among her husband's kin. It brings into unquiet history that one quiet thought, which peaceful death and burial offer through all glory and all strife.

The figure of Queen Euphemia, graven on her own seal, represents her under an open canopy, surrounded by heraldic devices;—a slender woman with a slender wand in her hand; a saddened face without beauty under classical folds of hair; simple, and few lines of drapery, which fall from her head to her feet, yet not serene lines, but unquiet, like the face of the queen;—not wholly a pleasing figure; yet, perhaps, she was happy and fair, and was falsified, unkindly, by the graver on the royal seal.

Elizabeth, the second wife of Robert, found the same sweet cloister resting-place. Desolately beautiful it must have been, with the vagrant winds coming in among the ruined pillars, through the long, roofless nave;—a place most fit for graves, yet where the monks were clinging still, in steadfast sorrow round their altars and their spoiled shrines.

As for Robert, the king, it is said he lived much beside the sea at his own Dundonald in Kyle, where the Abbey stretched her arms. "A comely tall man," says Froissart, "but with red-bleared eyes of the colour of sandal-wood. And it soon became evident that he himself preferred a quiet life to war; he had, however, nine sons who loved arms." His quiver, so bravely provided, the old man might well rest.

His reign is storied most of all by that chivalrous battle on the borders, which singularly the English and the Scottish ballads have preserved with equal pride.

"Of all the battles that have been described in this history," says the gay Froissart again, "great and small, this of which I am now speaking was the best fought." And "Chevy Chase" and "Otterbourne," on either side of the border, have preserved the romantic memory of that purple August day.

Robert was then an old man in the last autumn of his life,

> "When news was brought to Edinbro',
> Where Scotland's king did reign,
> That brave Earl Douglas suddenly
> Was with an arrow slain.
>
> O! heavy news, the king did say,
> Scotland can witness be,
> I have not any captain more
> Of such account as he."

But this is an English version of the king's dolour and extremity. Among the nine sons who loved war, the king had valiant and wise soldiers, as much trusted by his people, and feared by his foes, as the Douglas of Otterbourne.

In the spring of the year which followed, Robert Second died at Dundonald, and was buried in the Abbey of Paisley, beside his two queens, and his father, Walter, the Steward, and his mother, the Princess Marjory.

MONKS AS HISTORIANS.

PARCOUREZ l'histoire du vᵉ au xviᵉ siècle; c'est la théologie qui possède et dirige l'esprit humain; toutes les opinions sont, empreintes de théologie; les questions philosophiques, politiques, historiques, sont toujours considerées sous un point de vue théologique. L'église est tellement souveraine dans l'ordre intellectuel, que même les sciences mathématiques et physiques sont tenues de se soumettres à ses doctrines. L'esprit théologique est en quelque sort le sang qui à coulé dans les veines du monde Européen jusq' u' à Bacon et Descartes. Pour la première fois, Bacon en Angleterre, et Descartes en France, ont jeté l'intelligence hors des voies de la théologie. *Guizot.*

THERE is an intuition, a certain inner sense, by which we verify history; not in its details, but in its spirit, which is the true history. Details may contradict and falsify each other, yet in moods of pure thought, the present possess the past, by right of clairvoyant sympathy. A glance of quick sunshine, a word, an attitude, an act, flashing down the dim centuries, wins electrical response. We perceive! we comprehend!

This vision, which is moral, not mental, defies analytical treatment. Its source is in that human unity which suffers pain, throbs with pride, exults, though less intensely, with joy, over the being and doing of those yet removed by ages and continents; which does project its true self to the very heart of things, by intellect discerned dimly, and judged of only from far.

Imagination, not creative, but conceptive, is itself sympathy; and always, from its very nature, will embody in truest life those floating intangible forms, whose vagueness irritates the intellect, and provokes from it unwarranted strictures, definitions, speculations, generalisations. For wherever history recedes so far as to elude the tests of fact, it comes under the shelter of other laws, more benign, more merciful; laws none the less. Precisely where intellectual research becomes doubtful and thankless labour, does the moral feeling appropriate, as a perfectly inalienable right, the sphere thus tacitly abandoned to it, and which is properly its own.

There is a "divination of antiquity," a certain perception of truth, which is akin to faith, inasmuch as its knowledge is founded, not on apparent fact, but on that inner sense which is its own authority, and yet may never seek to be authority to any other mind.

The same faculty is exercised constantly in life. The closest analogy exists between biography and history. A quick flash of insight to character surprises us through dull eyes. It is direct, instantaneous, quite unmistakably true. No premises of knowledge here; no process of mental dissection; no acute analysis of motive to word, or action, or glance. It is a synthetic result in a mind unconscious of logic; the diviner is not shrewd, or only rarely so. And the surprise of delight glances on us like an unseen water.

The trial of years and friendship only had gained for us as much.

It is a distinct endowment, a "vision and faculty divine," a sort of undeveloped poetry with the element of sympathy interpenetrating every other. For it is the vocation of sympathy to interpret the unexpressed; to fill in, by intuitive knowledge, the left out lines of life.

Thus we must read history, in many of its most inviting pages, conscious that no research can ever retrieve for us the whole. The *whole*, the *unity*, the *entirety*—that is lost. We canot bring back the blooms of the summers faded long ago.

Perhaps a few people who love nature well, and have acquired the innocent habit of creating some second delights; of living again carefully, thoughtfully, the simple pleasures of their quiet hours,—have found how hard a matter it is to re-create a sky.

Perfume, outline, colour, come back, obedient to your sense. You know above what black bough of fir the Seven Sisters trembled out; you can yet count the wistful shadows which lay, green and brown, in the loch; before your eye, rises vividly that strange, beautiful, grotesque tower, which made you believe time a painter, picking out his lights skilfully, deepening in his shades, all and purely for effect, and to please his artistic soul; again, on that old, old wind, the odour is carried past, which you do not recall as a sensation, but as a sentiment, a thought, lost when it was born. But of the sky on which you looked as the happiest dream of all, can you recall the fairness? can you recall the gleam?

You can recall it none. No matter. Lift your eyes. Is there pale silver above you? Is there evanescent green? Are there bars of black and molten gold, fervid, burning, like youth's thoughts when they learn the first sorrowful meaning of *necessity?* When will hope, desire, faith, gleam into deadliest brightness ere life's first ideal sets?

This is enough. In such a sky you shall set your Seven Sisters; your tower of which time is so tender; your loch with the motley reflection; your black, wizened, elden fir. There is no inharmoniousness in it, with any landscape in your memory. The same heaven embraces all. Its infinity comforts you.

And in each individual personality, there is surely the same infinity,—an infinity which is for antiquity what to-day's sky is for the flowers and green sward of a life half a century old. If, through the vividness of our own intuitions and thoughts and imaginings, we cannot read the early centuries by the rushlight, in monkish fingers held, we are not likely to have lost much of either wisdom or delight.

The monks have falsified history, it is said, no less than the wandering minstrels; the monks in service to their church, as the minstrels to their chief and clan. But there happen to be no other chroniclers by whose records to correct those; to the ancient singers and the preachers, we owe all that our archives yield. When the sorrows and triumphs of the people had ceased in spontaneous song, when the harpers no more were historians, the pale-fingered monks took the pen. To the patient and faithful work of the old Benedictine Scriptorium, the learning (for all learning and genius the monasteries absorbed), the tireless devotion and labour, which had no reward on earth, which was all for God and the future, every treasure of the past is owed.

That the monks wrote simply in the light of their own time, that their faith is credulity, that their chronicles are full of such miracles as force even unwilling smiles, will not lessen the pleasure, and scarcely the confidence of the quietly receptive reader who brings to them that divining sympathy, which is, as the sky's infinity, to all the landscapes of time.

How the holy oil of Bishop Aiden calmed the sea for Eanfleda, the Kentish princess who sailed a bride to King Osuiu; how a light so bright, so sweet, that it filled with reverence all who saw, rested, like a glory, above the relics of King Osuald, as they lay in the open starlight before the convent gate of Beardaneu; of how sweet music was heard all night, played by unseen fingers, when the soul of the nun Earcongota was set free from its prison bonds,—these, and an hundred such legends, will not once disturb the faith of one who loves antiquity, its quietness and its grey; who loves to brood in the daybreak of his own culture and religion, among the wreathed mists and gossamers of that early and fair dawn.

Here he becomes a symbolist, not such as Rhaban Maur, nor Jean d'Avranches, but in a fashion of his own. His thought will scarcely stay to dissociate the legendary from the true, for both are rich, both are beautiful, and suggestive of more than enough.

That intuitive sense which discerns all kindred humanities,

which perceives the meanings unexpressed, or not guessed of, or wrongly interpreted, as the old rhabdomantist's rod discovered the clear hidden well; that quick sympathetic instinct which finds rightness in the heart of wrong,—it, and perhaps it only, reads clearly, and with no offence, the unfamiliar credulity of the mediæval chronicles.

Of how many things besides these must we cast the hard frame-work from us, and keep the essence only, the pure and sweet spirit which has struggled with hard necessities, with conditions foreign to its life.

Thought has its cycles. Sometime we shall go back, not to the mediæval superstitions, but, let us fervently hope, to some of the self-renunciation, the humility, the receptivity of soul, the work without thought of reward, the patience, the reverence, the submission, which these old historians teach.

And so we must follow the footprints of the devoted priest who gathered back what he could to the empty archives of Scotland.

CHRONICUS CLUGNIENSE.

———o———

IT is not from his form in which we trace
Strength, joined with beauty, dignity with grace;
That man, the master of this globe, derives
His right of empire over all that lives.
That form, indeed, the associate of a mind
Vast in its powers, ethereal in its kind;
That form, the labour of Almighty skill,
Framed for the service of a free-born will,
Asserts precedence, and bespeaks control,
But borrows all its grandeur from the soul.
Here is the state, the splendour and the throne,—
An intellectual kingdom all her own;
For her, the memory fills her ample page,
And truths poured down from every distant age.
                                                    Cowper.

SOMEWHERE on the east of the cloister, stood the Scriptorium of the Abbey. The monks of Paisley, it is said, were famed for their learning and industry;—a statement which we must take upon trust, like so many others in our history. Edward First, and long afterwards Cromwell, did their work as well as could be done. And nearly all vestiges of this industry, with that of most

Scottish Abbeys, have perished in hostile fires, or with the ships of King Charles Second.

There is no William of Malmesbury, no Venerable Bede, preserved for authoritative reference in involved questions of the times. Gildas, the royal Scot, the Herodotus of Britain, lived and died, happily for him, under the shadow of Glastonbury. But of the old monastic scribes and illuminators who wrote on the stained vellum—histories, gospels, psalters, the lives of the saints, the hymns of Fortunatus and St. Gregory—as they must have done, being Benedictines in the Scriptorium of Paisley—only one relic remains. This is the Black Book, or Chronicus Clugniense.

A manuscript, supposed to be the original of this *Chronicus*, is preserved in the royal library at St. James's. An authentic copy is reported to have been burned at Holyrood Abbey. "It was during the English usurpation," says Crawford, with significance distinctly sorrowful, and as if the affix of a date would be a species of tautology. But more exact annalists name the year 1543, which was by no means during any usurpation of the English. For the Earl of Arran then governed Scotland,—and the dowager queen, Mary of Guise, and the Earls Cassilis, Angus, Lennox and Glencairn, were filling all the northern arena. And withdrawal of the baby-queen's hand from the son of Henry of England, had brought that fiery king's armies north by land and sea.

John Knox's account of how the fleet came to Leith, and of the strange supineness of all the people there and around, is as picturesque as picturesque can be.

"Men assembled to gaze upon the ships, some to the castle-hill, some to the mountains and other places eminent; but there was no question, 'With what forces shall we resist?' And when the Admiral's flat boat shot out, and sounded from Granton hills, till by East-Leith, and there was divers opinions as to what this meant, still no credit was given to any that would say, 'They minded to land.' And so passed every man to his rest, as if the ships had been a guard for their defence." Then dawned the Sabbath May morning, and what was meant was plain enough. For "they ordered the ships so that a galley or two laid their snouts to the hills."

And the burning of Edinburgh lighted up the Braid hills and Borough moor, and was seen exultingly from the Frith, where the grey May mists were gathering. The Abbey of Holyroodhouse was wrapped in the general flame, and among all its other treasures perished the Chronicus Clugniense. Happily only a copy. The original Chronicus was left in existence for that abundant disputation, which occasionally honours the memory of men and of their works.

It is said to have been got by Lambert out of Sir Robert Spottiswoode's library, and given by him to Colonel Fairfax, who carried it off with him to England, in that second desolation of the Scottish archives.

And now comes the disputation; for Camden openly declares that all the Scottish historians are beholden to the Scotichronicon. He allows no peculiar Tree of Knowledge even to the Clugniac monks, who lived and wrote and laboured among the white orchards of the Cart.

And Stillingfleet, with bolder pen, is sceptical of the separate existence of any Black Book of either Paisley or Scone. Transcripts of John of Fordun might be made in many a Scriptorium—in that of Paisley among the others. And is that all?

Crawford will by no means admit so much. He struggles for the Chronicle, as eagerly as the Greeks for the body of Hector. "I shall give a few sentences of each," he says, "and then let the reader judge." "There was one Gathelus, (saith Fordun, in his Scotichronicon, L. I., C. 9,) son of Nicolus, one of the kings of Greece, who, having displeased his father, was banished his country, and went into Egypt, where he was married to Scota, the king's daughter . . . After the destruction of Pharaoh in the Red Sea, Gathelus is chosen king, but discontents arising, he and his wife Scota, with their company, put to sea, and made westward."

And so, not from the Book of Paisley, but an abridgment of it—(which in fair comparison ought not to be)—he quotes how this Gathelus "brought with him from Egypt the fatal marble chair which was first transported to Ireland, then to Albion, now called Scotland; wherein all their kings were crowned, until the time of Edward First, who transported the whole ancient regal monuments of Scotland, with the fatal marble chair, to Westminster, where it remaineth to this day.

The Scots shall brook that realm as native ground,
If wierds fail not wherever this chair is found."

The reasoning which from such quotations infers the independent source of the two chronicles, is somewhat difficult to follow; except that in a preceding sentence, *Cecrops*, and not *Nicolus*, is named as the father of Gathelus.

Gathelus, the son-in-law of Pharaoh, sailing westward and northward, and becoming the founder of the Scottish monarchy, is a picture over which we smile. But the monks, educated in wonder, with their grave and careful pens, wrote it down for history. Some youthful Clugniac, indeed, with a humour which would not be extinguished, even by the scapulary of his order, might give a naive turn to the tales of the Senachines, or less antique legends of the saints, even as a modern wit will hang his jest on the very science reared on facts which all the world owns. But for the most part we must believe that the annals of these monks were written in serene good faith. Scepticism was not a growth of the mediæval centuries.

As to the learned controversy for or against the originality of the Chronicus Clugniense,—Aikman, in his notes to Buchanan's history, makes a compromise which we may suppose to be just. The Black Book of Paisley, he admits, was a transcript, but it was also a continuation of Fordun. This granted, it is more than admissible that we take what glance we can of old John of Fordun and his "Scotichronicon."

The land was breathing again, in a space of freedom and peace, after the long, sorrowful desolation which Edward First of England had made. And, looking round, she found how solitary she was left in the midst of the ages—the marble chair of Gathelus gone—her treasured archives spoiled. There was no longer scroll nor volume to prove her kin with the past; that immortal kinship precious to nations, as to individual souls. For both alike recoil from loneliness, and are fain to strengthen their humanity by multiplying their ancestors, singling them out and embracing them from all the crowd of shades.

Besides, the archives of Scotland had been rich with peculiar wealth. The kings of whom they told, were no modern race, like the Norman dynasty of England. Their royalty had no beginning. It reached unto the darkness. The Bruce who bore the sceptre of Scotland, in A.D. 1314, was a child of those early Pharaohs who ruled when time was young.

The thought partook of the sublime. Yet annals there were almost none, to prove this far-reaching kith and kin with the first civilisations of the world.

Ideas group themselves in centuries. Froissart was in his zenith. He was riding with kings and princes over every famous battle-field in Europe, a gay poet and courtier, a Trouvere; present at every tournament, at every pass of arms; preparing, with a keen observation, and an ever gay and ready wit, his brilliant "Chroniques de Franc, d'Angleterre, d'Ecosse, d'Espagne, de Bretagne, de Gascogne, Flandres et lieux d'alentour."

Froissart had been in Scotland in the year 1364. John of Fordun may himself have seen him while he was the guest of King David—then but lately married to the beautiful plebeian Queen Margaret—who disgusted his proud nobles, the Stewards most of all. John Barbour, already famous for his epic of the Bruce, and living in court favour, was archdeacon of Aberdeen. John of Fordon was a secular priest, and a canon of the same cathedral,—an obscure man, whom his contemporaries scarcely so much as name.

But a brave and patient idea seems to have filled the priest's soul; perhaps a devout emulation of the worldly gallant Froissart. Not on mettled war-steed, in the glitter of proved mail; not like him to gather tales of knightly chivalry from all the ends of Christendom, must this humble priest go forth, but treading, foot by foot, every shire in England and Ireland, fen and wood and wold, he shall re-collect what scattered annals he can find of his native land.

The idea has in it that *longue patience* which Buffon makes the synonym of genius. Yet the Chronicle evinces, it is said, neither much genius nor skill. The simple ardent patriotism of the priest stood him in stead for both.

John of Gaunt, with his army, was haunting the border country, keeping the tireless raiders of Annandale and Cumberland in awe, when this solitary priest, with but his garb and mien to protect him, came among the green pastoral Cheviots, and across the little Sark. He would ford the tiny river which ran between the hostile lands, and stoop to drink of it, perhaps, as a summer traveller may.

And then for his weary way,—among the English woodlands and fens; resting in the guestan hall of some convent, Benedictine or Augustinian; receiving the scant hospitality of some hermitage, or wayside inn. Richard Second, a boy-king, was now on the throne of the Edwards, and the oppressions of Scotland were some decades old. But the deep animosities of two nations, brave and thoughtful enough both, a decade or two could not wear away as footprints are washed from sand. When the sun set behind Wales, or rose upon the Essex shore; when the sky reddened into dark behind the black, leafless forest boughs, or flashed into summer dawn on a whiteness of daisied lea,—the stranger's heart still was in the priest, who, with his one darling thought, travelled, foot-sore and weary, to his ever-shifting shrines. Every library, every scriptorium to which his priest's garb gave him access, was searched with eager, devout care, for some relic of his country's past. Many *on dits*, also, he would gather on his fervent way; talking with the old men, and the priests who had been old men's confessors. And then there were the poets and the chroniclers of England's own, with whom, it is possible, some kindred flash might bring him into brief contact.

He may have talked with Robert Rolle, "hermit of the order of St. Augustine," and doctor of divinity besides, who lived in his Yorkshire solitude, paraphrasing the poetry of the Bible, and writing, in dull Latin verse, his thoughts on morals and religion; or with Robert Longlande, the priest who slept on the Malvern hills, and saw through the vision of Piers Ploughman, mercy, faith, and the rest of the virtues, clothed maidenly, and allegorized in the child-fashion of that time. Perhaps beneath the oaks of Woodstock, where that courtly old poet was wont to muse, he may have greeted "blythe and merry Chaucer," with the ink-horn at his side.

And yet none tells us so. Fordun left no footprints behind him. Much spoil of history he took back across the border. In 1385, he was dead.

This is all we know. Of where or how he died, no record has been kept, no tradition lingers. He is said, in his earlier life, to have been incumbent of the parish of Fordun, a fair little nook which nestles not far from the Grampian hills, and whence posterity has given him the only name he bears.

In this parish, beside Fenella hill, is a glen which is called the Friar's. In the glen are the ancient ruins of a Carmelite house of religion. Where facts fail us, we lawfully resort to fancy. Might not the travel-worn priest, in this sweet double seclusion of glen and sacred edifice, find rest for his tired feet ? The banks are woody round Fordun kirk; and the Luther water sings matin and vesper melodiously as any choir; and the chapel of St. Palladius, to which pilgrims come from far, stands in the little kirkyard. Where so dear a refuge for the faint years before the end ?

No matter. Wherever father John's feet may have rested, his patient hand laboured still. Five books of the "Scotichronicon," in the too brief years, he wrote, bringing his history down to the close of the reign of David First (A.D. 1153). And closing the record of the canonised king's life, John of Fordun died.

Into strange oblivion has passed the personality of the old chronicler, but his work projects itself farther than the shadow of his patient life. Such old religious solitaries, from whose existence were omitted beauty and love, must have had a peculiar interest and possession in the lonely links which bound them in kin to the future.

These interests and possessions, John of Fordun was not

denied. Collections of various manuscripts, extending to the date of his death, were found among the priest's effects. And although the careful hands and fond eyes that had gathered these like dust of gold were for ever and ever at rest, with this pathos of unfinished work behind, the work would not cease; other scribes would resume the pen which had dropped from John of Fordun's weary hand.

In the year 1441, Walter Bower, abbot of Inchkeith, took up the chronicle. In eleven new books he brought the history down to his own time, and died while the events of which he wrote were still forming round him.

It was then the monks of Paisley assumed the task he left, and began, in their Chronicus Clugniense, a transcript and continuation of the "Scotichronichon."

THE ABBOT TARVIS.

Only through a life of self-devotion, is the Self, which is originally the vessel of selfishness, transformed into the image in the Finite of the Divine Love. . . . . .
The new Life which the new individual evolves in himself, is planted as a germ in the renovated humanity round him. *Bunsen.*

IT was the reign of James First, when, after the long disquiet, the king had come home to his kingdom; when at last "the key kept the castle, and the furze-bush the kye," as the prince had threatened in his proud wrath, coming back among the stormy nobles, who was each to his own vassals king, and fain to be king if he might to other vassals than his own.

And the Abbey, in pathetic ruins, had lain for nearly a century. None had had heart to re-build it, since the flames lit by the English army had rioted through the fair cloister, curled up window and roof and wall. Amidst the desolation, Walter and Marjory had been laid, and Robert Second and Robert Third and Queen Euphemia, for the dust was holy kin. All the early Stewarts were gathered there at rest. Neither fire nor sword could take from the sacredness of that old Clugniac fame. But none had thought to re-build it. A mournful ruin it stood, yet without the poetry of decay. There had been incursions of the English since the days of Edward First. And the battle with Donald of the Isles was but a recent story. It was elsewhere the golden age of painting, sculpture, architecture. Scotland had missed her day, and she knew it. How could she rear lovely stone on the straths which were battle-fields?

With the return of James, comes a sudden accession of strength. The swift, stern hand of the poet-prince, brought a sense of rest to the land. "The key for the castle, the bush for the kye," was no idle truism now. That this terse little saying of the king, has come down through so many generations, told and re-told unweariedly, shows what it meant for the land. The king was his people's darling, like so many of his name after. And in the glad breathing time, the old Abbey rose again.

One "Schort Memorial of the Scottis Chroniklis" records the restoration in an obituary of the abbot who ruled at that time:—

"On 29th June, 1459, Decessit at Paslay, Thomas
" Tarvis, Abbot of Paslay, the quhilk was ane right gud man,
" and helplyk to the place of ony that ever was; for he did
" mony notable thingis, and held ane noble hous, and was ay
" wele purvait. He fand the place out of all gud rewle and
" the kirk unbiggit. He biggit the body of the kirk, fra the
" bucht stair up, and put on the ruf, and theckit it with sclait,

"and riggit it with stane, an biggit ane great portion of the
"steeple, and ane statelie yet-hous, and brocht hame mony
"gud jowellis, and claithis of gold, silver, and silk, and mony
"gud bukis, and made staitlie stallis, and glasynnit meikle of
"all the kirk, and brocht hame the staitliest tabernakle that
"was in all Scotland, and the maist costlie. And schortlie
"he brocht all the place to freedom, and fra nocht till ane
"mighty place, and left it out of all kynd of det, and at all
"fredom till dispone as them lykit, and left ane of the best
"myteris that was in all Scotland, and chandellaris of silver,
"and ane lettren of brass, with mony other gud jowellis."

This building of church and steeple and gate-house, this adorning with stone, and enriching with jewels, and cloth of gold and silver and silk, must have been in the early days of the right good abbot's rule. The date of his death precedes by only one year that of King James Second. So he lived through the long feuds of the Crawfords, Chrichtons, and Douglasses; through the years of the famine and the pestilence; through the trusty, long imprisonment of the second boy King James; through the distressful obscurity of the beautiful queen-mother Joan, wedded in her widowhood to the Black Knight of Lorn, who wooed nor loved her none, nor comforted her like the Scottish King in Windsor Tower.

Set in his niche in history, the right good Abbot Tarvis assumes a certain shape and substance among the moving figures of his time. His care was directed to the material strength and beauty of the ruined Abbey which he governed. His passion was work, and the monastic rule provided with tender discretion for every passion and gift.

Bede had long ago praisefully recorded the story of Ouini, "a monk of great merit, having forsaken the world with the pure intention of obtaining the heavenly reward; worthy in all respects to have the secrets of our Lord specially revealed to him; and worthy to have credit given by his hearers to what he said, for he had come with Queen Aedilthryde from the province of the East Angles, and was her prime minister, and governor of her household. As the fervour of his faith increased, resolving to renounce the world, he did not go about it slothfully, but so fully forsook the things of this world, that, quitting all he had, clad only in a plain garment, and carrying an axe and hatchet in his hand, he came to the monastery of that most reverend prelate called Lastingaeu; thereby intimating that he did not go to the monastery to live idle, as some do, but to labour, which he also confirmed by practice; for as he was less capable of meditating on the Holy Scriptures, so he the more earnestly applied himself to the labour of his hands. In short, he was received by the bishop into the house aforesaid, out of respect to his devotion, and there entertained with the brethren; and whilst they were engaged within in reading, he was without at work, doing such things as were necessary."

And how Ouini was honoured in his labour, Bede continues to relate, in a passage so marvellous and sweet, we wrong the abbot Tarvis none by pausing to transcribe it here.

"One day, when he was thus employed out of doors, and his companions were gone to the church, as I had begun to state, the bishop was alone, busied in reading or praying in the oratory of that place, when, on a sudden, as he afterwards said, he heard the voice of persons singing most sweetly and rejoicing, and appearing to descend to the earth from heaven. Which voice he said he first heard coming from the south-east, that is, from the highest quarter of the east, and that afterwards it gradually drew near him, till it came to the roof of the oratory where the bishop was, and entering therein, filled the same and all round about it. He listened attentively to what he heard, and, after about half-an-hour, perceived the same song of joy to ascend from the roof of the said oratory, and to return to heaven the same way it came, with inexpressible sweetness. When he had stood some time astonished, and seriously revolving in his mind what these things might be, the bishop opened the window of the oratory, and making a noise with his hand, as he often had been wont to do, ordered him to come into him. He accordingly went hastily in, and the bishop said to him, 'Hasten to the church, and cause these seven brethren to come hither, and do you come along with them.' When they were come, he first admonished them to preserve the virtue of love and peace among themselves and toward all others; and indefatigably to practice the rules of regular discipline, which they had either been taught by him, or seen him observe, or had noticed in the words or actions of the former fathers. Then he added that the day of his death was at hand; for, said he, 'That loving guest, who was wont to visit our brethren, has vouchsafed to come to me also this day, and to call me out of this world. Return, therefore, to the church, and speak to the brethren, that they, in their prayers, recommend my departure to our Lord; and that they be careful to provide beforehand for their own, the hour whereof is uncertain, by watching, prayer, and good works.'

"When he had spoken thus much and more, and they, having received his blessing, had gone away in much sorrow, he who had heard the heavenly song returned alone, and prostrating himself on the ground, said, 'I beseech you, father, may I be permitted to ask a question?' 'Ask what you will,' answered the bishop. Then he added, 'I beseech you to tell me what song of joy was that which I heard of beings descending upon this oratory, and after some time returning to heaven?' The bishop answered, 'If you heard the singing, and know of the coming of the heavenly company, I command you, in the name of our Lord, that you do not tell the same to any one before my death. They, truly, were angelic spirits, who came to call me to my heavenly reward, which I have always loved and longed after: and they promised that they would return seven days hence and take me away with them.' Which was accordingly fulfilled, as had been said to him."

And so it was Ouini, the monk, who could not meditate on the Scriptures, who, while the others read and prayed, wrought alone with his axe in the forest; the monk, who could only *work*, to whom was vouchsafed this high privilege of hearing the Loving Guest's music when he came to call the bishop Ceadda home.

This legend of the Mercian convent would be well known among the Benedictines. It would cross the Border with the Clugniac monks who came to the White Cart in the days of Walter, the first Steward. It was many times rehearsed, perhaps, in the desolate locutorium, when the monks sought comfort of each other; while the fair wasted convent lands lay, lonesome enough, under the soft sun, and the broomy braes were lonesome too, and all the land mourned.

The story of the monk Ouini was in the true genius of St. Benedict, who had followers, by no means idle, in the first palmy years of his rule. But that was long ago. The languor of many centuries had, with its slow presage of death, already crept over unconscious Christendom.

Yet was the well-beloved abbot Tarvis none the less revered, nor less saintly, that his memory was not to descend, embalmed in legend and miracle, but in a homely manner, like Ouini's, the favoured monk, linked with the building of the buttress stair, and the roofing of the church with slate, and the raising of a stately lodge for the porter who kept the gate. And with all strength and humility the abbot did his work, leaving his labour behind him as the sole memorial he asked. After lying in rest and oblivion for more than four hundred years, the abbot Tarvis's memory, a year or two ago, was curiously enough revived.

The old, unbeautiful town had crept close up to the Abbey, had bridged the now grimy river, had invaded the orchard lands. Where the white May blossoms had fallen, where the monks had walked in the sunshine, the small, mean houses of the crowd had risen obtrusive and irreverent. They had come close up in front of the dim, receding doorway, of the beautiful mullioned window, under the shadow, once so dreamy, of buttress and pinnacle and spire.

And so the old Abbey had stood, stifled in its reverend beauty, till some late, kindly impulse was evoked to rescue and spare its charms.

And while the workmen were busy with excavations, demolitions, and repairs, they came upon a treasure-trove in the heart of the dim, common town. Some feet below the surface of the ground, was found a mass of old ashlar stone-work, which measured fifteen by twenty-one feet. It lay to the north-west of the north-west turret of the Abbey. The form, as well the position, of the foundation, made all who could judge of the matter agree, that this must be the remains of the "ane staitlie yet-hous," by the abbot Tarvis built.

As to the other work of this active and right good abbot, in lack of personal details, we must fill in from wider history. Happily, the monastic unity renders this a possible resource. The rule of St. Benedict was wide, and all who came under its sway, through the long middle ages, had a certain commonness of life.

Thus the life of the Saxon abbot, Benedict Biscop, who lived in the seventh century, may be used, without peril, as a helpful commentary on the life of the Scottish abbot who lived in the fifteenth.

Not, indeed, that through changes manifold, monasticism had not gone, losing much of its fervour and its purity, as it passed through the ages' crucible. But the similarity is greater than the difference, as from loose leaves of history we gather. And a page from this Biscop Benedict, who ruled on the banks of the Wear, has analogies full of interest, when taken with the brief, long after record of the abbot on the banks of the White Cart.

The "gud jewels" and cloth of gold and silver and silk, the many good books he brought home, how "he glassynit meikle of all the kirk, and brocht hame the staitliest tabernacle that was in all Scotland," recall that old journey to Rome which Benedict undertook. "He brought back," as Bede records, "great numbers of sacred books, hymns, gospels, and epistles, to enrich his convent on the Wear. These he had either bought at a price, or received as presents from his friends. Arriving at Vienne on his homeward journey, he received back the books which he had purchased, and which he had entrusted to their keeping. . . . Benedict crossed the ocean and went into Gaul, when he made inquiry for masons who could build him a church of stone after the Roman style, which he always loved. These he obtained, and brought them home with him: and such zeal in the work did he exhibit—out of his love to the blessed Peter, for whose honour he was doing this,—that in the course of one year from the time when the foundations were laid, the church was roofed over, and within it you might have witnessed the celebration of masses. When the work was drawing to a close, he sent messengers to Gaul to bring over glass-makers (a kind of workmen hitherto unknown in Britain) to glaze the windows of the church, and of its aisles and chancels. . . . Moreover, this religious trader

K

took care to import from the regions beyond the sea, if he could not find them at home, whatever related to the ministry of the altar and the church, and to holy vessels and vestments."

It was from France also that, in all likelihood, the abbot Tarvis sought masons for his work. Scottish architecture revived on Continental, not on English models. The breach between England and Scotland had been too recent and deadly and deep to suffer much fellowship or imitation, even in those fine arts, whose nature it is to soften asperities, and be, to all men who love them, as the green mosses to the forest, or their sweet odours to the flowers. But the architecture of this old Abbey must have one brief chapter of its own. And the good abbot Tarvis recedes among the fitful shadows, after all is said, scarcely more defined than the first founders of the house.

RENOVATION.

A CASEMENT high and triple-arched there was,
All garlanded with carven imageries
Of fruits, and flowers, and bunches of knot-grass,
And diamonded with panes of quaint device,
Innumerable of stains and splendid dyes,
As are the tiger-moth's deep crimsoned wings;
And in the midst, 'mong thousand heraldries,
And twilight saints, and dim emblazonings,
A shielded scutcheon blushed with blood of kings and queens.
Eve of St. Agnes.

THE arts introduced by the Normans, extending much further than their arms, came with the Saxon princess into Malcolm Canmore's kingdom. In the religious architecture of the two countries, there are no distinctive features at that early date.

But four hundred years lay between the Norman Conquest and the abbot Tarvis of Paisley, and many long sorrows and oppressions had come to disunite the peoples. When the abbot thought to rebuild the buttress stair and kirk and roof, he did not look to Henry's kingdom, which had abbeys enough, and fair enough. The stately, perpendicular architecture was then in the height of its reign, with its solemn and serene beauty, its transom, and arches, and sub-arches. If it had returned to the old Norman formality, and lost, in its very richness, the early English flowing lines, it had, as all who have seen an old church of that time must acknowledge, an effect supremely religious, which we do not care to analyse.

But not one such specimen is to be found in all Scotland; for a deep wrong and resentment lay between the two peoples now.

James First, it is said, ascended the throne of a realm less civilized than Alexander Third had left two hundred years before. The little mountain land had kept her life in the long unequal contest—her life, and that was all. For her native king, and the freedom which a mountain people draw like native breath, she had sacrificed everything else. And many generations of sons must be born in her straths and glens, ere she could forget this in the frank brotherhood of humanity.

So when her stern, much loved king won a breathing time to Scotland, it was across the sea that she looked for re-civilization, and not across the English border.

Long before this, indeed, Scottish students had flocked to France. They had crowded the court of Charlemagne, learned men of all degree. "Henricus, in his dedication of the life of Cesarius to that monarch, says: 'Why do I speak of Scotland? that whole nation almost, despising the danger of the sea, resort to our country with a numerous train of philosophers, of whom the most famous, abdicating their native soil, account themselves happy under your favour, as the servants of the wise Solomon.'" And now, a greater necessity would draw to every centre of foreign culture, those who loved learning and the arts, or who sought to restore to their own country the gentler graces which she had lost.

It was, probably, from some such tour, the abbot Tarvis had returned, when he brought home his costly jewels, and relics, and good books.

The first architect of Paisley was, indeed, a Parisian by birth, yet the monastery he erected was essentially early English. It had taken a century of war to draw those distinctive lines which, henceforward, appreciably exist between English and Scottish architecture. The Scots, like the mountain Swiss, were travellers by nature. And there were thoughts enough in stone to be gleaned over all Europe.

The Flamboyant of France, Spain, and Germany, contemporanious with the English perpendicular, was then in the first youth of its glorious exuberant tracery. Roslin Chapel, of nearly the same date, offers something of this splendour. Paisley, subdued and chastened—perhaps by its greater necessities—by the poverty which had come upon it through long and wasteful days of war, offers a suggestion of the same architectural beauty—a very faint suggestion—no more.

Abbot Tarvis, with his good jewels, would bring home many fair memories, and, not improbably, also some skilled French or German artist, who could turn these fair memories into solid stone on the banks of his own river.

The band of monastic workmen, for every abbey had such, would work with willing and devout hands to restore what Walter had founded.

Already a little village had gathered on the edge of the orchards, close to the religious house, seeking aid, and government, and protection, as other villages gathered round other abbeys, or round the baronial castles. The abbot, it is said, was usually a gentler lord than the knight. The greenest, wealthiest landscapes were those held in vassalage to the monks. So the people would watch gladly while the Abbey walls arose, slowly and patiently again, steeple and nave and choir.

The finest part of the abbot Tarvis's work is the southern window in the transept, of which there now only remains the great central mullion, its cusps partly broken, but the tracery in the head entire. Its effect is still wonderfully beautiful, situated, even as it is, in the common heart of the town, with no aid of black bough or green leaf.

The windows in the pier-story at this end of the nave, although less elaborate in detail, are yet in the same style, exhibiting two trefoil-headed lights, with a central mullion, and a quatre-foiled pointed main arch.

The interior of the nave is thus described :—

"Substantial piers composed of clustered shafts, with simple capitals, and supporting noble pointed arches, the mouldings of which, though plain, are delicate as well as numerous, divide the aisles from the body of the fabric. Above, resting on a wall, that fills up the interstices between the arches themselves, and rises a little above them, is a triforium, composed of a range of large semicircular arches, that spring from clustered columns, and are also enriched with many slender bands or mouldings. Beneath each of these finely sweeping arches, two pointed ones are formed, cinque-foiled at top, and divided from each other by a short but delicate clustered column, with a rather ornamented capital. The space between the heads of these minor arches, and that of the principal one above, is, as well as the latter, open to the body of the structure, and beautifully cusped. Masonry fills up the vacancies between the main arches of the triforium; but, from this masonry, between each pair of arches, there juts out towards the centre of the building, a semi-hexagonal projection, supported by two ranges of corbels, receding downwards. Each of these ends in a sculptured figure, contorted, and apparently groaning under the superincumbent weight. . . . Altogether, this triforium and its appendages are perhaps unique.

"Above it rises the clerestory, the arches of which, opening also into the interior of the nave, are plain pointed ones, rather narrow, but of just proportions, with clustered piers and plain mouldings.

"The present roof of the church is a simple coved one; but the original roof was, as the roofs of the side aisles still are, finely groined, with sculptured bosses at the intersection of the ribs. One such boss yet remains, towards the west end of the southern aisle. Not far from it, near the roof, are two very small trefoil-headed niches, in which images of the saints are supposed to have stood." *

* Swan's "Beauties of the Clyde."

Of the long choir, there only now remains a bit of wall, a few feet high, mixed with the grass and grave-stones, yet still encrusted here and there with the relics of its curious, crumbling sculptures. Discernible on the south side are traces of the graceful old Sedilia—four cinque-foiled recesses, each beneath its pointed arch, once the seats of officiating priests, beside the high altar,—now open to every wandering foot that treads the grass-grown graves. Near them is a small, plain piscina, one of those old water drains, often set beneath pediments, adorned with open wooden work, or rich in sculptured tracery. But no adornment now lingers round the old dismantled stone.

Two large pointed arches, long filled in with solid masonry, once opened from the choir to the chapel of St. Mirrinus. Between the choir and the nave are still the remains of strong clustered pillars, which supported the tower crowned by the abbot Tarvis's spire. This spire, which is said to have been very beautiful, and three hundred feet in height, stricken by lightning, fell some time in the sixteenth century. The exact date of its fall is not known; but it was shortly after the spoliation of the Abbey had begun—while the broken images lay in the open cloister court, and during the time that Lord Claude, the boy abbot, wore the last of the dishonoured mitre of Paisley.

LORD LYELL'S GIFT.

No life, my honest scholar—no life so happy and so pleasant as the life of a well-governed angler; for, when the lawyer is swallowed up with business, and the statesman is preventing and contriving plots, then we sit on cowslip banks, hear the birds sing, and possess ourselves in as much quietness as these silent silver streams, which we now see glide so quietly by us. Indeed, my good scholar, we may say of angling, as Doctor Boteler said of strawberries, "doubtless God could have made a better berry, but doubtless God never did;" and so if I might be judge, "God never did make a more calm, quiet, innocent recreation, than angling." *Izaak Walton.*

T is briefly recorded by Crawford,—" Robert, Lord Lyell, was a benefactor to the monks of Paisley, by the fishing of Crockat-Shot, in the year 1452." But the locality of this old fishery is hardly to be rescued from the years. The name, familiar to the ears of the abbot Tarvis and his monks, lingers no longer on any shady, near stream. On what mild, clear days, when the green was fresh upon the birks, and the early pure-veined wood-sorrel, whitened under the hawthorn hedge (for these little tiny things, known and loved and young through the centuries, help us to wonderful *realism* in living back the old days), the monks cast their patient lines on the still, brown water, contemporary history tells us—but not the monastic page.

The stillness of the convent life, the shadows of the dark, old Abbey, half ruined and half restored; the earnest, pious striving to revive the old dream of peace, beneficence, supreme sway, make just such contrasts as are needed to the stormy outside groups, which compose the warlike picture of James Second's reign.

"The truce with England being expired, the Scots made incursions into England, and the English into Scotland, accompanied by the usual devastation. In England, Alnwick was taken and burned by James, brother of the Earl of Douglas; in Scotland, Dumfries was similarly treated by the Earl of Salisbury; and Dunbar by the Earl of Northumberland; and the spoil in men and cattle was considerable. An agreement was, however, entered into by the commanders for an exchange of prisoners, as the captives on both sides were nearly equal both in number and rank. By these incursions, although the country was almost reduced to a solitude, the war was not brought to a crisis."

And then there was the battle of the Sark, which has no contemporary historian; but of which the French have delighted to tell how the English were *bien battus*. For the English had lost their brave leader, and lost heart beside the little stream,—the little and slow water which severed two lands.

And the earls of Douglas and Moray were at war in the wild north; and the earl of Crawford made an open raid on all the nobles loyal to the king. "James of the Fiery Face," and yet a true Stewart,—handsome and chivalrous, and wiser than his own day,—has round him the same setting of utter disquiet as his father.

In the summer of 1452, sentence of forfeiture was past against the rebel earl of Crawford,—"his gudis and gear confiscat, his landis dealt, and his name abolished and blotted out of the buke of armes for ever."

Lord Lyell was one of those who sat in this summer Parliament, when the Braid hills were broomy, and the May-mists from the sea were past. He moves among his stormy peers, once or twice across history. What his link with the monks of Paisley may have been, we are not told. But it is in the same year of this stern legislation against the house of Douglas, that lord Lyell grants the Abbey his quiet fishery, for thanksgiving and prayer.

And so we are taken aside into the conventual calm to the newly restored monastery, which the abbot Tarvis still rules—a placid revival of beauty in the midst of intestine wars. And the women come to church serenely, wearing curches by the king's command. For James has not disdained to legislate also for the simple women of his realm. "It is ordained that na woman come to the kirk or market having her face mussaled that she may not be kenned, under pain of the escheat of the curch." In their home-made curches they come, and their gowns blue and green and red; which gay tints, however, the king's grace allows only as holiday attire. And they kneel, with their homely, daily needs, before the old shrines re-carved; and they reverence the good Lord Abbot, who is nearer to them than the king.

"If the church was the one building of the priest, so was it of the people. It was the single safe and quiet place where the lowest of the low found security, peace, rest, recreation, even diversion. If the chancel was the priest's, the precincts, the porch, the nave, were open to all: the church was all which the amphi-theatre, the bath, the portico, the public place, had been to the poor in the heathen cities. It was more than the house of prayer and worship, where the peasant or the beggar knelt side by side with the burgher or the baron; it was the asylum, not of the criminal only, but of the oppressed, the sad, the toil-worn, the infirm, the aged. It was not only dedicated to God; it was consecrated to the consolation, the peace, even the enjoyment of man." *

And "the fishing of Crockat-Shot," the gift of Robert, Lord Lyell, adds one little mite more to the much-required wealth of the Clugniac Abbey, rising from the ruins which the English army had left behind it.

* Dean Milman's "Latin Christianity."

THE LORD OF THE ISLES.

AND yet these blottings chronicle a life,
A whole life, and my life.
Browning.

IN the end of the fifteenth century, the life of John, Lord of the Isles, was wasting slowly away within this Benedictine cloister.

He had led a stormy and almost royal life among his sea-dashed domains. His grim, old castle of Artornish was planted high upon the rocks, and the rocks overhung the waves. There were wierd Scandinavian traditions cherished in that old sea line. The Lord of the Isles held court apart from the Scottish king. Always between the Scottish king and the keep of old Artornish lay that dark, protecting arm of green water, which was better than a hundred charters.

But the lords of the isles aspired to more than independence; they would renounce allegiance to the Scottish king, and through some faint show of vassalage to England, not easily to be enforced, would themselves become kings. Little love or loyalty there had ever been between any king of Scotland and these island lords.

And so, on Edith's bridal-eve, the warder of the keep gives greeting to the unknown strangers who claim its hospitality :—

> "Be what ye will, Artornish Hall
> On this glad eve is free to all;
> Though ye had drawn a hostile sword
> Against our ally, England's lord;
> Or mail upon your shoulders borne
> To battle with the Lord of Lorn;
> Or, outlaw'd, dwelt by greenwood tree
> With the fierce knight of Ellerslie;
> Or aided even the murderous strife,
> When Comyn fell beneath the knife
> Of that fell homicide, the Bruce;
> This night had been a time of truce."

But many decades after the "bridal of the Maid of Lorn," the secret treaty was signed, for which Lord John suffered the monastic seclusion of Paisley.

John was the grandson of that "John de Yle" who, in the first year of the reign of Edward Fourth of England, drew out the treasonable treaty against his native prince, which Scott, in his notes to "The Lord of the Isles," has preserved from Rymer's Foedera.

"From this castle of Artornish, upon the 19th day of June, 1461, John de Yle, designing himself Earl of Ross, and Lord of the Isles, granted, in the style of an independent sovereign, a commission to his trusty and well-beloved cousins, Ronald of the Isles, and Duncan, Arch-Dean of the Isles, for empowering them to enter into a treaty with the most excellent prince Edward, by the grace of God, king of France and England, and lord of Ireland.

Edward Fourth, on his part, named Laurence, bishop of Durham, the Earl of Worcester, the prior of St. John's, Lord Wenlock, and Mr Robert Stillington, keeper of the privy seal, his deputies and commissioners, to confer with those named by the Lord of the Isles. The conference terminated in a treaty, by which the Lord of the Isles agreed to become a vassal to the crown of England, and to assist Edward Fourth, and James, Earl of Douglas, then in banishment, in subduing the realm of Scotland.

"The first article provides that John de Isle, Earl of Ross, with his son, Donald Balloch, and his grandson, John de Isle, with all their subjects, men, people, and inhabitants, become vassals and liegemen to Edward Fourth of England, and assist him in his wars in Scotland or Ireland; and then follow the allowances to be made to the Lord of the Isles in recompense of his military service, and the provisions for dividing such conquests as their united arms should make upon the mainland of Scotland among the confederates. These furnish such curious illustrations of the period, that they are here subjoined :—

"'Item, the said John, Erle of Rosse, shall, from the seid 'fest of Whittesontyde next comyng, yerely, duryng his lyf, 'have and take, for fees and wages in tyme of peas, of the 'seid most high and Christian prince, c. marc sterlyng of 'English money; and in tyme of werre, as long as he shall 'entende with his myght and power in the seid werres, in 'maner and fourme aboveseid, he shall have wages of 'cc. lib. sterlyng of English money yearly; and after the 'rate of the tyme that he shall be occupied in the seid 'werres.

"'Item, the seid Donald shall, from the seid feste of 'Whittesontyde, have and take, during his lyf, yerely, in 'tyme of peas, x. l. sterlynges of Englysh money; and when 'he shall be occupied and intend to the werre, with his 'myght and power, and in maner and fourme aforeseid, he 'shall have and take, for his wages yerely, x l. l. sterlyng of 'Englysh money; or for the rate of the tyme of werre.

"'Item, the seid John, sonn and heire apparent of the said 'Donald, shall have and take yerely from the seid feste, for 'his fees and wages, in the tyme of peas, x. l. sterlynges of 'Englysh money; or after the rate of the tyme that he shall 'be occupied in the werre; and the seid John, th' Erle 'Donald, and John, and eche of them, shall have good and 'sufficient paiement of the seid fees and wages, as well for 'tyme of peas as of werre . . . '"

But the lords of the isles wax bolder.

"'Item, it is appointed, accorded, concluded, and f.nally 'determined, that, if it so be that hereafter the seid reaume 'of Scotland, or the more part thereof, be conquered, 'subdued; and brought to the obeissance of the seid most 'high and Christian prince, and his heires, or successours, of 'the said Lionel, in forme abovesaid, descendyng, be the 'assistance, helpe, and aide of the seid John, Erle of Rosse, 'and Donald, and of James, Erle of Douglas; then, the 'said wages and fees for the tyme of peas cessyng, the 'same Erles and Donald shall have, by the graunte of the 'same most Christian prince, all the possessions of the seid 'reaume beyonde Scottishe see, they to be departed equally

'betwix them; eche of them, his heires and successours, to
'hold his parte of the seid most Christian prince, his heires
'and successours for evermore, in right of his crown of
'England, by homage and feaute to be done therefore.'"

Of the fate of John, the grandfather, history leaves us in
the dark. But Donald made a bold attempt to fulfil his
part of the treaty. He ravaged the lands of Athol; he
proclaimed himself a king. Always looking southward for
aid from Edward, he looks in vain, and sweeps on,
merciless in his triumph, dreaming of a conquered Scotland,
and a crowned Lord of the Isles.

And he came to pleasant Blair, and the lone little chapel
of St. Bride, where the earl of Athol and his wife had
found sanctuary when their castle was taken. Donald,
acknowledging no sanctuary, entered the sacred place,
seized the earl and countess, and sent them to a dungeon
in the Hebrides. And from that time, says old story,
misfortune tracked his steps. Some miserable years of
madness awaited him, and then came the dagger of a foe.

But John, the grandson, once more rose with his armed
vassals, renewed the league with England, and still saw the
vision of a crown before him.

Then there came a day when the secret treaty was no
more secret, when the rumour slowly crept through the
mountain-land—which had so faithfully held through its long
devasting minorities, to the little crowned king in the
cradle—that this western prince, with all his liegemen,
was pledged to England; that he had secretly divided
all its mountain and its moorland, and its shady green

straths—Kyle and Lennox, and Athol and Argyle—
and taken English gold for wages against his native king.

It was in the dull December of 1475, that the young
James Third convened in Edinburgh all the loyal peers of
his realm. And John, Earl of Ross, and Lord of the Isles,
was summoned to come and answer for the secret treason
and rebellion, which had lasted through the king's reign.

The Highland Earl failed to appear. To enter the grey
old capital, while the king was there, in his early, handsome
youth, with nobles still trusty and strong around him, would
surely not have been discretion, the better part of valour.
So, when the rebel chief came not, the king sent two loyal
lords, the earls of Crawford and Athol, to besiege his rocky
keep. And then John, the grandson, the old earl now,
after vainly looking to England for help, looking north and
south in vain, and bearing alone the burden of that paction
which his fathers had made, suddenly threw himself on the
king's mercy, and thus saved the lordship of the Isles.

He could not, however, save his earldom of Ross. This
was forfeited to the king. But his stormy old keep of
Artornish was left to him, beside the sea. And here for
twenty years more he lived an unobtrusive life, ruling his
own vassals, and holding his Island court. He lived
through the wars which cost James Third his life, and gave
to the troubled country another boy-king, yet he took no
part in them.

James Fourth reigned well. Song has not music, nor
has story words, to tell the love that was borne to him.

"In this mean-time," says old Pitscottie, "was guid
peace and rest in Scotland, and great love betwixt the king

and his subjects, and he was well loved of them all; for he was very noble."

And again the same chronicler asserts:—" Every man loved his prince so well, that they would on no ways disobey him." Which words have a nearly Arcadian sound of perfect order and felicity.

Soon, yet not first, to break the harmony, was this old Lord of the Isles, who, in nearly forgotten quiet, had dwelt so long at Artornish. The blame of the insurrection falls indeed, not wholly, on lord John—but rather on his restless nephew, Alexander of Lochalsh; for the forfeited earldom of Ross tempted the younger lord who had not yet experienced the disappointments and humiliations of defeat. Alexander was defeated by the Mackenzies near the little river Conan; and the penalty of his rebellion fell back upon the Lord of the Isles.

This old lord, who had lived through so many long wars and dark intrigues, was at length bereft by Parliament of his last remaining title and estates. It was on a January day of the year 1494, that, old and poor and landless, he came before the palace-gate to make a formal surrender of all he had had, to the king.

The king seems to have received him with the chivalrous courtesy and kindness of a very youthful conqueror to a grey-headed foe. Lord John remained sometime, we are not told how long, as one of the royal household, and was finally sent to life-long seclusion in the Clugniac Abbey of Paisley. The generous clemency of the king simply awarded this penalty—which seems indeed at the close of so fierce and stormy a life, to have in it no penal element, but to be what the human soul would most surely and fitly choose—a place of soft enclosing shadows, whence the look, back and onwards, might be cast—whence, perhaps, from the ashes of contrition, some sweeter hope might arise.

THE SCHAWES OF SAUCHIE.

> Too late for antique vows,
> Too, too late for the fond believing lyre,
> When holy were the haunted forest boughs,
> Holy the air, the water, and the fire.
> *Keats.*

ALREADY, through all Christendom, there is a trembling like the quiver of forest-leaves,—that quick, voiceless throb of motion, which all who love sylvan life have noticed, with a thrill of sympathy, in the *humanness* of the presage.

The storm will come anon; the little violets cower, fold their pale petals to the wind, show their stems and their tender green cups. There is a solemn stillness—a pause—a rest;—then the storm comes.

No more Crusades. The power of the Turks advances to the skirt of the Papal territory, near the very seat of the apostles. Eneaus Sylvius is pope. Eneaus, who wrote wonderingly of poverty-stricken Scotland; who went over the treeless wastes, and saw the blackened trunks in the mosses,—poor dumb vestiges of an earlier beauty and repose. Eneaus, pope Pius Second, comes down to his own sea-side, and lifts up his hands, like Moses, to move the gathered princes to some old religious enthusiasm, but the hands of the sick and wearied and eager pope are upheld in vain. The wind is already passing through the forest,—the first low presage of the storm.

Julius Second is in the near future; Julius the soldier pope, who reared the papal temporal power, and lost that Tarnkappe,—that invisible mantle of sanctity and purity, real, or always believed; which was, to the first tiaraed heads, a strength as true as was the fabled vesture of the hero in the Niebelungenlied.

Erasmus is not yet in England, nor has pope Innocent Eighth granted his fatal commission to the archbishop of Canterbury to make inquisition of the English monasteries. But Erasmus, who himself has worn a cowl, can laugh at the monastic life. And "the Abbeys which towered in the midst of the English towns, the houses clustered at their feet, like subjects round some majestic queen,"* are already judged of their subjects,—covertly judged, it may be. All outward homage is paid to the lord abbot and the monks; but a thought of askance broods beneath,—the first presage of the storm.

The work which has left the name of the abbot Schawe, of Paisley, to posterity, has a reference quite appropriate to the suspicions and unwhispered alienations of the time.

It happened to Paisley, fortunately, not in a spiritual

* Froude.

sense, but as preparing it for some worldly dignities, that in this reign its abbacy fell vacant. James Third was married to the young fair Margaret of Norway, whom even Buchanan confesses to have been "a woman of uncommon beauty and virtue." And the royal bearing of the king, his refined, if effeminate, tastes, conveyed no premonition of the long trouble and the tragic end which would come.

An act, newly passed by the Scottish Parliament, had empowered the clergy to choose their own dignitaries; the convents their abbots and priors. But James, in the true Stewart fashion, had scarcely attained his majority, ere he tacitly ignored this law, annulled the election of the monks, and appointed to the Abbey of Dunfermline an abbot of his own choice.

James Schawe of Sauchie, was castellan to the king. George, the future abbot, was a younger son of the castellan. It is but fair to suppose the choice was made by the king, and not by the Clugniac monks, whose election could scarcely have fallen on one whom the faint echoes of history lead us to suppose had but a small religious vocation.

The historical footprints of these old Schawes of Sauchie impress us with a vague distrust. We read, with a conscious antagonism, the obscure and meagre records of their gifts and schemes and deeds.

The ancient house of Sauchie, ruinous, dismantled now, was a fort of some consideration amidst its own domains. These domains were small indeed, but notable because of their neighbourhood. The old round tower of Bruce stood on the near land of Carnock; Sir John Graham's lonely castle, where Wallace had often slept—a still place among its woods and steeps—was also hard by. And then there was the Abbey Craig from which Wallace won his great victory; and the Bannock Burn, whose name was inspiration ; and the royal forest of Stirling ; and the shady woods of Dundaff. There were, too, the Lennox hills and the Ochils and the gate of the bold north, whence the shadowy tartans of the clans would emerge from the mountain fastnesses to levy their black mail. And, best of all, there was the king's castle on its picturesque storied rock, storied already by the reigns of the two earlier Jameses.

Here, at Stirling Castle, king James spent most of his time with his favourites, his musicians, and his architects; loving not war, yet continually doomed to it.

It was fine in the king's youth to see, from his castle of Stirling, that rich delightful carse of Teith, and those blue links of Forth among the meadows,—winding, winding, in and out, sunny, placid, slow—like quiet thoughts, or happy fancies. Had he only not been a king, or had there been no lords Argyle and Douglas and Hailes and Home, so that his vest of gold and robe of lilac and ermine he might have worn at leisure, listening to the sweet musicians, who were more to him than counsellors or knights ; while Margaret, also, in her spangled kirtle, very discreet and fair, bore him such fond company as report made her fit to yield.

But the king could not make his kingdom to his liking, nor could the kingdom make its king. The king was a Stewart. Never did one treasonable thought against his dynasty arise. But there was a little prince. Perhaps this little prince was bold and warlike as his father's nobles were, and as his father was not.

James Schawe, the castellan, must have won the favour of the boy, and the favour of the king also, for himself and for his sons. When Paisley became vacant, the king made young George Schawe its abbot; and committed to the abbot's tuition his second son, the Duke of Ross.

But the prince of Scotland was meanwhile much at Stirling with the king, and became the friend of the castellan; and was wooed long, and warily perhaps, through ambition or patriotism, or what passion was strongest in him.

The banished earl of Douglas has come back, across the borders, in arms; and Albany, the warden of the marches, has joined the old turbulent lord. And there is a fierce battle fought on St. Magdalen's day, at Lochmaben, where the vassals of Douglas were expected to rally. But the vassals of the Douglas remain loyal to the king, and the proud earl is taken. The king can be gentle to this old lord, whose years are nearly over. He condemns him to life-long imprisonment in the monastery of Lindores. Kirkpatrick his vassal weeps; but Douglas weeps none. "He that can do no more must be a monk," he says. And so he goes to the monastery on the chill sandy shores of Fife,—the convent which Prince David had founded when at last he came home from the Crusades.

And the Douglas dree'd his wierd; and the old league with France was renewed; and with England was made one of those many truces which were alway so quickly broken. The lords Evandale and Lyle returned from negotiations with Richard Third while the abbot Schawe was building walls round the orchard lands of Paisley. The lord Lyle was one of those numerous noble donators to the Abbey who unconsciously intertwisted the ecclesiastical and political threads of history. The fishing of Crockat-Shot was, as has been told, gifted to the monks of Paisley by lord Lyle, or by lord Lyle's father, in the abbot Tarvis's days.

But troubles thicken round the king. The boy prince James has been won to head an opposing army; and the nobles will listen to nothing but that the father shall resign his crown to the son. James looked despairingly for help across the sea, and across the border. "He sent also to pope Eugenius Eighth, beseeching him, by his paternal love for Scotland, to send a legate to oblige his refractory subjects, under pain of ecclesiastical censures, to lay down their arms and obey their king. The pope, in consequence, wrote to Hadrian of Castile, a man of uncommon learning and wisdom, at that time his legate in England, to use his endeavours for restoring tranquility to Scotland. These remedies, however, were too late."* The bitter, long-accumulated hatred between the nobles and the king could not be allayed by Hadrian, nor by any king of England or of France.

The king, timid, uncertain, was waiting in Edinburgh castle. The nobles were powerful and impatient. "For although they had the prince with them, both for ensuring the obedience of the common people, and to show that they were not arrayed against their country, but against a most

* Buchanan's History.

pernicious king; yet, lest the arrival of foreign ambassadors should shake the determination of the lower orders, they anxiously exerted themselves to end the contest by a final battle."

And soon enough the battle, so eagerly desired, was fought. For the king, anxious and weary, would again seek his favourite Stirling, which his trusted Castellan of Sauchie would keep for him against all comers. The king, with his little force, rode to the castle gates, and the gates were closed upon him; and he knew the treachery of Schawe.

And there beside the Sauchie-burn, on the land of his false vassal, his last battle was fought. The men of Annandale, with their long spears, put to flight the small royal force; and the king, on the grey charger, which, " whether to flee or follow, could waur every horse in Scotland," fled towards a little mill on the side of a neighbouring water.

The shrift of the priest, and the dagger of the soldier in that humble, lonely mill, this chapter may not stay to record; it contains no history of king James.

But Schawe of Sauchie, the castellan, whether by constraint or guile, had the young prince in his care when he took up arms against his father. And Schawe, the abbot of Paisley, had in his care the Duke of Ross. So that, for that brief time, the Schawe family was distinctly ascendant; not politically nor openly in any way so as to wound the nobles' pride or incur their displeasure, but by having such personal influence as could make all other dispensable.

It is significant enough of the sway which father and son

maintained, that two months after this date, the boy-king grants to the abbot, as an especial token of his favour, friendship, and gratitude, a charter, erecting the village of Paisley into a burgh, and investing him, "his very dear confessor," with a supreme power, (a charter signed in Stirling castle, which the father of the abbot kept.)

The signatures attached are those of notable rebel lords, Hailes and Douglas and Lyle and Drummond and Angus and Colin of Argyle.

Charter of James Fourth, to the abbot Schawe of Paisley :—

"James, by the grace of God, king of the Scots : Be it "known, that for the singular respect we have for the "glorious confessor, St. Mirrin, and our monastery of "Paisley, founded by our most illustrious progenitors, where "very many of the bodies of our ancestors are buried, and "are at rest, and for the singular favour and love which we "bear to the venerable father in Christ, George Shaw, "present abbot of said monastery, our very dear confessor, "and for the faithful service rendered us in a variety of "ways by the said venerable father, in times past, and "in a particular manner, for the virtuous education and "nourishment of our dearest brother James, duke of Ross, "in his tender age, we have made, constituted, erected, and, "by the tenour of our present charter make, constitute, "erect, and create, the village of Paisley, lying within the "Sheriffdom of Renfrew, a free burgh in barony; we have "granted also to the present and future inhabitants of said "burgh, the full and free liberty of buying and selling in

"said burgh, wine, wax, woollen and linen cloths, wholesale
"or retail, and all other goods and wares coming to it; with
"power and liberty of having and holding in the same
"place, bakers, brewers, butchers, and sellers both of flesh
"and fish, and workmen in the several crafts, tending in
"any respect to the liberty of the burgh in barony:
 "We have granted likewise to the burgesses and inhabi-
"tants of the said burgh of Paisley, therein to have and
"possess a cross and market-place for ever, every week on
"Monday, and two public fairs yearly, for ever; one,
"namely, on the day of St. Mirrin, and the other on the
"day of St. Marnock, with tolls and other liberties per-
"taining to fairs of this kind; of holding and having for the
"future the said village of Paisley, a real and free burgh in
"barony, with the foresaid privileges, grants, and all other
"liberties, as freely, quietly, fully, entirely, honourably, and
"well, in peace, in every time, circumstance and condition,
"as the burgh of Dunfermline, Newburgh, Aberbrothick,
"or any other burgh in barony in our kingdom is more
"largely endowed and held: And we have granted besides,
"to the said venerable father, and to his successors the
"abbots of Paisley, the right and power of chusing annually
"the provost, bailies, and other officers of said burgh, and
"of removing the same as need shall be, and of chusing
"others anew in their room. In testimony whereof, we have
"caused our great seal to be put to this our present charter.
".These reverend fathers in Christ being witnesses :—
"Robert, bishop of Glasgow; George, bishop of Dunkeld;
"our beloved blood relations, Colin, earl of Argyle, lord
"Campbell, our Chancellor; Archibald, earl of Angus;

"lord Douglas; Patrick, lord Hailes, master of our "household; Robert, lord Lyle, our justice; Andrew, "lord Grey; Lawrence, lord Oliphant; John, lord " Drummond.

"At Stirling, on the nineteenth day of the month of "August, 1483, and in the first year of our reign."

The duke of Ross was, however, removed from the care of the abbot Schawe, and intrusted to lord Hailes, now created first earl of Bothwell, and had granted him the old baronial castle and lands of that name. These feudal turrets, already clad in centuries of ivy-green, with their story past and to come, sheltered the royal duke.

But the abbot Schawe, proud and supreme, ruled his new-made burgh, and wrangled with neighbouring Renfrew, and still held the favour of the king.

And the wind, with its low presage of storm, was a whisper unheard far away.

THE ABBOT'S CHARTER.

---o---

THIS gift alone I shall her give:
When death doth what he can,
Her honest fame shall ever live
Within the mouth of man.
George Boleyn.

THE Burgh of Paisley was twelve years old when the abbot granted it a charter—a charter with a blending of ecclesiastical and nearly royal pomp. It is granted to "our loviles the provost, bailies, burgesses, and community," and defines with much exactness, and wise forethought for the rights of the Abbey, the privileges these *loviles* may exercise, the submission the abbot shall exact.

The lands, on the water of Cart, extending by the king's highway, the wood of Oakshaw, and a part of the forest of Espadair, "the tail of the Broomlands," and the Prior's Croft, and the Holm of Welmeadow, and the lands of Sneddon, the hedged-in Whitefauld, and a part of the pleasant common, and a part of the green moss, and a certain mustard-yard, are named in the abbot's charter, and defined with clear boundaries, as land to be let or feued to the burgesses under expressed reserves.

For pasture there shall be the common and the moss. And a fragrant broom-dyke is named, and "the marchdyke of Inch," which has a sort of story in it. . There are also rights in the peat-mosses, and the quarries, and the coal-*heughs*, bestowed and retained royally, always with conditions annexed. For whatever befall the burgesses, "where we please, in the said mosses and quarries," always the abbot may take. And "whoever shall find or gain a coal-heugh, or coal-heughs . . . we will and order . . . that we shall thence have our necessaries."

And there is a curious revival of the old mill right. "To our miln of Paisley, and not to any other mill whatsoever, paying there for mulcture to the thirty-one dish," the abbot requires absolutely that all the grain of his dependents shall be brought.

"Charter by the abbot and convent of the monastery of Paisley, to the provost, bailies, and community of the burgh of Paisley, 2nd June, 1490.

"'Jesus —— Maria,

"'To all and sundry who may see this indented charter, 'George Schawe, abbot of the monastery of Paisley, and 'convent of the same place. Of the Clugniensian order and 'diocese of Glasgow, wisheth safety in God everlasting. 'Be it known to your university, that forasmuch as we have 'the village of Paisley made and erected, by our most 'excellent lord the king, into a free burgh, to us and our

THE ABBOT'S CHARTER.

'successors, as is fully contained in a charter granted
'thereupon, under his majesty's great seal; therefor, we
'have diligently considered the premises, always providing
'for and wishing the utility of our said monastery: With
'advice and consent of our whole chapter, chapterly
'convened. To have given, granted, set, and in fen-farm,
'let, and by this our present chapter to have confirmed to
'our lovites the provost, bailies, burgesses, and community
'of our burgh of Paisley. All and whole our said burgh in
'barony, with the pertinents, lying in our regality of Paisley,
'within the sheriffdom of Renfrew, within the bounds and
'limits underwritten, viz., Beginning at the end of the
'bridge of Paisley upon the water of Cart, and extending by
'the king's highway towards the west of the vennel opposite
'to the Wellmeadow; and from thence equally ascending
'towards the north, by the dyke to the lands of Oakshawside
'to the wood of Oakshaw betwixt the said wood, as also the
'passage to the common of the said burgh, and the broom
'dyke which extends by the lands of Sneddon, from the
'common of the said burgh to the water of Cart on the
'north, and the said water of Cart: as also the forest of
'Espedair, on the east part; and the mustard-yard, and way
'extending on the south part of the house of John Murray,
'and so by the hedge extending above the west end of the
'Whitefauld, on the south part, and the said Whitefauld;
'as also a part of the common of the said burgh; and said
'Wellmeadow, and ditch of the said lands of Oxshawside,
'on the west part, upon the one side, and the other for
'erecting and building tenements, mansions, and yards to
'said provost, bailies, burgesses, and community, as is

M

'specially assigned, or hereafter shall be assigned to every
'one of them by us and our convents, by our said convent,
'by our charter of feu-farm, together with certain acres of
'the nearest lands, lying within the limits and bounds afore
'assigned or to be assigned to every tenement, mansion, and
'yard, according to the tenour of our said charter made, or
'to be made there upon. Moreover, we annex and
'incorporate the loft-house building, mansions, yards,
'and lands of Seidhill, to the liberty and privilege of our
'said burgh in barony of Paisley, to be possest perpetually
'in all time hereafter: as also we have given, granted, set
'in feu-farm, let, and such like, to the said provost, bailies,
'burgesses, and community of our said burgh of Paisley, and
'their successors for the time being, our lands under-written;
'whereof one part of the lands lies at the west end of our said
'burgh towards the south, betwixt the lands of Causeyside
'and the lands of Thomas Leith, called the Bank, on the
'east part, and the lands of Castlehead; as also the lands of
'Sir Henry Morris, John Whiteford, and the stabbs of
'Riccartsbar, on the south parts; and the bottom of the
'Ward, on the west part; and the tail of the Broomlands,
'as also Wellmeadow, and the Prior's Croft, on the north
'part.

"'And the other part of the said lands lies on the part
'of the said burgh, betwixt the lands of Oxshawhead and
'the wood of Oxshaw, as also the Croft of Robert, called
'the Slatebank, on the south part; and the lands of
'Sneddon, and water of Cart, as also the Holm of Ward-
'meadow, on the east part; and the march-dyke of Inch,
'and the moss of Paisley, on the north parts; and the said

'moss, on the west parts, upon the one side, and the other
'for the convenience of the said burgh, or for ever to be
'possest for the common pasturage of the cattle of the said
'provost, bailies, burgesses, and community : And such like
'we have granted, given free license and power to the said
'provost, bailies, burgesses, and community, and their
'successors for ever; and for gaining or taking their fuel,
'or whatsomever from our peat-mosses of Paisley, for sus-
'taining the said provost, bailies, burgesses, and community
'and their successors for ever; and for gaining and taking
'stones out of our stone quarries for erecting and building
'of the said burgh, as oft and so oft it shall be lawful for
'you, providing that we have what may be necessary for us
'where we please in the said mosses and quarries; and in
'case the said provost, bailies, burgesses, or community of
'the said burgh, shall find or gain a coal heugh, or coal
'heughs, in their said common of the said burgh, we will,
'and order that our successors shall, thence have our
'necessaries; we paying in our part of the expenses for
'the gaining of the said coal heugh, or coal heughs, as the
'said provost, bailies, burgesses, and community of the said
'burgh, pay for their part thereof, or shall be willing to pay.

"'And further, we give and grant to the said provost,
'bailies, burgesses, and community of the said burgh, a
'common pasture of the breadth of twelve ells, on the north
'side of St. Mirrin's Croft, extending from the said part of
'the foresaid common lands, even to the other part thereof,
'having and holding all and whole the foresaid burgh of
'Paisley in a barony, with the tenements, mansions, yards,
'acres of land, bounds and limits thereof, assigned or to be

'assigned by us to them, with the common pasturage of
'their cattle upon the moss of Paisley, and license in our
'peat-mosses and quarries aforesaid, as the same lie in
'length and breadth, to the said provost, bailies, burgesses,
'and community of the foresaid burgh, and their successors,
'in feu-farm heritable, for ever, by rights hereof, used and
'divided, limited or to be limited by us to them; with power
'of buying and selling, within the said burgh, wine, wax,
'cloth, woollen and linen, arts of crafts, and other goods
'and merchandize coming thereto, with the annual customs
'and tolls, and withal and sundry other liberties, commodities,
'profits, and easements, and righteous pertinents whatsoever,
'belonging, or which may justly be understood hereafter to
'belong to the said burgh in barony, with power of chusing
'and making burgesses and stallingers, according to the
'custom and laws, and statutes of burghs made thereanent:
'Which burgesses and stallingers, and every one of them,
'shall, at their entry, swear they shall be faithful to our
'sovereign lord the king, and his successors, kings of
'Scotland; as also to the Steward of Scotland, and his heirs
'and successors; and to us the abbot and convent, and our
'successors; and to the said bailies and community, and
'common utility of the said burgh, in the same manner
'as burgesses in other burghs do, or have been in use to
'do.

"'Moreover, we give and grant to the provost and
'bailies of the said burgh, to be elected by us for the time,
'and their successors, full and free power of holding,
'convening, and fencing of burgh courts, of the said burgh,
'and of continuing the same so oft as it shall be needful;

'and of uplifting the issues and amercements of the said
' courts, and of fining the absents, and of punishing trans-
'gressors and delinquents according to the statutes and
' laws of burghs ; and of chusing serjeants, officers, ministers,
' tasters of ale and wine, and appretiators of flesh, and other
' servants, whomsoever necessary for a burgh, and as it is
' statuted and ordained in other burghs, according to the
' strength, form, and tenour, so far as concerns the extension
' of the foresaid liberties, as is at length contained in the
' charter of the said burgh in barony, and privileges thereof,
' granted by our sovereign lord the king to us and our
' successors : And further, we give and grant to the bailies
' of the said burgh, to be chosen by us and our successors,
' full power and a faculty of taking and receiving resignation
' of, and sundry lands, acres, and tenements, lying within the
' said burgh, and to give and deliver heritable state and
' seisin, as is the use in burghs, to the wives of the possessors,
' or their true heirs, providing they seisin to no other
' person, neither receive resignations without our consent,
' and assent had, and obtained thereto.

"' It is also our will, that the said provost and bailies
' of the said burgh be annually chosen by advice of us and
' our successors, at the term and court limited by law; and
' that they shall be deprived of as oft, and oft as needs be,
' without any abstract whatsoever.

"' And further, we will, and grant, that the said provost,
' bailies, burgesses, and community of the said burgh, shall
' for ever have, for sustaining their burgh, profits of the said
' burgh, the fines of all burgesses and stallingers of the said
' burgh, to be made in all time coming, together with the

'ancient customs and tolls of the said burgh, as is the
'custom of other burghs; rendering yearly the foresaid
'provost, bailies, and community of the said burgh, and
'their heirs and successors, to us and our successors,
'furth of the tenement, mansions, yards, and acres of land,
'within the bounds and limits of the burgh, before written,
'the barony farm and service of court, used and wont, with
'the yearly rents due furth thereof, according to the tenour
'of our rental and register, and is at more length granted,
'or to be made and granted, upon the feu-farm tacks of the
'said tenement, mansions, yards, and acres. And that the
'said provost, bailies, burgesses, and community of the said
'burgh, and their successors, shall come with their grain
'whatsoever, in so far as they shall grind, to our miln of
'Paisley, and not to any other miln whatsoever, paying
'therefor to us mulcture to the thirty-one dish, only as men
'abiding of our lands for all other burdens, exaction,
'question, demand, or secular service, which can any
'manner of persons furth of the said burgh in barony,
'tenements, mansions, yards, and acres, lying within the
'said burgh, with the pertinents.

"'In witness whereof, the common seal of the chapter of
'our said monastery, as appended to this present indented
'charter, remaining with the said provost, bailies, burgesses,
'and community of the said burgh; and the common seal of
'the said burgh of Paisley, is appended to the present
'indented charter, remaining with the said abbot and convent,
'at the monastery and burgh, aforesaid, the second day of
'June, 1490. Before these witnesses, viz. :—

'JAMES SCHAWE of Sauchy.   'JOHN RALSTON of that ilk.
'DAVID SCHAWE, his son.   'JOHN SCHAWE.
'THOMAS STEWART of Craigenfeoch.   'SIR ALEXANDER JUGSTON, and
'ROBERT SEMPLE.   'JAMES YOUNG, public notary.'

"Extracted from an English translation of the original charter lying in the burgh of Paisley charter chest."

In the oath administered to the burgesses, there still lingers a relic of the supremacy of the old lord Stewards, who founded the Clugniac monastery, and ruled feudal chiefs in Strathgryfe.

"Burgesses and stallingers, and every one of them, shall, at their entry, swear they shall be faithful to our sovereign lord the king, and his successors, the kings of Scotland; *as also to the Steward of Scotland, and his heirs and successors;* and to us the abbot and convent, and our successors."

So supreme in the convent and the burgh reigned the abbot Schawe.

A VASSAL OF THE ABBOT.

> We feel within ourselves
> His energy Divine; he tells the heart
> He meant, he made us to behold and love
> What he beholds and loves, the general orb
> Of life and being; to be great like him,
> Beneficent and active.
> *Akenside.*

HE has not an historical name, or only very locally so. James Crawfurd was a kindly tenant of the abbot Schawe and his monks;—that is, held his lands from the Abbey, not by bargain, but on simple favour, a common feudal tenure, and one which his fathers had enjoyed for many generations back.

He was not a peasant-vassal, but the cadet of an ancient house, descended from the family of the Crawfurds of the castle and barony of Achinames, which lands passed from father to son, from the fourteenth century to the eighteenth, when it was broken up, and finally sold, castle and lands, by Patrick, the last lord of the soil who bore the name of Crawfurd.

And the Crawfurds of Achinames were a branch of the notable Crawfurds of Louden, hereditary sheriffs of Ayr in the days of Alexander Second. "Reginald Crawfurd, Sheriff of Ayr, and Hugh, the son of Reginald," are witnesses of the sorrowful transfer, by Walter High Steward of Scotland, of the lands of the convent of Dalmulin to the mother Abbey of Paisley.

The family from this distant date have some links of interest in the Abbey.

The Crawfurds of Achinames were devout. Long ago, gentle, graceful Robert Second had confirmed to the kirk of Kilbarchan, a grant made by the Crawfurd of that time.

The kirk, among its low mosses, and pretty knolls, and strips of wood, and the sleepy, tranquil shimmer of the Gryfe, and the shiny cascades of the Locher coming down from the Munebrock moor, was already a dependency of Paisley, a *cell* of the great Abbey, and dedicated to St. Barchan, an obscure member of the Kalendar.

In this little kirk one of the Crawfurds endowed an altar to the Virgin. The chartulary of the Abbey of Paisley records his grant of "the lands of Lyndocht and Glenlean, with their pertinents, and an annuity of three merks out of the land of Achinames for the maintenance of a chaplain to celebrate Divine service at the altar of the Virgin Mary, in the kirk of Kilbarchan. This he grants for the health of his own soul, and for the soul of his wife, and for the soul of Sir Reginald Crawfurd, his grandfather, as also for the souls of his father and of his mother."

A later Crawfurd is named as one of the arbiters in the dispute between the abbot Schawe and the burgh of

Renfrew. And his history is followed in a few brief words, and no comment, as one in the crowd of chivalry who went out to Flodden with the king, pressing close on the royal banner, and who never came back again.

So this Crawfurd who fell beside King James was a cousin, by some removes, of James Crawfurd of Kylwynnat, the kindly tenant of the monks.

Of these lands he had thus held, James Crawfurd afterwards became the possessor. And on the erection by James Fourth of the village of Paisley into a burgh, James Crawfurd was appointed, by the abbot Schawe, one of the bailies of the place—one of the first bailies of the little new-made town, with its five and twenty lieges, and the abbot Schawe for its lord.

The low lands of Seidhill lay round the Abbey. Wellmeadow lay on the ridge, towards the old Roman prætorium, looking out towards the green braes. These lands of Seidhill and Wellmeadow had passed to James Crawfurd, with consent of the abbot and convent, on the sixteenth day of May, in the year 1490. But one year earlier than this, James Crawfurd had acquired land from " John Stewart, Earl of Lennox, and Lord of Dernlie."

The document is still preserved, " whereby we gave and " granted to our well-beloved James Crawfurd of Seidhill, " and Elizabeth Calbrayth, his spouse, all and sundry, our " land of Kylwynnat and pertinents, lying in the earldom of " Lennox, within the sheriffdom of Sterlywing, which " belonged to John Blair of Adamton, and Elizabeth " Colquhoun, his spouse."

Respecting this transfer of land from John Blair of

Adamton, to James Crawfurd of Seidhill, and Elizabeth Calbrayth, his spouse, nothing more than this has been preserved. Lennox was one of those rebel lords who disturbed the close of the reign of James Third, and the beginning of the reign of James Fourth. He had formerly been leagued with Schawe of Sauchie, the father of the abbot George; and sometime this same year was defeated at the green Tala Moss, not far from Stirling, by lord Drummond, and the king's troops.

An event which was largely personal to the new burgess of Paisley, was but small in the stormy adventures of the lord of Lennox and Darnley. The historical name gives but a brief glimpse into the time, into the passionate settings of certain homely lives; casts one glimmer upon obscurity, and having done this, has done all.

James Crawfurd, for ten years, remains in the happy shade, and then emerges once. His life is near its close. The late, long, silent shadows, stealing across the Campsie glen, deepening in the green gares among the hills round Kylwynnat, warn him how soon the long, long sleep may creep over him.

Sons or daughters has he? There is Master Archibald Crawfurd, vicar of pleasant Erskeyne, in the broad bend of the Clyde. Master Archibald Crawfurd, from his vicarage, may see the fair lands of Lennox; see Dumbuck, where St. Mungo stood, looking down, with his sandals and staff, on the wondrously fair solitude he must win for God and the church; see Dumbarton, already storied with tales of Wallace and Bruce, and of its own lords of Lennox, and of many more beside; or see the purple splendour of Argyle, far-off, in the August noons,—while walking and musing where the oaks of Erskeyne meet the sunny shallows of the Clyde.

James Crawfurd and Elizabeth Calbrayth are well contented with their lot. And they will raise a chapel to be both thanksgiving and prayer, "for the souls of all their friends, benefactors, ancestors, and successors, and salvation of all the faithful dead." Very wide grows their benevolence, very large their tenderness; for "goodness and mercy have followed them all the days of their life." They could not comfort themselves, perhaps, with David's most sweet psalm, and so they will rear a little chapel which will dumbly plead and praise.

The charter of foundation, well preserved on vellum, and written in abbreviated Latin, is addressed thus:—" To "all the sons of Holy Mother Church, present and to "come." It then narrates by what divine impulse the granters have been moved, by what desire of pious devotion, and increase of the worship of God. The grant is with consent and license of a venerable father in Christ, George, by divine persuasion, abbot of Paisley, and of the convent there. It has also been confirmed, ratified, and approved by a reverend father in Christ, Robert, by divine mercy, archbishop of Glasgow, and his chapter there. The grant is to raise one chapel for the altars of the saints and confessors, Mirrinus and Columb; and to provide, for ever, one chaplain thereof. The chapel was to be built on the south side of the Abbey; and was built, it is expressly said, " by the granters from their own industry, in praise of " the Almighty God, Son and Holy Spirit; the glorious "virgin and mother Mary; and the blessed Peter and Paul, "the apostles; and in honour of all the saints: Also, for "the souls of that excellent deceased prince, James the king "of the Scots; and likewise for our illustrious prince, king "James the Fourth; and their predecessors and successors: "and for the souls of them, the said James and Elizabeth "Crawfurd, and Master Archibald Crawfurd, vicar of "Erskeyne; and for the souls of all their friends, bene-"factors, ancestors, and successors, and salvation of all the "faithful dead."

For the sustentation of the chapel, altars, and chaplains, which the granters had erected, founded, constituted, and ordained, they gave, granted, and in pure alms perpetually mortified, all and sundry, that Burgall tenement, and whole Burgall lands of Scheidhill, with their pertinents, lying in the burgh of Paisley, in the south part thereof, near the mill of the said lord abbot and convent of the monastery of Paisley. And also, all and sundry, the outfield land of the aforesaid land of Scheidhill, with pertinents, as the same were more fully contained in the charters, instruments, and evidents thereof: as also, all and sundry, the lands of Wellmeadow, with pertinents, lying in the west part of the foresaid burgh, upon the public highway, on the south part thereof; and likewise as more fully contained in the charters, instruments, and evidents afore mentioned.

The bailies of the new-made burgh were appointed patrons of the chapel when James and Elizabeth Crawfurd had passed, as they must soon pass. And James Crawfurd, careful still of the little town in which he himself had ruled, made a special provision regarding all future presentations,

If born within the young burgh, there could be found a priest, with clerkly and pious gifts which would adorn such an office, no stranger from old Wenlock, nor even from Lennox or Kyle, or any other foot of Scottish soil which was ruled by good king James, should be preferred as chaplain before the said priest, whose first qualification lay in his being a native of the town.

If twenty days within the time when the chaplaincy became vacant, the bailies of Paisley should fail to present another chaplain to the Abbey, through such neglect the right should pass from the bailies to the abbot and monks, for that time, and that time only, as the charter carefully expresses. For the rights of the town were guarded jealously from all ecclesiastical encroachment.

The chàplain, whoever he might be, must become a monk of Paisley; and daily, in the new transept chapel, say masses for the souls of the dead; for the soul of king James the Third, and the soul of the reigning king; for the souls of James and Elizabeth Crawfurd, and of Master Archibald, the vicar of Erskeyne; for the souls of all their friends, benefactors, ancestors, successors.

And if, for fifteen days, the chaplain should absent himself, and none should plead for those whom the founders loved at the altars of St. Mirrin and St. Columb, he must be deposed from his office, and another chosen in his stead, that the souls of the faithful dead might not suffer by neglect of the living.

The charter was signed at Paisley, on the fifteenth day of July, 1499, and had these seals appended, viz. :—

"ROBERT, ARCHBISHOP OF GLASGOW.
"THE CHAPTER OF GLASGOW.
"THE ABBOT AND CONVENT OF PAISLEY.
"THE BURGH OF PAISLEY.
"JAMES CRAWFURD.
"ELIZABETH CRAWFURD."

The formal presentation of the deed took place six days later. It is recorded that "at ten o'clock forenoon, within "the council chamber of the Town House of the burgh of "Paisley, James Crawfurd and Elizabeth Calbrayth, his "spouse, appeared personally, and in the presence of two "bailies, and the town clerk, and others, ratified the "mortification and appointment of the patrons of the chapel "and altars of St. Mirrin and St. Columb."

And in that same year, when the trees were wierd and bare, and the snow lay white on the Abbey roof, and the drifts were deep among the braes, James Crawfurd of Kylwynnat lay at rest in the sacred earth. An inscription may be seen still, in the south gable of the Abbey, which, in Latin, entreats of the reader a passing prayer for his soul.

Two kinsmen of unnamed degree, whom tradition scarcely follows, survived James and Elizabeth. James, the elder of the two, held by birthright the green lands of Spango, and lived a quiet, nameless laird through the troublous Reformation times. And Robert, the younger and less richly portioned brother, became a soldier, says the history, "either of Scotland or of France." An unrenowned Quentin Durward he in the train of Francis First, fighting in fair Savoy against the emperor Charles; or hearing amiable gossip of the joyous, worldly pope Pius Fourth, when Pavia was forgot in Cerisolles, and the victors had leisure to be amiable, and to smile at the borken treaty of Nice, and at the busy, peaceful, gay old pope. Or, perhaps, there was no such wide field for the adventurous Scot; and instead of Bayard and Bourbon as his compeers, there were Lindsay and Argyle and Douglas, and the quondam abbot, Claude Hamilton; and instead of the bright vales of Savoy, the straths of Stirling and Lennox. However that may be, fame and honour he got none, as is told by his quaint, praiseful epitaph on the Abbey wall of Paisley:—

"Heir lyis ane honorable man, caiptane robert crawfurd,
"granter of Paslay, i ye sepulture of James Crawfurd of
"Sedil, quilk decessit ye fourt of Julii, ye zeir of God, 1575.

"quha neuir rasevit honors
"of na man, and has maid to
"mony sundry."*

* Who never received honours of any man, and has bestowed honours on many.

THE CHAPEL OF ST. MIRRINUS.

*This peace to a propitious God I owe;
None else, my friend, such blessings could bestow.
Him will I celebrate with rites divine.*
                        Beattie.

AND the little chapel arose, stone by stone, very fair to see. The masons, as they paused in their labour, might rest above a green grave—six feet of daisied turf—where James Crawford, the founder, lay. But the chapel, in its sweet chaste beauty, rose slowly like the prayer of the dead.

Men might question and wonder far away across the sea, when Cæsar Borgia laid aside his cardinalate, and became a soldier and a duke. And Savonarola's passionate denunciations of the sinfulness and apostacy of the time, might echo still through his convent of San Marco, or among the Damascus roses where the people had heard him preach.

But in the little northern kingdom, far from the unholy war of papal and imperial interests, of heresy and faith, rose, with belief and devotion, this chapel to the saints. Saints, no longer a possibility on the skirts of the Papal sway, might have shrines raised to them, in all sincerity, in the realm of James Fourth.

There were the Lollards of Kyle, indeed; but the laughter of the gay young king had averted a persecution which might have spread seed far and wide. And neither Cæsar Borgia's wickedness, nor Savonarola's lofty zeal, had in wavelets, however little, touched the island yet.

The beautiful small chapel, in the southern transept of the Abbey, rose under the eye of the abbot Schawe without faltering or delay. Michael Angelo, in his yet undreamed glory, works among the antique marbles, all the splendour of his life before him, and his great gifts still his own. But the nameless architect also, to whom splendour never came, wrought serene thoughts into the sculptures of the shrines of Saint Mirrin and Saint Columb.

The chapel is very little—only forty-eight feet long; twenty-four feet broad at the westerly portion, and twenty-two feet broad in the east. But the roof is of great height; bossed, and ribbed, and groined, the ribs springing diagonally from slender triple shafts in the south, and uniting and terminating in simply carved corbels, between the two large arches in the opposite wall.

These arches, eighteen feet high by eleven broad, simply moulded, and supported on pillars still more simple, once opened from the little oratory into the Abbey choir. But in the ruthless days of demolition, which came when the chapel was but sixty years old, some hand, more tender than wont, must have cared for the shrines of St. Mirrin and St. Columb. The arches through which the priests passed from the beautiful choir, to offer their daily masses for the souls of all the faithful dead, have been filled in with solid ashlar-work, to shut out the green grass which grows among the roofless ruins and broken sculptures beyond.

A flight of four steps, crossing the whole floor, leads to the eastern end of the chapel, where the altars of the saints stood. Extending along the lower part of the wall behind the altar, is a frieze of one foot, eight inches deep, placed between eight-inch cornices. The frieze is divided into compartments, ten of which are filled in with sculptures in half relief, so curiously worn and defaced, that their meaning can scarcely now be deciphered. They have, however, been supposed to represent the seven sacraments of the Romish Church — Matrimony, Communion, Extreme Unction, Ordination, Confirmation, Penance, and Baptism. The remaining compartments of the frieze have been left uncarved. When the order had gone forth from John Knox, and the lords of the congregation, to "pass incontinent to every kirk, and bring forth the haill images, and burn them openly," there could be no more such adornment of niche or frieze. The series of curious ecclesiastical carvings, and then the rude blank, are a significant note on the iconoclasm of the time.

A plain font still stands against the southern wall, and near it a small niche obediently dismantled.

Behind the altar was a pointed window, twenty feet high and twelve feet broad, and composed of four trefoil-headed lights. Only a faint suggestion of the old placid beauty is obtained from the slender mullions, now filled in with solid brick.

Opposite, in the western gable, is a window similarly arched, but smaller, being only seventeen feet high, and nine and a half feet broad, and having no tracery, but only plain mullions, simply crossed in the head, like the easternmost windows of the nave.

A very plain doorway leads from beneath this window into the cloister-court. This is now the only entrance to the chapel, but probably was not opened till after the great arches had been filled with masonry to shut out the ruined choir.

And so imagination must be used to restore the pristine beauty; for a sense of disappointment seizes you in this little fair chapel of St. Mirrinus.

You must see (as the monks long ago would see) through the two great arches the clustered pillars of the choir, and the light, warmed and softened by the coloured glass, falling on the altar from the great window above, or blent harmoniously on the pavement with the meeting rays that stream through the smaller western window;—the eye must obtain from these distance and colour both, all the mystery and delight of perspective through the grey wreathed shafts beyond; and, from the storied windows, those warm tones which pervade the air like scent or sound, which seem to embody emotion, or etherialize thought,—those semi-spiritualistic attributes, which do, like the mythic sylphs, belong wholly to neither earth nor heaven, but partake of and unite both.

In the chapel, as it now stands, the intense whiteness of

light, for which there are no distances, nor nooks to give refuge to shadow, troubles and fatigues the eye. It is like a constant protest on the worn unfinished frieze, on the broad bared altar-steps, on the one little desolate niche; like intellect obtruding on a region which was only meant for faith; like the eye of the arch-iconoclast exulting in the ravage he has done. For decay claims always the tenderness of shadow to make it fair.

And yet the great window above the altar is closed,—the window where the glad sunrise came with rays from Bethlehem! The light, no longer diffused and soft, but hard, concentrated, intense, through the clearness of the one white sheet of glass,—is it an unwitting symbol which the Protestants themselves have set, of some divine element, and many sweet humanities also, omitted from the rigid system they carved above the ruins of the old?

But the interest of the stranger gathers round a large altar-tomb, placed in the centre of the aisle, and invested with much fond tradition.

Certain history it has none. It is called Queen Blearie's Tomb. But who is this old queen Blearie, whose effigy, placid and sweet, lies quiet, with folded hands, above her tomb; and still, fair, chiselled face, looking eastward, as in waiting, or in hope?

Traditions all unite in declaring her Marjorie the daughter of Bruce,—that chase-loving princess Marjorie who wedded the brave young Steward. Persistently they assign this effigy to the daughter of Robert Bruce, giving no reason why; for Marjorie never was queen. And her son, Robert Second, called king Blearie from defective sight, as has been told, found graves for his two wives within the precincts of the Abbey. Naturally we should give to queen Euphemia, the daughter of the earl of Ross, or Elizabeth, that still less renowned queen, the soubriquet her husband bore. But tradition passes both by, and will have only Marjorie Bruce, the daughter of the hero-king, to keep in serene effigy.

Two paragraphs from Billings' Antiquities shall serve for description here :—

"The main object of attention is that mysterious monument known as Queen Blearie's Tomb. It is the monument of a female, whose effigy lies at full length on a large altar sarcophagus. The figure is graceful and simple, and the drapery well developed. Over the head is a large canopy of the richest pendant Gothic work. But the large sarcophagus is itself both the most remarable and most beautiful portion of the monument. It is divided into compartments, characteristically enriched with quatre-foils and raised mouldings, profusely decorated. It exhibits many ornamental devices, partly of an ecclesiastical, partly of an heraldic character.

"The character of the whole of this work of art, as well as the edifice in which it lies, is heightened by the deep mystery in which its history is involved. Although it did not originally belong to the chapel, which indeed is evidently of a somewhat later date, yet its present position is happily chosen at least for effect; as from the great size of the monument, the chapel stands so proportioned as if it were a niche suited to contain it." *

* Billings' "Baronial and Ecclesiastical Antiquities of Scotland."

In the spoliation of the Abbey, this effigy was torn from its place, and lay long uncared for in the open cloister court. But wondrously through rain and shine, unmarred the fair face looked up, and the hands lay serenely folded in their long prayerfulness. The pure carved-stone lineaments, exposed among the rank grass, were at length rescued, about the year 1770, and laid, by the marquis of Abercorn, in the chapel where they rest.

The burial vault of the family of Abercorn is now beneath the old altar of the chapel of St. Mirrinus. And the noble name is fast superseding the saintly name. The Abercorn Aisle it is called; and there lingers not one tradition round it of Mirrinus and Columb, the early tutelary saints.

The little chapel has another name, locally the most familiar of all. A name which it well merits, although in a less degree now than when Pennant, an hundred years ago, in the days when tourists were few, made his "Tour in Scotland," and wrote enthusiastically of this wonderful Sounding Aisle.

"The echo is the finest in the world. When the end door, the only one it has, is gently shut, the noise is equal to a loud peal of thunder. If you strike a single note of music, you hear the same gradually ascending with a countless number of repetitions, until it dies away, as if in an immense distance, and all the while diffusing itself in the circumambient air. If a good voice sings, or a musical instrument is well played upon, the effect is inexpressibly fascinating, and almost of a celestial character. The deepest as well as the sharpest tones are distinctly reverberated, and at regular intervals of time. When a musical instrument is sounded, it has the effect of a number of instruments, of a like size and kind, playing in concert. When a number of different instruments in unison sound the same note, a good ear is able to distinguish the individual sound produced by each. A single instrument sounding a particular note, and then instantly its fifth, or any other concordant note, both sounds can be heard, as it were, running into and uniting with each other, in a manner peculiarly agreeable. But the effect of a variety of instruments playing in concert is transcendantly enchanting, and excites such emotions in the soul as to baffle the most vivid description."

Since Pennant came north across the border, and stood in the Sounding Aisle, and heard that "transcendant enchantment" which baffled his pen to describe, changes have been made, renovations and reconstructions, which have somewhat diminished the spell. Yet still very lovely and strange is the long sweet echo through the lofty vaulted roof, like the lingering gathered voices of the many poor striving souls, who here, through four centuries, prayed and laboured and taught, waiting and longing to see God, and who died and were buried namelessly within the cloistral ground.

VISIONS.

I WHO was fancy's lord am fancy's slave:
Like the low murmurs of the Indian shell,
Ta'en from its choral bed beneath the wave,
Which, unforgetful of the ocean's swell,
Retains within its mystic urn the hum
Heard in the sea-grots, where the Nereids dwell;—
Old thoughts still haunt me; unawares they come
Between me and my rest, nor can I make
Those dreadful visitors of sorrow dumb.
Aytoun.

TO Innocent Eighth in the Vatican, with behind him the stormy, ambitious pontificate of Sixtus Fourth, and round him the unholy memories of Imoli and Forli, his tiara already reft of much of its spiritual power, and all the unquietnesses and profanities of beautiful Romagna at his feet,—this remote and little province of the church was an easy thing to sway.

One imagines the touch of scorn with which the Medici and Colonna, fighting revengefully in the shadow of the Papal chair, will hear the reverential prayer of the fervid young Scottish king, who, safe far away among his rude, brave people, yet cannot live at peace without the benediction of the pope. Any Italian prince will be more easily content. Ringing through St. Celso are the words of the mother of a dead Colonna:—

"Behold the head of my son! Such is the truth of the pope. He promised if he had Marino I should have my son. He has Marino; I have my son—dead!"

Happy little far-off mountain land, that does not yet know the miserable disenchantments of its loyalties and its faiths.

James Third, in the distress of the civil war, had appealed to the pope for aid. And the pope's response to this appeal was a sentence of excommunication passed against the rebel prince and lords. After the battle of Sauchie-burn, when James Third was dead, and the nobles, one and all, had rallied round their now unquestioned king, the token of Papal displeasure lay heavily over the land, and another appeal from king and nobles was made to Innocent Eighth.

The Schawes had been insurgents. The Schawes were James's friends; acknowledged by the boy-king with especial honours and favour; and one of them wore the mitre of the rich illustrious Clugniac house. We half expect to read his name, as we do, in the pope's responsive bull.

It was in the last year of his pontificate, on the 27th of June, 1491, that Innocent issued from the Vatican this peace to the troubled consciences of the Scottish king and his lieges. The abbot of Paisley is one of three, expressly empowered by the pope, to absolve and restore the penitents to the privileges of the church.

But the absolution of the pope never took away from James Fourth the sorrow, the passionate remorse for his unfilial rebellion.

> "June is to our sovereign dear
> The heaviest month in all the year;
> Too well his cause of grief you know,—
> June saw his father's overthrow.
> Woe to the traitors who could bring
> The princely boy against his king!
> Still in his conscience burns the sting.
> In offices as strict as Lent,
> King James's June is ever spent." *

And the iron girdle worn round his waist, never laid aside in either war or pleasure, Scott has also remembered in his "Marmion":—

> "I said he joyed in banquet bower;
> But mid his mirth 'twas often strange
> How suddenly his cheer would change,
> His look o'ercast and lower,
> If in a sudden turn he felt
> The pressure of his iron belt
> That bound his breast in penance pain,
> In memory of his father slain."

And this remorse mingled with an intense belief in the supernatural,—that deep kinship of poetry, that all but inevitable accompaniment of quick susceptibilities and the genius of music and song,—has left passages of romance in history which verse can scarcely idealize. The story of the warning spectre seen in the chapel of Linlithgow, told in the simple prose of Pitscottie, is nearly as picturesque as can be.

* "Marmion."

"The king came to Lithgow, where he happened to be, for the time, at the council very sad and dolorous, making his devotion to God to send him good-chance and fortune in the voyage. In this meantime there came a man, clad in a blue gown, in at the kirk door, and belted about him in a roll of linen cloth. . . . His forehead was bald and bare. He seemed to be a man of two and fifty years, with a great pike-staff in his hand; and came first forward among the lords, crying and speiring for the king, saying he desired to speak with him. While, at the last, he came where the king was, sitting in the desk at his prayers; but when he saw the king, he made him little reverence or salutation, but leaned down groffling on the desk before him, and said to him in this manner as after follows:—'Sir king, my mother hath sent me to you, desiring you not to pass, at this time, where you are purposed; for if thou does, thou wilt not fare well on thy journey, nor none that passeth with thee.' . . . By the time this man had spoken these words unto the king's grace, the even-song was near done; and the king paused on these words, studying to give an answer; but in the meantime, before the king's eyes, and in the presence of all the lords that were about him for the time, this man vanished away."

Buchanan, too, relates the vision :—

"This declaration of war being brought to Scotland, one evening whilst the king, who was on the point of setting out for his army, attended the vesper service, as he was wont, in the church at Linlithgow, an old venerable looking man entered the cathedral, bare-headed—his hair of a bright golden lustre, flowing over his shoulders, but thinly scattered on his smooth bald forehead; clothed in a long azure-coloured robe, and girt about the middle with a linen girdle—who, pressing forward to the king through the surrounding crowd, when he reached him, bending over the the chair in which he sat, thus addressed him with emphatic simplicity :—' I am sent to warn thee against proceeding in thy present under-taking; which admonition, if thou neglectest, it will not fare well, either with thee, or with those who may accompany thee. I am besides ordered to warn thee to beware of using any familiarity in associating or advising with women; but if thou dost otherwise, it will occasion thy destruction and disgrace.' Having spoken thus, he mingled with the crowd; and after the service was ended, when the king enquired for him, he could nowhere be found. What rendered the occurrence more astonishing was, that all those who stood nearest him, and who observed him, and were desirous of putting many questions to him, no one perceived how he disappeared. Among these was Sir David Lindesay of the Mount, a man of unsuspected probity and veracity, attached to literature, and during life invariably opposed to falsehood, from whom, unless I had received the story, as narrated, vouched for truth, I had omitted to notice it as one of the commonly reported fables."

Scott seems to have gleaned from both versions, and introduces the story in his poem as, "Sir David Lindesay's Tale."

Already familiar to readers of poetry, some excuse is perhaps required for introducing it here; but these desultory pages may only plead the liberty accorded by their name.

Sir David alludes to the vision having been seen in James's fateful June:—

"When last this ruthful month was come,
And in Linlithgow's royal dome
　　The king, as wont, was praying;
While, for his royal father's soul,
The chanters sang, the bells did toll,
　　The bishop mass was saying;
For now the year brought round again
The day the luckless king was slain.
In Katherine's aisle the monarch knelt,
With sackcloth shirt and iron belt,
　　And eyes with sorrow streaming;
Around him, in their stalls of state,
The Thistle's Knight-companions sate,
　　Their banners o'er them beaming:
I too was there, and sooth to tell,
Bedeafened with the jangling knell,
Was watching where the sunbeams fell
　　Through the stained casement gleaming;
But while I marked what next befell,
　　It seemed as I were dreaming.

"Stepped from the crowd a ghostly wight,
In azure gown with cincture white;
His forehead bald, his head was bare,
Down hung at length his yellow hair:
Now, mock me not, when, good my lord,
I pledge to you my knightly word,
That, when I saw his placid grace,
His simple majesty of face,
His solemn bearing and his pace
　　So stately gliding on,—
Seemed to me ne'er did limner paint
So just an image of the saint
Who propped the Virgin in her faint,
　　The loved apostle John.

"He stepped before the monarch's chair,
And stood with rustic plainness there,
　　And little reverence made;

> Nor head, nor body bowed nor bent,
> But on the desk his arm he leant,
> And words like these he said,
> In a low voice, but never tone
> So thrilled through vein and nerve and bone:—
> 'My mother sent me from afar,
> Sir king, to warn thee not to war,—
> Woe waits on thine array;
> If war thou wilt, of woman fair,
> Her witching smiles and wanton snare,
> James Stewart, doubly warned, beware;
> God keep thee as He may!'
> The wondering monarch seemed to seek
> For answer, and found none;
> And when he raised his head to speak,
> The monitor was gone.
> The marshal and myself had cast
> To stop him as he outward pass'd;
> But, lighter than the whirlwind's blast,
> He vanish'd from our eyes,
> Like sunbeam on the billow cast,
> That glances but, and dies."

Another story, still more wierd, is told by old Pitscottie. It has not attained the poetical celebrity of the vision in the chapel of Linlithgow, and is probably new to most of those readers who love not to plod through ancient annals, cumbered by unfamiliar words, and as unfamiliar ideas.

It was on the eve of Flodden. The fated army of the king was gathered on the Borough moor, then "delightful," says Drummond of Hawthornden, "by the shade of many stately and aged oaks." There were gathered to the king's banner, "all his earls, lords, barons, and burgesses; and all manner of men between sixty and sixteen, spiritual and temporal, burgh and land, islemen and others, to the number of a hundred thousand, not reckoning carriage men and artillery men. . . ." And the king had left queen Margaret, and was himself come to Holyrood, ready, at the head of his army, to march for the Borders on the morrow :

"When there was a cry heard at the market cross of Edinburgh, at the hour of midnight, proclaiming as it had been a summons, which was named and called by the proclaimer thereof, 'The summons of Plutock,' which desired all men to compear, both earl, lord, and baron, and all honest gentlemen within the town (every man specified by his own name)—to compear within the space of forty days before his master, where it should happen him to appoint, and be, for the time, under the pain of disobedience: . . . Mr Richard Lawson, being evil-disposed, ganging in his gallery stair forenent the cross, hearing this voice proclaiming this summons, thought marvel what it should be, cried on his servant to bring him his purse; and when he had brought him it, he took out a crown, and cast it over the stair saying, 'I appeal from that summons, judgment, and sentence thereof; and take me all whole in the mercy of God, and Christ Jesus, His Son.' Verily, the author of this, that caused me write the manner of this summons, was a landed gentleman, who was at that time twenty years of age, and was in the town the time of the said summer; and thereafter, when the field was stricken, he swore to me there was no man that escaped that was called in the summons, but that one man alone who made his protestation, and appealed from the said summons; but all the rest were perished on the field with the king. . . . The news spread through the town on the morne, and came to the king's ears."

The discreet twenty years of the certain landed gentleman are needed to verify a tale so circumstantial and so wierd. Such stories at least mean that remorse had wrought upon the poetical temperament of the king, and made him keenly superstitious, a fact which all his realm knew. And none knew this better than queen Margaret, who could not share his remorse, and does not seem to have shared either much of the fine temper of her husband. "We lak naething," she had written to Henry Eighth a few months earlier than this, "our husband is evir the langer the better to us, as knawis God." But she can work relentlessly on the secret passion of the king. He will not quail for any muster which all the power of England may bring; but the tremor of a leaf may move him, Margaret has discovered long ago.

How James's religious observances led him a repeated guest to the Clugniac Abbey, founded by his ancestors, another chapter must show.

A ROYAL RECLUSE.

WHY hast thou made me so weary, O day,
With the pitiless blaze of thy dazzling ray,
With thy lights that flash through the quivering trees,
With thy never-ending melodies?
Thou'rt welcome, O night, so sad and pale,
Come drop on the weary world thy veil;
Away with the splendour, the glory, the din,
Let nothing intrude on the quiet within;
And let me slumber alone with thee,
And dream of the heaven high over me.
From the German of Julius Sturm.

IN August of the year 1503, James Fourth was married.

The most recent delineations of the juvenile bride Margaret are by no means amiable. Yet the old chronicler speaks of her with some kindness. Never indeed with enthusiasm, as he does of his native prince, nor as of Magdalene, the French bride who shared for three little months the throne of Margaret's son. But always with that measured approval which, perhaps, her dispassionate mediocrity deserved. She was a Tudor princess, and had no genius to the Stewarts.

All who care for such matters, may become familiar with the meeting of bride and bridegroom. For such the graceful person of the king is vividly drawn,—his form of middle height, his velvet jacket, and his long curled beard and hair. They know how the hawking-lure was flung across his shoulder, how skilfully he played upon the lute. They know how he leaped upon his "right fair courser" without the aid of the stirrup. They know the lowly reverence he made to the queen, how he kissed her and all her ladies; and how he took the princess apart, and talked with her "a long space." That James's love for the queen did not equal his outward devotion, was not his fault, but his sorrow.

The summer after his marriage, James came to the Abbey of Paisley; became a guest of the new abbot, who was also a Schawe of Sauchie, and kinsman of abbot George, the king's early friend, and his brother's tutor. The queen was not with him. There is little recorded of his visit. It was in the fateful month which he kept for solemn memories. A brief monastic retirement, in the season of the year when remorse was deepest, is consistent with all we know of James, and in keeping with habits of an earlier time.

We trace with strange pathetic interest the footprints of the haunted king,—among the fallen blooms of the Abbey lands; by that slow and quiet water, which was still a place for pearl-fisheries and sedges and cool broad-leaved lilies, where the shy heron might come; and where, beyond the verge of the orchard, might be seen, here and there, the mossy, decayed stumps of oaks, relics of the old forest. The uses of the old monastic life come back, like a mellow autumn wind, laden with decay of riches, yet wistfully, mournfully pervaded by something we fain would keep.

That James's devotion to his father's faith, and especial tenderness towards the monastery founded by his fathers, did not turn him from justice and tenderness towards those of alien faith and sympathies, one illustration has been kept.

It seems not inappropriate to insert it here, in this brief pause of history, where conventual silence is round the king, and we picture him one of the devoutest sons whom the Romish Church has nurtured. The narrative was written in the year 1531, by Alexander Aless, in defence of the private reading of the Bible, and was addressed to James Fifth.

It relates how John Campbell, laird of Cessnock, and one of the Lollards of Kyle, was ensnared into religious troubles by those whom his roof had sheltered. For he was a good man, and kept a priest at home, who read to him and his family the Bible in their native tongue. Secretly the priest read to him; but the laird kept an open hall, to which all wayfarers came, and welcome, and the wandering friars among the rest. And round the winter fires, chance words were spoken which kindled suspicion among the hooded guests.

"At last," says Aless, "his mind having been often sounded, the monks violating the law of hospitality, and, as it is said, passing by the eating-table and the salt, they carried his name to the bishop, and accused him of heresy. In that suit, when, after a long disputation, it appeared that both he and his wife were in danger of their lives, Campbell appealed to the king. Although the monks were grievously offended that the king should call the cause before himself, still he thought it belonged to his good faith and humanity, that to good and noble men he should not fail to do his duty. He therefore graciously heard the cause on both sides; and when the husband, from natural reserve, and not a little agitated by fear of the monks, answered with modesty, the king commanded the wife to plead the cause."

The king has pity on the bashful laird. And so Dame Campbell of Cessnock, a good wife, and a wise woman — we must believe a fair woman too—"quoting the Scriptures, refuted the charges brought against them so distinctly and wisely, that the king not only acquited the defendants— Campbell, with his wife, and the priest—but also, rising up, he caressed the woman, and extolled her diligence in Christian doctrine. Having severely reproved the monks, he threatened that, if ever after they created trouble of this sort to such honourable and innocent persons, he would punish them severely. To Campbell himself, indeed, he presented certain villages, that there might remain an honourable token of his decision, and of his good-will towards him, lest there should be supposed to lurk in his (the king's) mind any suspicion against Campbell· because of the accusation of the monks." *

This case of Campbell of Cessnock was a few years old when the king came to Paisley Abbey, in the year 1504.

* "Pictorial History of Scotland."

The larger kindness of the king triumphs over his religious zeal,—perhaps, also, the charity he had learned through penitence.

And James leaves behind him in the cloister only the memory of his love of harp and lute. The sweet-stringed instruments had comforted him, as David's harp had charmed another king. There is, among the royal accounts of the time, this brief entry :—

"1504—Item, the last day of June, in Payslay, to lord "Sempille's harper, xiiijs" (14s).

Lord Sempille, whose harper's gentle skill introduces him to these pages, was then sheriff of Renfrewshire, and one of an old knightly family,—vassal to the first High Steward for lands round the loch of that name.

He was created a baron by James Fourth in 1488, when the near village of Paisley was presented a burgh to the abbot Schawe. His little but fair barony lay in a wooded strath,—"the very vale of Tempe, of Renfrewshire," it was called by a late historian. In its centre, on the edge of the loch, like the barony, little but lovely, the ruined, roofless, ivy-grown walls of an old church may still be seen.

It was built by this first lord Sempille in the year after the brief sojourn of James in Paisley, while the grateful presence of this king, who took captive the hearts of his lieges, was still fresh and fragrant in the shady vale of Castle-Semple.

The charter of foundation declares it founded by John, first lord Sempille, "in the year 1505, to the honour of

"God, and the blessed Virgin Mary; and for the prosperity "of king James the Fourth, and Margaret, his queen; and "for the soul of Margaret Colvil, his former spouse: also, for "the salvation of his own soul, and Margaret Chrichtoun, "his present spouse; of all his predecessors and successors, "and of all the faithful dead."*

The following year this charter was confirmed at Edinburgh by the king; and a large revenue was granted for the maintenance of the little church beside the loch— "the lands of Upper and Nether Pennelds, and the mill "thereof; and the lands of Auchlodmont; as also the tiends "of Glasford were annexed to it."

A few years later, lord Sempille, the founder, fell on Flodden-field with the king.

* Anno 1505 : In honorem Dei et Beatae Virginis Mariae; et pro prosperitate Jacobi quarti Regis, et Margaretae, Reginae suae; et pro anima Margaretae Colvil, quondam spousae suae, nec non pro salute, animae suae et Margaretae Chrichtoun, spousae suae modernae, omnium Antecessorum et Successorum suorum et omnium fidelium defunctorum.—Crawfurd's "History of Renfrewshire."

QUEEN MARGARET'S PILGRIMAGE.

> BLAME not my lute! for he must sound
> Of this or that as liketh me:
> For lack of wit, the lute is bound
> To give such tunes as pleaseth me.
> Though my songs be somewhat strange,
> And speak such words as touch my change,—
> Blame not my lute!
>
> *Sir Thomas Wyatt.*

AN unbeautiful country, rich in neither hill nor shadow, with whinny knowes and woodless streams, and moors without the charm of moorland;—in the midst of it, a little old-fashioned town, as still as still can be; its churchyard on a tiny height, at the western end of the street; in the midst of the old churchyard, some bits of broken sculpture and masonry,—the insignia of the bishops of Galloway, and the old worn arms of Scotland: also, one fair Saxon arch, very nearly entire, the fairest and completest, it is said, within the four seas; one or two later pointed arches; and that is all of Whithorn!

A certain pure, truthful life, lived in the fourth century, made it a shrine for Christendom, and gave it its glory. For St. Ninian died here, where he had taught and prayed, and was buried somewhere in his own church,—the first church in Scotland built of stone.

It was James Fourth's favourite pilgrimage. Once at least every year, he came to pray at St. Ninian's; and left offerings on the altars, and bounty for the poor. In a perilous illness of the queen, he had made this journey on foot; and Margaret's health had revived, it was said, from the hour when the king had knelt at the shrine.

So when the queen was recovered, a pilgrimage of thanksgiving was made by king and queen together, with a great retinue of state.

This pilgrimage has often been described, but not the incident in it, which gives it a place among the memories encircling the Abbey of Paisley. The journey was long from Stirling, among the pleasant summer fields, and across those bright veins of streamlets, which in Scotland, like happy wayfarers, make an unceasing song. And rest was grateful to the queen. The Paisley abbot was the king's friend,—a friendship, perhaps, knit closer by that royal retreat three years ago. So at this monastery, also linked by peculiar ancestral bonds to the king, the pilgrim retinue halted, on their journey to St. Ninian's shrine.

The pale queen, in her litter, was borne to the Abbey gates, and received by the hospitable abbot on a day in the early July. The guesten hall was crowded, for the king and queen were attended by a very regal retinue in no pilgrim-guise. The "chapel-graith" of the queen was held in two coffers; three horses carried the wardrobe of the king, and seventeen pack-horses were necessary for the various appurtenances of queen Margaret. Never had the old cloister rang to such sounds before.

The abbot of Paisley then was in the zenith of his power, reigning like a king over the king's gift,—the little new-made burgh, which lay at the abbot's feet, enjoying all the privileges which his predecessor had won, with escape of all the opprobrium which that winning may have cost.

That he was not the strictest of his order, certain old notices of his surroundings lead us to divine. As the population of the burgh gathered closer round the convent walls, the abbot built himself a summer house some few miles from his Abbey. The grounds of this summer dwelling touched the edge of Blackston Moss. And the house took its name from the moss, and had in this same moss various rights of its own. It had also round it pleasant orchards, and wealth of shady trees; and the river Black Cart partly encircled it, as the White Cart encircled the Abbey.

How the abbot divided his residence between his private chosen Blackston, and his house in the cloister court among his monks, we are only left to surmise. But it was in the Abbey gateway that he received his royal guests in July, 1507, when the queen's pilgrimage was made. And it was in the old Abbey the royal train abode, leaving some few faint traces behind them for curious historians.

There appears in the royal accounts :—" 1507—Item ix " day of Julii, to ane man to pass fra Paslay to Dumbartone " with ane letter to Andro Bertoun ijs."

In his galley from the Abbey orchards, down the quiet, clear Cart, between the cornfields and the oaks; past lonely, woody Inchinnan, with its Templars' graves three centuries old, and its legends of the Knights of St. John; cross the broad, solitary Frith, with its sandy reefs reaching far among the blue patches of water, to the grim old fortress rock, outlined in rugged grey and purple against the green Kilpatrick hills,—the king's messenger would pass on that errand, the purport of which none has told us.

This royal visit was brief; for, eleven days later, the king and queen are again at Paisley, returned from St. Ninian's shrine. And again there are little broken bits of history—suggestions, and no more—made by entries in the treasurer's account of the king's expenditure.

"Item, xxiiij day of Julij, to the workmen in Paslay to "drinksilver, xiiijs."

"Item to the maissounis in drinksilver xxiijs."

So they were working still at that late time of monasticism, working still with a brooding downfall so ominously near. Perhaps the great hewn-stone wall, in which the first abbot Schawe had set his ostentatious distich, was still incomplete. With the tireless patience of devotion, they were still carving here and there, finial and moulding, round the shrines, and mottoes in unknown Latin, before which the humble burghers could only kneel and be silent.

On Saturday, 20th July, the king and queen returned to Paisley; and on the day following, when high mass was said, James made his accustomed offerings. There are none recorded to have been made by queen Margaret.

" Item, the xxi day of Julij in Paslay, to the offerand to "the reliques xiiijs: item, that day to the kingis offerand to "ane priests first mes in Paslay, xxiiijs: item to the kingis "offerand at the hie mes, xxiiijs."

And a later entry records another and separate offering, made on St. Anne's day, at the altar of the saint. The date is 26th July—"item that day, saint Anne's day, to the " kingis offerand at the mes xiiijs: item, to the kingis "offerand on the bred to saint Anne's lycht, xiiijs."

Saint Anne's altar was one of the seven, that sacred number of the church, founded in Paisley, and richly endowed in lands by various givers.

Eight days after their return from Whithorn, the retinue left the Abbey. It was on the twenty-seventh of July, and again an account of the king, having no reference to Paisley, nor the royal visit there, helps us to fill in the picture of busy ecclesiastical life—not always a gentle nor devout life, but sometimes strangely the reverse.

" July 27th, 1507—Item lent by the king's command to "the abbot of Tungland, and can nocht be gotten fra him : " £33 6s 8d." *

And so we take and gather story round the linking of these two old names, king and foreign abbot, in this

* " Pictorial History of Scotland."

Benedictine house, with that quick interest by which we group historical incidents,—the sort of artistic impulse which makes pictures wherever it may ;—or rather, perhaps, the sympathy which claims the *humanness* of the Past, and always, whether we will or not, goes beyond the titles and names, and seeks for some traits of love or goodness; or, failing these, the motives which were instead of these in propelling the soul's destiny.

We seem to know how this abbot of Tungland has travelled in the king's company, from his Galwegian Abbey, not remote from Whithorn Priory. The king delighted in his skill. "French Maister John;" "Maister John, the French Medicinar," he was called before he was abbot. He was physician and alchemist, and both physics and alchemy were practised with eager interest by the versatile king. So he took to this "French Maister John," who was yet no Frenchman, but an Italian from Lombardy, and had only studied in France.

In 1504, the year in which James had previously visited Paisley, the abbot of Tungland died, and the Italian had been immediately appointed his successor by the king. As to qualifications for the duties of the abbacy, he had made not even so much as a pretence. He was neither good nor wise; but he was the king's favourite. Dunbar satirized him in his ballad of the "Fenyist Friar of Tungland;" but the king comforted him with gifts and honours, and the Italian was content.

"By the king's command, to Bardus Altovite Lumbard, "twenty-five pounds, for Maister John, the French medi-

"cinar, new made abbot of Tungland, whilk he aucht to the "said Bardus."

The king's generosity was unfailing; and the abbot was always his friend.

"Maister John," says bishop Lesley, "caused the king believe that he, by multiplying and otheris his inventions, wold make fine gold of other metal, quilk science he callit the Quintessence, whereupon the king made great cost, but all in vain."

A mine opened on Crawford Moor; a furnace built at Stirling; stillatours, brass mortars and vessels of all degrees, were put at the Italian's disposal. What if Maister John failed? The king still believed. The king believed, and in a modified way he practised the churchman's magic, and sought the philosopher's stone; or he was too devout and too humane and whole-hearted, to become either victim or adept in these occult arts.

And so a glad farewell, old magician and abbot! and a willing parting of company, as thou with king and queen at these Benedictine gates.

P

THE YEAR OF FLODDEN.

> TRADITION, legend, tune and song
> Shall many an age that wail prolong;
> Still from the sire the son shall hear
> Of the stern strife and carnage drear
>   Of Flodden's fatal field,
> When shivered was fair Scotland's spear,
>   And broken was her shield.
>
> "*Marmion.*"

THE abbot Schawe was succeeded by a son of the house of Lennox, a kinsman of the first earl, a descendant of Robert De Croc. The date of his accession is untold. It must have been only a year or two later than the king's last visit to his abbey. For in 1511 and afterwards, he is found making grants to his vassals, in the grave, supreme abbatial style, "with full consent of the convent."

Of this abbot Robert Stewart, there is not much to tell. Nothing indeed. He lived within the convent quiet. He makes no part in history.

But the history which environed his life is full, too full

of sorrow. The national tragedy absorbed, and contained, all minor tragedies. The abbot, like each of his vassals, had a kinsman on Flodden-field. And the king, himself, in the heart of his people had a kinsman's place. If he were romantically dear to his subjects of all degrees, he had peculiar claims upon the love of the Clugniac monks of Paisley.

The figure of king James had grown familiar in their green shady orchard walks, familiar in their still cloisters, so seldom touched by outside life. The monks had raised their eyes from their breviaries to answer the royal greetings; had been charmed, unwittingly, beneath their black cowls by the chivalrous smiles of the king. Where household love might come never, loyal love had come instead. James Fourth had been a gracious presence, beloved in the old monastic pile.

And on a September day, there came to the convent gate —worse even than the tidings of defeat—tidings that the king was slain.

How the wave of that great sorrow overflowed the land, mournful song and ballad unweariedly have told and told again.

"We have not taken sorrow by the hand
 With witting carefulness; none reckon'd this;—
The sorrow that hath fallen o'er the land
 Hath touch'd us, through extremity of bliss.

"O ring, sweet bells, that in the belfry-tower
 Hoard up your music—never anywhere
Was asked the burden, craven by this hour—
 Shed forth your passion on the tired air.

"Air grows so very weary of this grief,
 Hearing the constant echo of its pain,
Like a sick child that craveth some relief,
 And craveth still in vain.

"The very human faces have a sound—
A sound of sorrow through their dumbness heard,
O human brows that are with sorrow crowned!
O life of ours that is so strangely stirred!"

And a ballad, claiming no paternity, seems in some way to record or commemorate, on the banks of the White Cart, Flodden and the death of James. The local poets are many; it would be almost strange if none had touched that old story of loyalty and sorrow and devotion,—if none had followed the footprints of the royal penitent from the cloister to the battle-field.

"Saith the abbot, 'Lord James our king
 To-day is dead,
He is dead on Flodden field,
 Let mass be said.'

"It was to the monks of St. Bennet,
 Whose beads were told,
In that cloister built in the forest
 In the days of old.

"The abbot spake with his hand
 On his broidered hem;
Before the altar he stood,
 As he spake to them.

" As he spake, through the painted glass
 The red light stole,
Like the coming and flitting forth
 Of the royal soul.

" And the bloom of ungathered fruit
 On each orchard tree,
Paled for a moment, 'twas said,
 (Though none could see.

"The fruit that was red before
 On each orchard tree,
Grew green and pale with its sorrow,
 Though none could see.)

"Saith the abbot (his jewelled hand
    Made sign of the cross),
  'A vision hath come to me
    Of dool and loss.

"'I have seen the red hill-side
    At set of day,
  And the king's unshriven soul
    Passing away.

"'Great gifts he laid on our shrines,
    By the Holy Rood!
  And our cellarer's stores were filled,
    For the king was good.

"'Since the days of lord Walter, the Steward
    (Rest his soul!),
  None gave with so royal a grace
    For mass or bowl.

"'All over the purple Lennox,
    And green Strathgryfe,
  Much moan shall they make for the shedding
    This royal life.

"'But deeper than glen or turret
    The grief we shed
  For the king, who loved our convent,
    The unshrived dead.

"'Shrived or unshriven, I say,
    Our convent place
  Was ever the holier
    For the light of his face.

"'And, as my sire rules the Lennox,
    I hold no kinglier king
  Touch'd ever shrine or altar,
    Or abbot's ring.

"'I have seen, in a dream, red Flodden,
    And the battle flames;
  Say mass for the royalest Stewart,
    For the soul of James.'

THE YEAR OF FLODDEN. 231

"And a flood of luried amber
Round the abbot's head,
Confirmed to the monks of St. Bennet
That the king was dead."

But over all the land many utterly refused to believe the tidings. The king was not dead. He must fulfil his vow; he had gone to Jerusalem; he would come back again. There were those who had seen him riding forth when the battle was hopelessly lost, riding forth a solitary man from among the heaps of slain. He had gone to the Holy Land to pray for the souls of his men.

"He will come back to us," said the poor people, who had loved him well.

And Buchanan, with a wise reserve, yet not scorning it, explains this long hopefulness, for it was a people's prayer:—

"There are two accounts of the fate of the Scottish king. The English affirm that he was killed in battle. The Scots, on the other hand, assert that there were many that day clothed in armour similar to what the king usually wore, partly lest the enemy should chiefly aim at one alone, on whose life hung victory or the issue of the war; or, if the king should chance to be slain, that the troops might not be disheartened, or think they had lost him, so long as others, armed and accoutred like him, were seen in the field witnessing their brave or cowardly conduct. . . . There is one thing, however, I must not conceal, which I heard from Lawrence Telfer, an honest and learned man, then one of the king's pages, who was a spectator of the battle; he said, that after the day was lost, he saw the king cross the Tweed upon horseback. Many other persons affirming the same thing, a report was current for many years, that the king was alive, and would appear afterwards, having gone to Jerusalem to perform the religious vow which he had sworn. A report equally vain with that spread by the Britons respecting Arthur, and by the Burgundians respecting Charles."

But there was no reason for doubting that it was indeed the king who was found lying slain among a heap of slain, in the centre of his nobles. Only fondness and ignorance could credit any contradictory story.

Leo Tenth, beginning his pontificate, wrote to Henry of England, enjoining him to give the Scottish king burial in the Abbey of St. Paul's. For, strangely enough, this religious king had been under the ban of the pope. Excommunicated by Julius Second, he had no right to Christian burial. And Leo finds it necessary to explain his injunction to king Henry, by the fiction of late repentance, shown in battle or before it, by king James. No such honour was ever paid by Henry Eighth to his foe.

The abbot, Robert Stewart, of Paisley, survived the grief of Flodden for many years; he lived a hidden life in his cloister, and died an unrecorded death.

THE ABBOT JOHN.

AND let no man be deceived, as if the contagions of the soul were less than those of the body. They are yet greater; they convey more direful diseases; they sink deeper, and creep on more unsuspectedly.

Petrarch.

"MISERICORDIA et Pax," with the arms of the Hamiltons, and the initials "J. H.";—these, graven on the western wall of the north transept of the church, are all the memorials here of the late-day abbot John. Happy, indeed, for him, were these his sole memorials.

But the abbot John played a long and signal part in Scottish history. Not under this title; for before 1546 he had resigned the abbacy to his little nephew Claude. And his bishopric of Dunkeld was but a brief step to the highest church dignity in Scotland—the archbishopric of St. Andrews.

Here he moves very darkly across the cumbered page; and to write his history is no part of what this chapter proposes. It would be to tell of the keen warfare of a phase of faith struggling up to triumph; and another, which had served, with long benignity, the wants of preceding generations, succumbing, as it must succumb; but not graciously nor well. It might be to forget the kinship, sweet to claim beneath all difference, with its perennial sources of hope and joyfulness. And the gladness of deep-lying unity, like the hand of God through the dark, comforts the soul in perplexity, as the outcome of divinest life.

But ever in goodness, and not in evil, kinship and unity lie. And this abbot John, and such as he, are separating facts in history. The abbot rises up unkindly, wrapped in Rembrandt-like shade. We would not willingly evoke his spirit from the old darkness. As we can never yield to the good too fond an immortality, nor love too well the fragrance which floats above their graves; walking in the convent stillness with so many serene souls, we would fain forget and ignore this late archbishop Hamilton.

"Misericordia et Pax."

So rest old abbot, and the evil and the good rest with thee!

Who would follow with willing memory such a track as thine? who would go a summer pleasure-seeking through the camps of Murray or Argyle, or on a march with the Regent, suppressing the border clans? who would meet, for delight, the poor queen in extremity on the heights behind Musselborough, and hear the haughty speech of Glencairn, "they had come to grant pardon—not to ask it"? or see the long gaze of Mary, waiting for the archbishop and his vassals, and feel, with sympathetic instinct, how the hope all dies out of her heart? or hear the scoffer in the crowd,—"You need not look for the Hamiltons; there are no armed men within many miles"? Alas for this poor queen, who does not know her friends, nor how a heart beat beneath the dark Genevan gown, warmer than under the lawn!

A fine clear foil to the archbishop is this Reformer; as national and strong as the crags of Salisbury, or the castle-rock, set against his own sky. There are rare mosaics of steadfastness, and some tenderness and wit, set in his unconscious history, which readers will long come and gather,—gather out of their hard setting for various beneficent uses, and find, with a sort of willing surprise, how gentle this Reformer's soul.

"What have you to do," said the queen, "with my marriage? Or what are you in this commonwealth?"

"A subject born within the same," said he; "madam, and albeit neither earl, lord, nor baron within it, yet hath God made me (how abject soever I be in your eyes), a profitable and useful member within the same; yea, madam, to me it pertaineth, no less to forwarn of such things as may hurt it, if I forsee them, than it doth to any of the nobility, for both my vocation and office craveth plainness of me. . . . John Erskine of Dun, a man of meek and gentle spirit, was present, and did what he could to mitigate her anger, and gave unto her many pleasant words, of her beauty, of her excellency; and how that all the princes of of Europe would be glad to seek her favour. . . . The said John stood still, without any alteration of countenance, for a long time . . . and in the end he said, Madam, in God's presence I speak, I never delighted in the weeping of any of God's creatures. . . . But seeing I have offered unto you no just occasion to be offended, but have spoken the truth, as my vocation craves of me, I must sustain your Majesty's tears, rather than I dare hurt my conscience, or betray the commonwealth by silence."

But Mary remembers those tears on a certain December evening, when the news passes through the steep streets, and stirs the heart of old Edinburgh, that the queen, in her palace of Holyrood, has sent for John Knox. And how the young queen sat in state between her lords Maxwell and Lethington, how she whispered, and how she smiled, Knox has himself told. He, the Reformer, removing himself to some outside platform of view, looks down and sees the group, and simply tells his story.

"Her pomp wanted one principal point, viz., a womanly gravity; for when she saw John Knox standing at the other end of the table bareheaded, she first smiled and then laughed; whereunto her Placebos' gave their *plaudite*, assenting with like countenance. This is a good beginning, she said; but know you whereat I laugh? Yon man caused me to cry, and shed never a tear himself; I will see if I can cause him to grieve."

And so Knox is presented with a letter of his own, in which the queen reads sedition.

"Let him acknowledge," said she, "his own hand-writing."

"I acknowledge both the hand-writing and the diction."

"You have done more," said Lethington, "than I would have done."

"Charity," said the other, "is not suspicious."

"Well, well," said the queen, "read your own letter; and then answer to such things as shall be demanded of you."

. . After we say that the letter was read, the queen, beholding the whole table, said, "Heard you ever, my lords, a more despiteful and treasonable letter?"

While that no man made answer, Lethington addressed himself to John Knox and said, "Master Knox, are you not sorry from your heart, and do you not repent that such a letter hath passed from your pen, and from you hath come to the knowledge of others?"

John Knox answered, "My lord secretary, before I repent, I must be taught my offence."

"Offence," said Lethington; "if there were no more but the convocation of the queen's lieges, the offence cannot be denied."

"Remember yourself, my lord," said the other, "there is a difference between a lawful convocation and an unlawful; if I have been guilty of this I have oft offended, since I last came into Scotland: for what convocation of brethren hath ever been unto this day, unto which my pen hath not served? And before this no one laid it to my charge as a crime."

"Then was then, and now is now," said Lethington; "we have no need of such convocations as sometimes we have had."

John Knox answered, "The time that hath been is even now before my eyes; for I see the poor flock in no less danger than it hath been at any time before, except that the devil hath gotten a mask upon his face. . . "

"What is this?" said the queen; "methinks you trifle with

him. Who gave you authority to make convocation of my lieges? Is not that treason?"

"No, madam," said the lord Ruthven; "for he makes convocation of the people to hear prayer and sermon almost daily; and whatever your majesty or others think thereof, we think it no treason."

Then the queen reverts to that late offence committed by the preacher in her cabinet.

"You speak fair enough here before my lords; but the last time I spake with you secretly, you caused me to weep many tears, and said to me stubbornly, ye cared not for my weeping."

"Madam," said the other, "because now the second time your majesty hath burdened me with that crime, I must answer, lest for my silence I be held guilty: if your Majesty be ripely remembered, the laird of Dun, yet living, who can testify the truth, was present at that time, whereof your Majesty complaineth."

And then in that dark old chamber, standing up with uncovered head, before queen and nobles, so bravely and so earnestly the preacher makes his defence, rehearsing his own speech, and the queen's speech also, ending—"These were the sharpest words I spoke that day."

Said the secretary, "Master Knox, you may return to your house for this night."

"I thank God, and the queen's majesty," said the other.

Statuesquely simple in the gloom, stands this old Scottish Reformer.

And the archbishop in the shadows, not confronting him nor courting contrast, moves with evil disquiet across the troubled page, the shadows of his old Abbey lying far behind him, and, between him and them, a court life in France, and intrigues with the Guises, and plots and counter-plots. Yet not true to the queen, perhaps much less her friend than the stern Genevan-gowned minister, who draws tears from her eyes, and who is arraigned before her council, and there pleads his cause with rude assertion.

When Mary fled to Elizabeth, the archbishop might indeed go down and, standing waist-deep in water, hold the boat with both hands, and, moved partly by motives of prudence, and partly by a sting of remorse, pray her not to trust to the Protestant queen of England. But there is no soil in his nature for either friendship or loyalty.

The death of the regent Murray, who was shot in the open street, drew suspicion on the Hamiltons, especially on this old abbot John. And, a few months later, the retribution of his enemies overtook him, when Dumbarton castle was taken by the new regent.

For the archbishop abode in fancied security within castle walls. "This castle seemed impregnable. The rock is very hard, and is with difficulty shaped by any iron tool; but when broken by force, or falling down of itself, it diffuses widely a strong sulphureous smell. . . . On the south, along which the Clyde flows, the rock, precipitous on every other quarter, slopes a little, and, stretching out two arms, embraces a small spot, which, partly from the nature of the place, and partly by human industry, is so enclosed, that it affords space for several houses on the transverse sides, and forms a roadstead in the river, commanded by the batteries, sufficiently safe for friends, but dangerous for enemies. Small boats may approach to the very castle gates."

It was here, in safe guilt, the abbot John slept on that moonless spring night, when the castellated rock was scaled. Fortune favoured the assailants; for lest "the sky which was clear with stars, and the day which approached, should discover their attempt to the watchers above, . . suddenly a thick mist covered the heavens, but so that it did not descend beneath the middle of the castle rock, but involved the upper part in such darkness, that it hid from the garrison the view of everything that was going on below."

And through this opportune mist, the castle walls were scaled, and a drowsy garrison surprised, and the archbishop made prisoner. Lest any attempt should be made to spare his life, he was carried in haste by his captors to Stirling.

Meanwhile, in the brief space between his apprehension and his death, some dreadful proof was adduced of the guilt of this former abbot. One of the assassins, haunted day and night by the deed that had been done, and wasting under his mental torture, bethought him of a last relief. The confessional was no longer open throughout the land, with its some-time healing, or at least the opiate it might bring. But there lurked here and there a few constant yet timid souls, who adhered in fervent devotion to the faith which they might not own.

The assassin remembered one of these, "a school-master at Paisley, a simple man," and a priest. To him in his despair he went, confessed his crime, and named his accomplices.

The simple soul of the priest, who had hitherto only

been used to hear the daily confessions of erring thoughts and hard words, was suddenly stricken and appalled. Through his own utter trembling of conscience, he spoke hope to the assassin,—spoke of the mercy of God with a thrill of heart, and a doubt whether mercy were large enough for this. And the penitent read his thought, and refused to be comforted.

Only a few hours after his confession, and in the priest's sight, he died, in such remorse and despair, as filled his confessor with terror. The dying words of the assassin would not cease to ring in his ear. While he taught the little children, the schoolmaster heard them still. He heard, beneath the lisping voices, his penitent's agonized voice, not pleading, not asking,—only confessing his crime. And, under the spring stars, he saw the glazed despairing eyes; he saw them in the cold, brown water, that flowed under the orchards to the sea; he saw them everywhere, and saw not the little bright flowers, nor the glad green grasses, upspringing with their burden of the love of God. He saw those eyes, deathliest of all, when before him, in the ghostly twilight, rose the shattered, grey, old convent, where the abbot John had ruled.

The priest's secret overcame him. He dropped strange words to the neighbours, dropped them unwittingly, scarce knowing what he said; and the neighbours gathered them up, one by one, and put them together.

Then strange stories floated round the Abbey, and down the whispering streets. And they grew more definite and minute as they passed from lip to lip. And the guileless, terror-stricken schoolmaster, confronted with his own words, could neither deny nor evade; and the whole story thus became known.

The report reached the regent, that under the walls of the Abbey, where Hamilton had ruled long ago in his less guilty power, a poor priest had discovered to the people all that the lords were so eager to learn. And the schoolmaster was hastily carried to appear with the archbishop at Stirling.

His story was still the same. He had nothing else to tell. The assassin was hired by the archbishop; the assassian told all in his despair. The priest had no subtilty, no wisdom to guide his words.

"Was this told you under the seal of confession?" asked the archbishop of the priest.

And the priest could make no defence, but acknowledged the assassin was his penitent.

"Then," said the archbishop, "you are not ignorant, I suppose, of the punishment awaiting those who divulge confessions."

And he asked no more respecting the accusation. This simple priest, not long afterwards, suffered death for celebrating mass in defiance of the laws of the Reformed Parliament.

The archbishop was executed. Neither lords nor people were then in any mood to be tender of bishops or abbots. And it does not seem that this abbot John's life had drawn round it pity or fondness. The simple, serene motto carved, in his earlier days, on the transept of his own Abbey, all his later life belied. One reads the worn letters wondering what they mean, wondering whether some primal light, which died soon and utterly away, for a brief space lit the cloister life of the future unrighteous man.

TWO HARPS.

———o———

HEAVEN needs not to take pains when it would teach:
How easily two harps can sound in tune!
How easily an outstretched hand drops gifts!
So easily high Heaven can guide our souls.

Ancient Chinese Hymn.

A GREAT crisis has come. Great crises make us sympathetic. There are but a few minds self-contained, self-reliant enough, to dispense with the aids of custom, of usage,—which means with sympathy. Where custom is ignored, there is but the eagerer outlook for some otherwhere kindred touch to strengthen, to re-assure our humanity. Therefore, we take our motto from a distant land and distant age, prizing the more its sentiment, because of its foreign setting.

We do not live our lives in mosaic. We cannot detach their parts. Of every step forward we are but half convinced till some outside creation supports us with distinct and separate authority. For every note of progress, there is an echo of regret.

Not to all indeed. There are minds which, in all ages are, and must be, antiques. Their faith falls with plastic sweetness into those old forms which their fathers wrought out with infinite diligence and love and prayerfulness. Conceived for the requirements of other times, these forms startle all the proprieties of a more reasonable age. And the few who cannot smile at such anachronisms are forced to curious introspection, wonderment, and seeking within for that common human need which has had, in defiance of all surrounding growth, a bloom so strange and prodigal.

"The still, sad music of humanity" seems thus continually to plead its own right and necessity to worship with free will, with or without symbol, as each separate instinct claims. And so the "two harps" of the Chinese hymn has a touch of joyful truth. All time must listen to both. Well if it listen fairly, and perceive the blended harmonies which the master-hand evokes from the strings; and how, through the subtle intricacies which are discord to the untrained ear, God guides the waiting human soul to light, to immortality.

Through a duality of consciousness, the world unceasingly moves through antagonistic powers, which, acting each upon each, like the physical forces of nature, propel its destiny. It is through no imperfection that we are hindered from possessing both. God's gifts are thus disposed, that so the beauty and the strength, the light and the shade, the poetry and the science, may each be called forth into being.

All our knowledge of matter is knowledge obtained by spirit. It is the spirit which *knows*. Only of spirit itself can we have an intuitive certainty. And the world, the old brooding world, so rich in its faiths and its mysteries, did homage to this unavowed truth, in the simple manner of its childhood.

For then all creation was indeed but the embodiment of spirit. And every pale spring flower, and red or snowy autumn fungus; every moist dripping cavern, or glistering shelly creek; every grove of oak or pine; the carmine streak of morning in the sky, or the tremor of the first little star that came out in the wake of the moon,—had some tutelary spirit of its own, which conferred on it beauty and significance;—rather, was, itself, the manifestation of intelligence, or energy, or passion; and was loved not simply, as now, for its fragrance or its light.

And so, through the stillness of the water, men turned to the genii of the waves, to Thetis, the fair queen. And it was not the unresponsive liquid, with its shadows and its gleams, with its opal and cobalt and purple, which filled the old poet's mind, but the beautiful pervasive spirit, which was actually a presence and a power, a being to be propitiated, to be even, after human fashion, loved and wooed. And far beyond philosophies, in the stillness of the woods, in the old primæval forests, where the Red Man bent his bow, with a strange unconscious prefiguration, he made the cross over his lakes, and cast, at the point of intersection, his offering to the god of waves.

And were there not Woden and Thor, and Balder the Beautiful? The teeming myths of the south, the sterner genii of the Scandinavian seas, the subtle oriental faith, with the half-truth of its Trinity, its Brahma, and Vishnu and Siva; all spoke of the out-stretched hand of man, the worshipper, into the spirit world, of his nearness of kin to those whose veil is invisibility.

Then by a natural inversion, all spiritual truth was crystalized—*fossilized*, it may be, when its early keen vitality the ages had worn away. And that other strong human motive was springing out of its decay. Science was repudiating faith. The one harp was silencing the other.

The Church which grew with the ages was no separate life. It took what these brought, what Pagan culture also brought. Yet, with its sweeter humanity, took not physical nature for shrines, but lives that had been lived purely in the holy light of God; and not these lives alone, but all that they had touched, and touching, in subtle re-action, conferred upon, as they received from. The quickness of human sympathy produced those vivid forms, the vitalizing, passionate apprehension of tremors, and faiths, and convictions to which these common outward accessories had ministered in daily ways. And so quick the apprehending sympathy, the mode was scarcely perceived, the mode which would offer so many temptations to a less spiritual, or at least a less imaginative age.

In the slow rhythm of history that age came, a self-aggrandizing generation with no mental or moral impulse to raise them through the symbol to the real. And so there became idolatry in the forms which were once beautiful significant rites. And matter was no longer the expression of some out-breathing spirit, but spirit was itself materialized in the rude thought of the people. The age required some other guiding hand than that lovely and restful and beneficent faith of early mediævalism born. Its very richness had darkened while it beautified its growth, like the shadow of flower petals upon their own green leaves.

Every age with quick precision responds to its own necessities. The vigorous and keen life of the sixteenth century in Scotland, was the triumphant vindication of the ecclesiastical destruction and revolution out of which it arose.

Long afterwards, Schlegel, who was born a Protestant, philosophising in his unworldly goodness, clinging to the unity of the earlier faith, concludes, in that fond hopefulness which the purest spirits cannot lose—" The church was destined, by the losses it experienced, to learn the danger of its too worldly policy." And it may be that in quiet parishes, hidden away among the Scottish hills, there were priests who comforted themselves with the same unbreathed thought.

Men cannot scaithlessly doff their faiths, like the fashions which Van Dyk painted. Superstitions even may be possibly worn too lightly. For superstitions usually have a half that is true, and it is much to lose half a truth; while to many, even now, it seems a small ill to accept the mediæval rites with the hallowed mediæval crown. But to Knox and Murray and Argyle, the nimbus was long paled away; and the church, into which they themselves were baptized, was discrowned by its own perversities. There was no thought of purification or renewal, but only of destruction, which would not flinch in the hearts of the Reformers.

WARNING.

———o———

Evil still shall end in evil!
On the rude marauding race
Zens turns his frowning face,
And striketh those in sin that revel.
Schiller's "Feast of Victory."

A CURIOUS letter or proclamation has been preserved by John Knox. Its date is 1558. So the very youthful lord Claude wears then his Culgniensian mitre; and the stern pope Paul Fourth in Rome nears the end of his brief pontificate; and beautiful bright queen Mary is a new-made bride in France; and Mary of Guise in Scotland, subtle and gracious and fair, upholds her daughter's right and faith as best she may, against the leagued nobles of the land.

Through the bridal rejoicings there comes a clamorous, assertive voice, a protest, a threatening, an appeal. Not the Lords of the Congregation, not Argyle, not the gentle laird of Dun, so brave beneath his courtesy, have cast down defiance like this :

"The Blind, Crooked, Lame, Widows, Orphans and all
"other Poor, so visited by the hand of God as cannot work.

"To all the flock of friars within this realm, we wish res-
"titution of wrongs past, and reformation in times coming,
"for salvation.

"Ye yourselves are not ignorant (and though ye would
"be, it is now, thanks unto God, well known to the whole
"world, by His most infallible Word), that the benignity or
"alms of all Christian people pertaineth to us alone, which
"ye, being whole of body, strong, sturdy and able to work,
"what, under pretence of poverty (and yet nevertheless pos-
"sessing most easily all abundance), what, through cloaked
"and hidden humility (though your proudness is known),
"and what through feigned holiness (which now is declared
"to be superstition and idolatry), have these many years,
"expressly against God's Word, and the practise of His holy
"Apostles, to our great torment, alas! most falsely stolen
"from us. And as ye have, by your false doctrine, and
"wresting of God's Word, . . induced the whole people,
"high and low, into a sure hope and belief, that to clothe,
"feed, and nourish you, is the only most acceptable alms
"allowed before God; and to give a penny or a piece of
"bread once in a week is enough for us; even so ye have
"persuaded them to build you great hospitals, and maintain
"you therein by their force, which only pertains now to us
"by all law as builded and given to the poor, of whose
"number ye are not nor can be reputed, neither by the law
"of God, nor yet by any other law proceeding of nature,
"reason or civil policy. Wherefore, seeing our number is
"so great, so indigent, so heavily oppressed by your false

"means, that none taketh care of our misery, and that it is
"better for to provide there our impotent members which
"God hath given us; to oppose to you in plain controversy,
"than to see you hereafter (as ye have done afore) steal from
"us our houses, and ourselves in the meantime to perish
"and die for want of the same: We have thought good;
"therefore, ere we enter with you in the conflict, to warn
"you, in the name of the great God, by this public writing,
"affixed at your gates where ye now dwell, that ye remove
"forth of our said hospitals, betwixt this and the feast of
"Whitsunday next, so that we, the only lawful proprietors
"thereof, may enter thereinto, and afterward enjoy the com-
"modities of the church, which ye have hereunto wrongfully
"holden from us; certifying you, if ye fail, we will, at the
"said term, in whole number (with the help of God, and as-
"sistance of His saints in earth, of whose ready support we
"doubt not), enter and take possession of our said patrimony,
"and eject you utterly forth of the same.

"Let him therefore that before hath stolen, steal no more;
"but rather let him work with his hands that he may be
"helpful to the poor.

"From all cities, towns and villages of Scotland.

"January 1st, 1558."

The friars were an old discord. Over all Christendom
the priests had scorned, disowned them. There was no
poetry in their order. And be it acknowledged or not, there
is a *conservatism* in poetry which stands stead for strength
and truth both.

Dean Milman's description of these Mendicants, as they

were found over France, Spain, Italy, as they were seen over all Europe, is a comment on this Scottish proclamation:—

· "There was absolutely nothing to limit the number of the monks, still less that of the friars in their Four Orders, especially the disciples of S. Dominic and S. Francis. No one was too poor or too low to become a privileged and sacred Mendicant. No qualification was necessary but piety, or its semblance, and that might too easily be imitated. While these Orders in the Universities boasted of the most erudite and subtle and all-accomplished of the school-men, they could not disdain or altogether reject those who, in the spirit of at least one of their founders, maintained the superiority of holy ignorance. Instead of being amazed that the friars swarmed in such hordes over Europe, it is rather wonderful that the whole abject and wretched peasantry, rather than be trampled to the earth, or maddened to Flaggelantism, Jacquerie, or Communism, did not all turn able-bodied religious Beggars; so the strong English sense of Wickliffe designates the great mass of the lower Franciscans in England. The Orders themselves, as was natural, when they became wealthy and powerful, must have repressed rather than encouraged the enrolment of such persons; instead of prompting to the utmost, they must have made it a distinction, a difficulty, a privilege, to be allowed to enter upon the enjoyments of their comparatively easy, roving, not by all accounts too severe life. To the serf, inured to the scanty fare, and not unfrequent famine, the rude toil and miserable lodging; and to the peasant, with his skin hard to callousness, and his weather-beaten frame,—the fast, the maceration, even the flaggelation of the friar, if really religious (and to the religious these self-inflicted miseries were not without their gratification), must have been no very rigorous exchange; while the freedom to the serf, the power of wandering from the soil to which he was bound down, the being his own property, not that of another, must have been a strong temptation."

They had proved themselves brave in times of great peril; but they were despised, the Mendicants, and most of all by the churchmen. And when, in the fifteenth century, a Franciscan friar became pope, and honoured and privileged his beloved order, all the church had resented his bull.

Delegates had gone from Paris to see with their own eyes the leaden Papal seal attached to the incredible document. Ostentatiously, scornfully, they had professed to disbelieve. And when disbelief became impossible, they had defied the pope. On all the convent gates in Paris, a proclamation, by the king's command, forbade priests and curates to permit the friars to preach or hear confession in their churches.

And that was a hundred years ago. Scotland had borne long, had been patient and reverential. But the end must come. After their long patience, the people rose with bitterness proportioned to their patience. "The beginning of the end" was now.

It was but a few months after this that Walter Mill suffered martyrdom. Yet the risk was already small to the lieges who offered these insults to the friars. At Edinburgh, four weeks earlier, the first Scottish Covenant was subscribed by the powerful lords Argyle, Glencairn, Morton, and Lorn, pledging themselves open enemies to "superstition, abomination and idolatry." And already the baronial castles sheltered here and there throughout the land, as trusted and revered chaplains, preachers convicted of heresy, who expounded to chief and vassals their own Reformed faith.

The Abbey on the White Cart was no convent of friars. It had never affected poverty. Its wealth and far-reaching authority were its uncloaked glory and temptation. Still, in the ancient gateway, the eleemosynar stood, with the free, gracious bounty of Mother-Church, for all her poor children. The corn which the Clugniac monks cultivated on their fair fertile strath, was corn for "the widows and the orphans, and all the poor so visited by the hand of God, as could not work." They had never asked, but always given alms. We do not read that this bold proclamation touched the Clugniensian house.

When its day came, the angry people would find enough to plead against the jewelled mitre and ring, and the fine vestments, and the carved images. Proud wealth would be no less a charge to bear than proud poverty. The pathetic plea on the gates of the friars—"none taketh care of our misery"—bore perhaps a reassurance of its own to the abbot of Paisley and his monks, with their hundred and twelve bolls of meal, set against it as the yearly dole.

Yet the first sacriligious attack is made on the ecclesiastical retreats, and there are but two little years more for the abbot Claude to reign.

A LETTER TO MARY OF GUISE.

I OUGHT to bear the burthen of my rank.
George Elliot.

IN May-time, a year later, the Reformers write to Mary of Guise, the perplexed queen Regent, who rules in her daughter's name. Not as to the "flock of friars" threatening defiant, but with some tone of pleading, "God move your princely heart."

"Because we did not utterly despair of the queen's "favour," writes John Knox, "we caused to form a letter to "her Majesty, as followeth :—

"To the Queen's Majesty Regent,
"All humble obedience and duty promised.

"As heretofore with hazard of our lives, and yet with "willing hearts, we have served the authority of Scotland, "and your Majesty now Regent in this realm, in service to "our bodies dangerous and painful; so now, with most "dolorous minds, we are constrained by unjust tyranny pur-

"posed against us, to declare unto your Majesty, That ex-
"cept this cruelty be staid by your wisdom, we shall be
"compelled to take the sword of just defence, against all
"that shall pursue us for the matter of religion, and for our
"conscience' sake, which ought not, nor may not be subject
"to, mortal creatures, further than by God's word man is
"able to prove that he hath power to command us. We
"signify, moreover, unto your Majesty, That if by rigour
"we be compelled to seek the extreme defence, that we will
"not only notify our innocency and petition to the king of
"France, to our mistress, and to her husband, but also to
"the princes and council of every Christian realm, declaring
"unto them, That this cruel, unjust, and most tyrannical
"murder, intended against towns and multitudes, was, and
"is the only cause of our revolt from our accustomed obed-
"ience; which, in God's presence, we faithfully promise to
"our sovereign mistress, to her husband, and unto your
"Majesty Regent, provided that our consciences may live
"in that peace and liberty which Christ Jesus hath purchased
"to us by His blood; and that we may have His word truly
"preached, and holy sacraments rightly ministered unto us,
"without which, we firmly purpose never to be subject to
"mortal man; far better, we think, to expose our bodies to
"a thousand deaths, than to hazard our souls to perpetual
"damnation, by denying Jesus Christ, and His manifest
"verity; which thing not only do they who commit open
"idolatry, but also all such as seeing their brethren pursued
"for the cause of religion, and, having sufficient means to
"comfort and support them, do, nevertheless, withdraw from
"them their dutiful support.

"We would not your Majesty should be deceived by the
"false persuasions of those cruel beasts, the churchmen,
"who affirm, That your Majesty needeth not greatly to
"regard the loss of us that profess Christ Jesus in this
"realm. If (as God forbid) ye give ear to their pestilent
"council, and so use against us, this extremity pretended, it
"is to be feared that neither ye, neither yet your posterity,
"shall at any time after this find that obedience and faithful
"service within this realm, which at all times ye have found
"in us.

"We declare our judgments freely, as true and faithful
"servants. God move your princely heart favourably to
"interpret our faithful meaning: further, advertising your
"Majesty, that the self-same thing, together with all things
"that we have done, or yet intend to do, we will notify by
"our letters to the king of France. Asking of you in the
"name of the Eternal God, and as your Majesty tenders the
"peace and quietness of this realm, That ye invade us not
"with any violence, till we receive answer from our mistress
"and her husband, and from their advised council there:
"And thus we commit your Majesty to the protection of
"the Omnipotent. From St. Johnston, the 22nd of May,
"1559.

"Sic subscribitur,

"Your Majesty's obedient servants
"in all things not repugnant to God,

"The faithful Congregation of
"Christ Jesus in Scotland." *

* Knox's History of the Reformation.

John Knox has but returned twenty days from France; and St. Johnston (Perth) has been the scene of most ominous disquiet. And among those who fan the flame of resentment in the Regent's mind, is singled out as specially obnoxious to the Protestants, the old abbot Hamilton of Paisley.

John Knox is not choice in his epithets. He was no finer than his times. "No man," he says, "was at that time more frank against us, than was duke Hamilton, led by that cruel beast, the bishop of St. Andrews."

But John Hamilton, abbot and bishop, cannot yet learn to fear, however the old duke Hamilton might waver and temporize.

LORD CLAUDE, THE LAST ABBOT.

DISDAINED the golden fruit to gather free,
And lent the crowd his arm to shake the tree.
Dryden.

UNIQUE interest surrounds the last abbot of Paisley. His history is linked with that of queen Mary; and every history so linked, seems enhanced with some glow of poetry from that most sorrowful of queens' lives.

There is another hush amid the darkness and sadness which again and again overtakes this little land, doomed through centuries to struggle for very life. "The considerate," writes George Buchanan, watching his poor country from distant collegiate quiet, "foresaw a tempest overhanging Scotland, dark and gloomy beyond conception; for the king had not made a will, and had left a girl only eight days old as his heir."

And then there is the strife of wily cardinal, and simple unambitious earl, unhappily placed by greatness at the head of a family unlike himself. The cardinal is fain to make the best of many absent lords, to make haste—in the darkness—and himself to head the headless realm. And the Hamiltons would also make haste with eager counter-moves, if their chief would only stir from his inactivity, and perceive the glory and the prize.

"Hamilton, the unambitious chief of the other party, appeared willing to remain quiet, if his relations, more anxious for their own aggrandizement than his honour, would have allowed him; but they incessantly stirred the hopes of the young man, and urged him not to suffer an advantage, which thus presented itself, to slip out of his hands; for they would rather have had the whole kingdom in flames, than have been compelled to live an obscure life in a private station: besides, hatred towards the cardinal, and the disgrace of bondage under a priest, procured them many associates. To all which was added a prospect— uncertain, indeed, but not without influence in procuring them adherents—that as there was only a girl a few days old, between Hamilton the next heir and the crown, she might be cut off during her minority by some fortuitous accident, or through the treachery of her guardians; and therefore, in present circumstances, the most promising method of procuring lasting advantage, was to calculate upon the increasing power of the Hamiltons; for if they should be deceived, it would not be difficult afterwards to procure pardon from a young princess desirous of popularity in the beginning of her reign." *

So already the tangle is weaving round the little

* Buchanan's History.

unconscious queen; and ventures are cast into the future, to be so sorrowfully redeemed. And there bloom for the baby princess the first spring daisies of her life, while Hamilton, earl of Arran, is made the regent of her realm.

The regent has governed but some few months, when lord Claude, his third son, is born. And in the same year his brother, the absentee abbot of Paisley, returns from France to share in the flush of the family power.

And then there are years of history when the boy lord Claude's life is hidden; but the little queen Mary's life is ruthlessly open to all the world. And the child-queen sails for France; and the Hamiltons grow haughtier than before. And the country is wasted with foreign troops,—Julian Romero with his Spaniards, the three thousand Germans of the Rhinegrave, and the boastful Frenchmen of D'Essy. In its worst times Scotland had never seen such waste. The Hamiltons totter on their height, and grasp their power the closer.

It is in the midst of this disquiet that the abbot John, laden with office, state preferments, and ecclesiastical dignities, cedes his mitre to the regent's son. That the power and wealth of this old foundation may not pass away from the Hamiltons, lord Claude, at ten years, is made the abbot of Paisley.

Ten years! and lord Claude wore the mitre, and held, in his boy-hand, the crozier of the famous Clugniensians, venerable in lore as in centuries. The bull of pope Julius, which invested him with his dignity, indeed adds four years to the life of the abbot, designates him as fourteen. The difference was little, but it served to remove lord Claude beyond the term of infancy. Pope Paul made his cherished Montorio a cardinal at eighteen. And his predecessor, Julius Third, loved the love of all men; and, spending retired days in his gardens of Papa Giulio, was not likely to trouble himself much regarding this remote island abbacy, and the exact years of the candidate for its mitre.

So lord Claude Hamilton was abbot of Paisley before boys dream of their lives; surrounded by grey-haired monks and scholars, whom, according to the rule of monasticism, he may control with a perfectly absolute sway. What provision was made for such a case, where the abbot must still have his nurse, is not recorded in history; yet it was not a solitary case.

The abbot Claude grew up in the monastic air, formed, on the one hand, by the cloister, with its traditions honoured faintly, its requirements unfulfilled, with its already anachronism of vows of seclusion and obedience; and, on the other hand, the vivid and varied, if not brilliant, interests of outside social life. And as we always assimilate with an unconscious selection, not knowing that we choose yet choosing nevertheless, drawing to ourselves with certainty the elements most akin, the young abbot grew up a soldier, and no monk!

The sweeping acts of the summer Parliament of 1560, made lord Claude an abbot no more; and made of the fair old Abbey, which slow centuries had reared, in one August day, a mediæval memory.

That unprecedented manifesto, which passed like wildfire through the land, and let loose the passions of the people on their venerable sacred piles, came with all speed to Paisley; and the work was done!

"Traist Friends. After maist hearty commendation, we "pray you faill not till pass incontinent to ye Kyrk of —, "and tak doun ye haill images yrof, and bring furth till ye "kirkyard, and birn them oppingly, and syklyk cast doun "ye'alteris and picturis, and purge ye said kirks of all kinds "of monuments of idolatry : and this ye faill not to do as ye "will doe us singular empleasance, and sae committis you "till ye protection of God. From Edinburgh, ye xii of "August, MDLX.

"Signed— "ARGYLE.
"JAMES STEWART.
"RUTHVEN."

The example had already been set. A letter, written by Kirkaldy of Grange, a year earlier, on the eve of some such destruction, explains what it meant :—

"The manner of their proceeding in Reformation is this: they pull down all manner of friary, and some abbeys, which willingly receive not the Reformation. As to parish churches, they cleanse them of images, and all other monuments of idolatry, and command that no masses be said in them; in place thereof, the book set forth by godly king Edward is read in the same churches. They have never as yet meddled with a pennyworth of that which pertains to the church ; but presently will take order throughout all the parts where they dwell, that all the fruits of the abbeys, and other churches, shall be kept and bestowed upon the faithful ministers, until such time as a further order can be taken."

An utter silence reigning in regard to the demolition of Paisley, we have only the history of other spoliations to form the picture for us.

Buchanan relates the effect of a sermon by Knox at Perth, when the multitude broke the altars and pictures of the church in which they were gathered :—

"With the same impetuous fury, several ran to the monastery of the friars, the rest of the common people continually flocking to them; and although the friars had prepared a guard to provide against any such accident, no force could resist the headstrong fury of the multitude. The first attack was made upon the idols and the holy apparel; and next, the poorer sort ran upon the plunder. There was found in the Franciscans' Convent not only plenty, but a superabundance of household furniture, sufficient to have supplied ten times their number. The Dominicans, although not quite so opulent, were yet sufficiently so. . . . All this property was left as booty to the poor, while the rich, to avoid even the suspicion of avarice, suffered some of the monks, particularly the prior of the Carthusians, to depart loaded with gold and silver plate. Nor was the abstinence of the soldiers from plundering more remarkable than their celerity in demolishing so many buildings; for the extensive monastery of the Carthusians was so quickly laid in ruins, not only demolished, but even the stones taken away so completely, that within two days, scarcely a vestige of their foundation remained."

At Crail, a little town "situate at the extremity of Fife, they overturned the altars, broke the images, and destroyed all the apparatus of superstition; and what was almost incredible, the abhorrence of the common people overcame their avarice. Thence they proceeded to St. Andrews, where they spoiled several churches, and levelled the monasteries of the Franciscan and Dominican Friars with the ground. These things were done before the very eyes of the archbishop, although he had a strong body of horse with him, such as a little before he thought sufficient to have protected the town; but when he saw the zeal of the people, and the crowd of volunteers, he withdrew with his troops from the fury of the multitude, and went to his clans and relatives at Falkland."

This archbishop is the former abbot John Hamilton, the uncle of the abbot Claude. How his old Abbey of Paisley fares, we may guess from these memorials.

But everywhere the wrath of the people burns hottest round the convents of the friars mendicant, the men who had shirked the common duty, and despised the strength and glory of work; the men who had concealed their ill-gotten riches in the semblance of unbeautiful poverty; the idle men "sturdy and able to work;" the men "of cloaked and hidden humility."

DEMOLITION.

THERE comes a time when the discovery is made, a golden moment of silent expansion and enlargement. Then the reason of all the discipline to which he has submitted becomes clear to him, the principle reveals itself and makes the confused and ill-apprehended multitude of details in a moment harmonious and luminous. But the principle at the same moment that it explains the rules supersedes them. They may be not less true than before. But they are obsolete; their use is gone.

"*Ecce Homo.*"

> THE minster stones grew old and grey,
> The minster worship died away
> In soulless forms, and senseless rhymes,
> And ringing of unmeaning chimes,
>   And florid gauds of art,
>   And preaching with no heart.
>
> The tool had turned its edge; the brand
> Had broken in its maker's hand;
> The shadow on St. Peter's chair,
> No power divine was anywhere:
>   And God for His intents
>   Needed new instruments.
>
> *Rev. W. C. Smith, D.D.*

THE silence is eloquent enough. The ruined *sedilia*, the broken bases, the half-erased inscriptions, tell all that words can tell. A century ago the cloister-court of

Paisley was filled with the beautiful debris of shrines and altars and images destroyed by command of the Reforming lords.

The scenes of that August day we cannot bring back again, how the monks fled from their convent through the eager streets, out through the ripening corn fields and over the meadows and the moss; grey old men who had almost forgotten how the outside world fared, whose grandfathers remembered Paul Crawar, the Bohemian, and his burning at St. Andrews cross; and men in their early prime, who were youths when Wishart, the gentle laird, preached on the Mauchline moor, among the broom and the May-flowers, and whose beautiful face had haunted them when they took the Benedictine vows, and almost averted the tonsure and kept them for strong life; young men, also, perhaps, who did not belong to their times—one or two, more there could not be—whose separate individualities were not touched, to whom the cloister offered all they needed, and, as yet, the cloister only.

And as vainly we ask how the young abbot demeaned himself amongst his flying monks; this bold young abbot Claude, with his history all before him; how he brooked to see the crowd of townsmen assail his convent gates, and to hear his voice derided and ignored within his own Abbey walls; how he saw with helpless hands all the wealth of the shrines scattered, and scorned by the meanest there as an unholy thing—scorned by the poor weak men and women who had often crept to the gate of the monastery, and taken the dole from the hands of the monks, and asked their blessing and their prayer,

DEMOLITION. 271

Axe and hammer and crowbar, and arch and buttress fall. Slow work and hard, but the men have willing hands. Patient men reared the loveliness with glad long labour and life, praying and building for the future, not weary for love's sake. Zealous men dispense with long labour. One day outdoes the years. O the crumbling and crushing of inwreathed flowers which the patient chisel wrought! And the stately pillars broken, and the unfinished chapel spoiled; and the clamour and the ring through the cloisters, of destructive, not creative work!

Yet other churches over all Scotland were faring worse that day. It may be that the authority which the family of the abbot, distinct from his office, gave him, shielded the monastery of Paisley from a more complete demolition.

For the nave was left untouched. The work of that August day laid choir and north transept in ruins, shattered the house of the abbot, the guestan-house, library, scriptorium, filled the cloister-court with the debris of the beautiful still retreat; but it left the long nave entire, desolate, profaned, indeed, but with no mark of violence. It left a church for the people; a church for worship in the new form amidst the ruins of the old.

Blame is so easily given when three centuries lie between, and the fever is past and the fervour too, and the ruins are wrapt in peace; when the lichens are folding round and clasping the scars of that long ago, and we have leisure to wonder and separate and contemn.

An impulse sufficient to warm and propel future generaations of men, must have in it some destructive element; so history seems to mean.

As for its iconoclasm, the Protestant church stands not alone in this. It is no peculiar out-come of that form of faith taught by the sixteenth century Reformers. Vasari stands mournfully among the ruins of Pagan art, and protests that even the destruction of the Goths and Vandals was out-done by the early Christians. The marble columns of the Tomb of Adrian were removed to build a church. Paintings, sculptures, mosaics, all the beautiful products of the antique Greek art, which could never be revived, which was long dug up in fragments and hopelessly imitated by the moderns; it was not the rude Northern warriors, but the Christians, had despoiled the world of these.

Yet the Christian church, for centuries, was the mother of beauty and art.

Perhaps in the disturbed shadows, when the people were tired of destruction, and slept in the little town at the feet of the dishonoured Abbey; when the autumn moon was rising behind the shattered spire, and silvering the broad corn-fields, and touching dark Ben Lomond, which leaned a low dense cloud against the furthest sky ; when stillness once more brooded over the deserted place,—some monk, uncowled, came back, and wandered among the broken shrines; some old reverend man in whom the love of God was deepest, who had waited and hoped and believed in the silence of his Benedictine cell, looking in that sinking despair, which all good men have sometimes felt, as on the triumph of evil at the desolation around.

But the good could not die. The Present learns from the Past, and wins hope from its perplexities and faith in God and in the future. This was no "golden moment" to the homeless Clugniac monks. Yet, with silent generations gathered between us and it, history writes it *golden*, even in sight of spoiled abbeys, torn parchments, and ruin and decay.

OUTSIDE THE CLOISTER.

---o---

ALL places that the eye of heaven visits,
Are to a wise man ports and happy havens,—
Teach thy necessity to reason thus;
There is no virtue like necessity.
Think not the king did vanish thee,
But thou the king.
                            "*King Richard Second.*"

WITH his mitre left behind him, and his unfulfilled vows, we greet the lord Claude in history when seven years have past.

There has dawned that sweet hopeful May-time, when the queen is a queen once more; and the fisher-boat, with its precious freight, comes into the ancient little jetty; and one more happy sunset gleams on Mary's white veil, and on the mail of the fifty cavaliers who are loyal to her for love.

It was at the little port of Queensferry that lord Claude, with his fifty armed Hamiltons, met the escaped queen, in her flight from Lochleven Castle. The ferry was very old, and already inwrought with history. Another queen, Saxon Margaret, had passed often to and fro, and shed over it those sacred memories which her presence left everywhere. And her great-grandson, Malcolm Fourth, had granted the right of the ferry to the favoured monks of Dunfermline, a spot which Margaret loved. He had also, this same king Malcolm, granted a similar right to Scone, "to the abbot, the monks, and their men," of free passage at Portoun Reginæ. The footprints of the old monks were already set deeply in the soil here, where the young quondam abbot of Paisley, with his vassals, waited for the queen.

Her biographers have traced, sympathetically, that last scene bright to the queen. Queen Mary is the heroine of many pages; lord Claude is the hero of this. He exacts a large meed of interest even in the charmed presence of the lovely discrowned princess, whose story all the world has hung upon.

A night at Niddry Castle, and the Almond water near, and near it, too, old Elieston, a hunting-tower of the kings; and the wearied queen finds rest and honour and hospitality under the roof of lord Seton,—a moment of the "Chamber called Peace," one little interlude of gladness in her long tired way.

But we turn, with a soft askance, from this queen wrapped in story, and link her journey, in a dim romance, with the distant bridal of lord Claude. Some patient years after this, he wedded Margaret Seton, a younger daughter of the house where he rested that night with his vassals. Through the tremors and disquiet of history, imagination claims still the right to listen for, and the sense to hear, these soft under-tones of life, which are always glad through sorrow, and always restful through pain. They are needed to take from broader story the sense of harsh inequalities, of power triumphant, and of power crushed; of the better striving through the worse, and the worse absorbing the better; and always of strife which is itself evil, unkindly to pure effort, unkindly to gentle thought.

To greet a simple pure emotion on any beaten track of history, charms us like a loved little wayside flower on a foreign battle-field. The emotion is not recorded; we fill it in of ourselves, this and much more which none have thought worthy to tell us.

One May-night, and again the queen is abroad in her unquiet country. But the Hamiltons are loyal and strong, and the queen hopes. And when lord Claude next appears, it is at Langside, commanding the queen's vanguard on that fatal day for poor Mary.

Lord Claude, with his royal descent, proud youth, and accustomed supremacy, hotly contests with the earl of Argyle for the command of the whole army. And Mary must decide the contest, very hard to decide; and because of nearer kinship, she prefers the earl of Argyle. And so, as so often occurred among the barons of Scotland, there was dispute and jealousy, without any show of concealment. Lord Claude would not brook that the Hamiltons should yield to the Stewarts. He had not learned the church's lessons of self-abnegation and meekness. He must have been a haughty abbot, even with his eighteen years.

And Mary saw it all, under the white hawthorn; saw the

battle lost, saw her army scattered, this poor queen. And then across the Lowland country, flying sixty miles the first day, and "sleeping three nights with the owls," as the queen herself wrote to France; flying in her white taffety through the chill bright vagaries of May, and her faithful friends drawing round her, closer because of her despair.

Again lord Claude appears when Mary is immured at Carlisle, keeping as near her as he may, paying her royal court, relieving her tedious hours. He is with her when she rides out "hunting the hare;" "riding so swiftly with her ritinue," that her keeper, Sir Francis Knollys, is afraid. To this queen, who escaped a guarded castle, with deep Lochleven round it, the level lands of Carlisle may be an easy highway where she will. And always there are closest round her those few faithful lords of her own. Sir Francis means hereafter to hold himself excused, "if such riding pastimes be required."

But if the queen may not hunt, she has still her young cavalier to talk with her between times; to beguile those frequent hours, when the red walls of Carlisle grow a weariness, and even the green May meadows, and that pleasant slow Eden water winding through them voicelessly. And she does not think of French lilies, but would fain be again queen at Holyrood, and see that grim grey fortressed outline against the Lothian sky. Lord Claude in his bright youth, even with a lost battle behind him, can talk of hopes and certainties, of which the young oftenest can talk in pure sincerity.

Sir Francis Knollys writes to Cecil displeased, perplexed, conciliatory: "Now the lord Claude Hamilton, the laird of

Skirling, and young Mr Maxwell, with divers other gentlemen and their servants, do lie in the town at their own charges, to the number of thirty or forty more, which gentlemen do, between meals, come in to see the queen; because we found that usage, and would be loth to grieve them with alterations until we know of her Highness' pleasure."

And again he writes a little later: "My lord Scroope and I have moved her Grace that these young lords and gentlemen of hers, that lie in the town here at their own charges, might be placed from the borders more within the realm."

But Mary will not have it so, and lord Claude abides still at Carlisle, till in early July, a more distant prison is decreed by Elizabeth for Mary. Mary enjoins lord Claude and the laird of Skirling to return and comfort her friends. And so, on the summer morning, the last farewell is said between fated queen and fond vassal, and they part within Carlisle wall; part, and never meet again. Here the two lives diverge. But the queen's fate colours ever afterwards the fate of lord Claude Hamilton.

Lord Claude was indeed included in the amnesty granted by the regent. But there could be no real amnesty in that too bitter quarrel. And there is the gathering of the clans round the walls of Edinburgh Castle; and the death of Murray at Linlithgow, and the fatal suspicions it cast. Then the inroad of English soldiers, and the nobles in arms again; and Strathclyde, and the country of the Hamiltons, lying waste for miles on miles; all that rich orchard land, famous even when Mary was queen, and the corn-fields, and wavy meadows, and shady haunts of the deer. And lord Sussex has entered Teviotdale against the Kers and the Scots; and lord Scroope, on the Annandale border, is plundering the Johnstones' land. And the new regent Lennox, who rules for the child-king, calls in vain his Parliaments, and issues his defied commands.

The regent held the Tower of Paisley. There is now no trace of such a tower; but story, for a moment, gathers round it in that unhappy time. And a mean little low-built street, which retains the name of Castle street, seems to fix the otherwise forgotten locality of this scene of struggle for queen Mary. The tower, as well as the despoiled Abbey, belonged of right to the lord Claude. He is named in history indifferently, the *abbot of Paisley* and *lord Claude*. And the tower was retaken in a spring month, March or April, while the distraught regent was settling his hard difficulties, by arms, or legislation, or in what way he could. The quondam abbot came down by the edge of the brown river, past the desolated monastery, to retake his own; "this gallant lord, supported by his faithful tenants,"[*] in that strange sweet charm of youth which works through the sternest history. His vassals loved him well; loved him best, perhaps, without his mitre. "He was a brave and gallant gentleman," say the Memoirs, "of steady honour, and unspotted integrity; who, by a series of virtuous actions, reflected lustre on his great ancestors, and enobled the illustrious blood that ran in his veins." But the faith and fondness of his vassals was not enough to save his lands. The old regent Lennox, with his grandson's

[*] "Memoirs of the House of Hamilton."

power in his hands, made haste across the country, leaving Parliament alone. He "marched in person to Paisley, and having summoned only the nobility of his own party, besieged the tower; when the water being cut off, the garrison were forced to surrender." *

This is but one small advantage; but the queen's party have a halo of sentiment, which keeps an eternity of youth in the unsuccessful cause.

The next appearance of lord Claude is in a night escapade, made with a Scot and a Gordon, on the nobles of the king's party at Stirling. In the grey early dawn they rode up the steep streets, while the slumbrous town was so still that "not even a dog barked at them," while the curling morning mists lay white on the Links of Forth, and the "gowlin' braes" beneath the rock were sodden with the morning dew. They took with them three hundred foot, and two hundred horse, having laid all the open country under tribute as they went. And the threats of Claude Hamilton, who is singled out as leader of the band, are recorded by an adverse historian in no gentle tone. That he was different from his peers in any traits of greater clemency, or in that benign charity we would fain ascribe to cloister life, we gather from no story which tradition or history brings us.

The cloud, which, from the time of Mary's flight, hung above the house of Hamilton, broke in the regency of Morton on the heads of all its members. The estates of the family were confiscated. Insanity shielded the eldest brother from the reach of human vengeance; but

* Buchanan's History.

on John, the abbot of Aberbrothock, and Claude, the abbot of Paisley, it broke with all the untempered rigour of brief power, and jealousy long pent up.

Disguised in a sailor's dress, lord John fled on foot into England. Lord Claude, less fortunate, lurked many days among the border wilds, in the green lonely places, where queen Mary, some short years before, had also sought shelter in her perilous flight.

At length the brothers met in Northumberland, and together sought shelter in France, where there were many to welcome them, for the love they bore to their queen.

As for lord Claude's Abbey, with all its rich appurtenancies, it was gifted to lord Sempil, a protestant nobleman, and a friend of the regent Morton. Dismantled, discrowned, but with wide lands, and wealth of teinds, the saintly old Clugniac house, the foundation of the first Steward, thus passed away from its abbots; passed for ever from the spiritual dream-land of consecration, of present divinity.

But lord Claude, in disgrace and forfeiture, was tenacious still of his rights. The ancient records of his Abbey—the book which was patiently written by many generations of his monks, within that spoiled Scriptorium, where pen will write no more—he will not have pass away with the meadows and the moors and the fisheries, and the forests and the churches and the mills, to an alien in family and faith, without making an effort to reclaim it. In 1574, he pursued lord Sempil in the civil court for delivering to him "ye Black Book of Paisley." Whether or not he gained his suit, and won back, in his early impoverished manhood, this precious monastic chronicle, the historian has not informed his curious readers. But we learn that his banishment at least was short, and that, while the king was still a child, he was once more in Scotland.

Again this restless lord Claude appears as a leader on the raid of Ruthven; that raid making one of those distinct pictures in which Scottish history abounds. The Athol lands and the hunting, and the castle and the stern group of nobles, clustered round the tearful boy, and exacting promises as another group had done from queen Mary years ago; and the words of the master of Glammis, "better bairns weep than bearded men;" and the studious outward respect, and the relentless constraint: they compose such a blent scene as only Scotland could furnish, of feudal independence and power, and traditional reverence for the king, who, with but his twelve years, and with none of the native kingliness of his race to be instead of years and make him a true monarch, is yet required by force or fraud to ratify the acts of his nobles.

To justify this lawless raid to the General Assembly in Edinburgh, the abbot of Paisley is appointed by his confederate peers. And James, through fear or discretion, himself upholds lord Claude's reasons, and forgets the tears he had wept, and declares lord Claude did well.

The year after Mary's execution, while some filial tenderness in the king still moved him to his mother's friends, he restored to lord Claude Hamilton all the possessions of the Abbey, erected into a temporal lordship by an act dated July 29th. But under the title of lord Paisley, Claude Hamilton is scarcely known. He still lived for nearly forty years; but his busy life was past. There were no cloister vows for him now, but there might be cloister quiet; and Ruthven and Stirling became old memories with the days he spent with Scotland's queen. The shadows of the grey ancient Abbey, a second time despoiled, might once more yield repose at the close of a late, long chequered day.

A mural tablet, which looks down on the tomb of princess Marjory, may be seen in the chapel of St. Mirrinus, inscribed with these words :—

"D.O.M.

"PIÆ . INFANTVM . MARGARETÆ .
"HENRICI .'ET . ALEXANDRI . HAMIL
"TONIORVM . MEMORIÆ . CLAVDI
"VS . HAMILTONIVS . PASLETI . DO .
"MINVS . ET . MARGARETÆ . SETON .
"EIVS . VXOR . PROLI . CHARISSIME.
"CVM . LACHR : POSS : OBIERE .
"MARGARETA . ANN : SAL : 1577 X
"KALEN : IAN : NATA . MENSES TR
"ES . DIES . XXII . HENRICVS 1585
"ID : MAR · NATVS · MENSES .
"TRES . DIES . DVOS . ALEXAND
"ER . 1587 . XI . KAL DECEMB . NA
"TVS . MENSES . OCTO . DIES TRES.

"FELICES . ANIME . VOBIS . SVPR
"EMA . PARENTES
"SOLVVNT . VOS . ILLIS SOLVERE
"QUÆ . DECVIT."

" Translation.
" To God the Best and Greatest.

" In Memory of the loving infants, Margaret, Henry, and " Alexander Hamilton; the mostly dearly beloved children of " Claude Hamilton, lord Paisley, and Margaret Seton, his

" wife. They died much lamented. Margaret, the 23rd of
" December, in the year of salvation 1577, aged three
" months and twenty-two days. Henry, the 15th of March,
" 1585, aged three months and two days. Alexander,
" the 11th of December, 1587, aged three months and eight
" days.
   " Blessed souls, to your death this is devoted.
   " He that hath taken you hath done what beseemeth him."

And so the gentleness of love had solaced this the last abbot's days; and when his youth's fire was spent, and his life lay far behind him, with his raids and his loyal devotions and his faded monastic honours, there were the little babes to remember, always to remember sweetly, and the tablet to carve and inscribe to those who had died long ago.

The fiery soul of that same lord Claude who rode up the steep Stirling streets, breathing vengeance through the summer night on poor queen Mary's foes, is tempered with strange resignation in the twilight of its eighth decade.

Lord Paisley died in 1621, and with him passed the last link which bound, within the precincts of the spoiled cloister, the old faith to the new.

JAMES SIXTH AT THE "PLACE."

> BUT, as of old, all now be gold,
> Move, move then to the sounds;
> And do not only walk your solemn rounds.
> *Ben Johnson.*

LORD Claude and his successors dwelt in the Place of Paisley. The distasteful name was ignored; there were the Place and the Kirk—the Abbey was no more. Among the ruined cloisters had dwelt the married abbot Claude, with his wife Margaret, and the children who died in infancy, and the sons who grew up and made part of history when lord Claude was gathered to his rest.

But with the name of the Abbey had also passed the power of the abbot. There was the lordship indeed; but the lordship was not like the abbacy, which conferred such benign unquestioned sway over soul and life. The abbot, despoiled, dwelt among his cloisters, despoiled like his own authority. And the little town council, hitherto content to rule under the shadow of the church, starts into sudden importance, and assumes discretionary power.

It is no more the reverend lord abbot who extends a princely hospitality to kings and queens and ambassadors within his own guestan-hall. A royal visit is projected. The king has been some years married, and has not yet brought his Danish princess to visit his mother's faithful lieges, and his fathers' ruined graves. James has had his bit of romance—unkingly James, with his king-craft—who, yet being a Stuart, must be touched by some moment of poetry. He cannot wait for his bride, whom the stormy seas have driven back, but must himself cross these seas in haste to meet her, whether his nobles will or no.

Great thanksgiving is offered when royal bride and bridegroom come home in safety; and, at the queen's coronation, three sermons in Latin, French, and English, are preached. And the king, at the first service they attend together in the High Kirk, rises up after the minister to thank him for his sermon and his prayers. With lifted hands he praises God he is king in such a kirk. "The kirk of Geneva," he exclaims, "keepeth Pasch and Yule; what have they for them?—they have no institution. . . I charge you, my good people, ministers, doctors, elders, nobles, gentlemen and barons, to stand to your purity; and I, forsooth, so long as I brook my life and crown, shall maintain the same against all deadly!"

James may not be false, but only a changeling, when years later on the throne of England, he declares to a prince of Lorraine, that "he sees slight difference between the two confessions, and that if the pope would make but one step in advance, he himself would make four to meet him."* Augustine and Bernard have become more to him than Luther and Calvin. But they read together with some interest these phases of the learned king's faith.

This first Presbyterian king is about to visit the dismitred abbot, to bring young Anne of Denmark to the old ruined Clugniac house. And the Town Council makes an entry in its records, 8th July, 1597.

"The quhilk day the said bailies and counsall, under-
"standing perfytly that the queen's Majesty is to be
"shortlie in the Place of Paisley, and in respect thereof for
"decoration of the kirk, and portes of the said burgh, in sic
"sort as may be gudlie done for the present, they haf
"concluded that there be ane pyntour sent for to Glasgow,
"for drawing of some drauchts in the *kirk* as salbe thocht
"maist necessar for the present; Secundlie, that ane wricht
"be conducit with for bigging and mending, and repairing
"of the portes of the said burgh."

And so the undoing of the people must be again undone. The kirk which was despoiled, and the gates which were thrown down scarce forty years ago, are restored by the cautious council, as the abbot Tarvis restored them, after that earlier destruction of these fated Clugniac walls. Not indeed as the abbot had done, with the "mony gud jewillis, and the claithis of gold, silver and silk," brought home across the seas with the stately tabernacle, and the silver candlesticks, and the rare books. The discreet town

* Ranke's "History of the Popes"

council sought only the skill of the neighbouring provincial town, not much at the best; but there was no Abbey now. O the waste of that old abbot Tarvis, who "glassynit meikle of all the kirk;" the waste on the "staitlie stallis;" the waste on the "mitre and the shrines!" Why should he have brought Flemish workmen with their unfamiliar ways, with their "unkent speech" and their idolatries, to the verge of their homely town? Was a fair carved flower a sermon?—was a lofty arch a prayer?—was a chisel the hammer of God to break the rock in pieces? The people have heard master Knox. Not all of them perhaps. But they have heard the preachers he has sent throughout the land. And did not the good Regent, the lord James Murray, long at peace, himself command the righteous work of breaking down the haunts of profanity? Profanations had clustered like rooks among the dim delicate shadows, the carvings with their fair symbolism misinterpreted, wrongly explained. And the town council, wise in its way, shall be no abettors of such. "Ane wricht" shall big and mend and repair the gates and kirk, that is all. Nor shall there be any pride, nor tender far thought for the future; what "is thoucht maist necessar for the present," shall be done, and is enough. So is slowly dying out the beauty which was nurtured in the arms of the church; that far-seeing, unselfish beauty, which is patient to wait and to grow as the oaks grow, and be tended by those who planted them not.

 The king and queen came to Paisley, and dwelt in the "Place" with "grey Paisley's haughty lord," when abbot no more. The visit was brief, and no record of it is kept.

There were not now the shrines, before which James Fourth had knelt, and on which he laid his devout offerings as he journeyed from Whithorn with queen Margaret. Nor was there any harper to charm the pedant king, even if he could have been charmed by sweet music like the earlier scions of his race. " The Lay of the Last Minstrel" was already sung. And that serene effigy of the royal huntress, Marjory, lay out in the open cloister, worn by thirty-seven years' sun and rain. Did young Anne of Denmark wonder over its placid lines, or listen in the wistful summer amid the beauty and decay, to the story of that early princess, the mother of the Stuart kings? Romance was fading fast from the cloister, when these, the last king and queen who were Scotland's own and no other, passed from the Abbey walls.

James paid them another visit. He was king of England then.*

---

* Since this chapter was written, and after the lapse of more than two hundred years, another royal visitor has been received within the precincts of the Abbey. The tombs of his Stewart ancestors were visited by prince Leopold, in the autumn of the present year (1875). And the visit of his royal highness has had a consequence immeasurably pleasing to all who love the old pile by the first Stewarts founded.

With a graceful reverence for the long neglected dead, it is announced that here the queen will raise a memorial to Robert Second. And the passionate loyalty of Scotland to her early native kings, blent with that tender sentiment which motherhood and queenhood wakes, is glad in this royal recognition of the fond family ties. For Scotland is eager to hold, through the long links of Tudors and Guelphs, those old strong golden links which bind her to her own past, to join in ancestral union the early story with the late, and in the beloved Sovereign, who fills the throne to-day, find kin with David, her sainted mediæval king; and with Bruce, her hero of a hundred stories; and with her young royal huntress, Marjory, the mother of the Stewart line.

THE LAIRD OF BELTREES.

———o———

TRUST me, sweet,
Out of this silence yet I picked a welcome;
And in the modesty of fearful duty
I read as much as from the rattling tongue
Of saucy and audacious eloquence.
Love therefore, and tongue-tied simplicity,
In least speak most of my capacity.
"*Midsummer-Night's Dream.*"

THE king loved the laird of Beltrees. He sent him on many honourable missions. He sent him to England when Elizabeth grew old, and the Scottish king's thoughts were full of his accession to the English throne.

The laird of Beltrees' lands lay near the lands of the Abbey. They sloped to the opposite edge of the loch which skirted the lands of Castle-Semple. The concerns of the laird of Beltrees were the neighbourly concerns of the abbot. The coming and going of the laird are told by the abbot's historian. And in a side-long way, as the greater throwing light upon the lesser, is inserted a mandate of queen Elizabeth regarding this gentle Sir James.

"Whereas the laird of Beltrees, being sent ambassador
"from the Scottish kinge unto her Majeste, ys now to
"make his departure againne into Scotland. This is
"therefore to will and command you in her Majestie's
"namme, and not onlie to see him furnished of good able
"poste horses for himselfe, his servants and guides, from
"place to place, to the town of Berwicke, but also to see
"him in his said journey used with all favour and courtesy.
"Whereof faille ye not as ye will answer to the contrarie.
"From the court at Richmond, the 23rd of February, 1599.

"To all mayors, sheryvis, justyces, bailyfes,
"constables, headboroughs. and all other her
"Majestie's officers, and others to whom it
"may appertain, and to every one of them.

"Sic Subscribitur—

"THOMAS EGERTON.   "THOMAS BUCKHURSE.
"GEORGE HUNSDAY.   "ROBERT HORTH.
"WILLIAM KNOLLYS.   "ROBERT CECYLL."

So the Scottish laird travelled safely under the queen's commendation, through the green flowery heart of England, to old battered Berwick-upon-Tweed. Two years later he goes upon another journey, a new created knight, under the same favour.

"Whereas Sir James Semple, knight, servant to the king
"of Scots, is to make his speedy repair into France for

"some specyal servyce of the sayd king, these are there-
"fore to will and require you and every of you, not onelie
"to suffer him and his servants quyetly to passe without
"any unnecessary lett or interruption, but also to see them
"provyded with sufficient and able poste horses, together
"with guydes from stage to stage to the town of Dover, at
"such reasonable pryces as are accustomed to be payd in
"lyke cases; and thereof not to faille, as you will answer
"to the contrary at your peril. From the court at
"Richmonde, the 4th October, 1601.

"To all her Majestie's sherifes, justyces of
"peace, bailyfes, constables, postmasters, head-
"boroughs, and all others her Majestie's officers
"whom it may concern.

"Sic Subscribitur—Robert Cecyll." *

What befell the laird on his journey south, and his voyage from Dover to Calais; what welcome met him at the French court, and what service he did to king James, the Renfrewshire historian does not know, or has not told. Neither has he told us at what time the laird came back from his travels, when he settled again at pleasant Beltrees beside the deep loch; whether James and Anne were yet reigning on Elizabeth's throne; or whether the king was still at Holyrood, writing his odd books, and descanting in his pure Latin with that curious garrulous mixture of wisdom and weakness and folly, the compound nature had given him in lieu of the beauty and chivalry of the earlier Scottish kings.

* "History of Renfrewshire."

We infer, though not with certainty, that his sojourn was long in France; and that there was no more a court at Holyrood, when the laird of Beltrees came home. But, dwelling by the side of his loch, he built in the little near town a great house at the cross of Paisley, which he meant to be the king's own. The king, among his English courtiers, had little thought of such; but the laird, among his oaks and elms, a very loyal gentleman, eager to do the king honour, had thought of it much and long. He had married "dame Giles Elphinstone," as loyal as the laird himself, and it pleased their fancy to raise this house in waiting for king James.

The king was long of coming. He had reigned fourteen years in England ere he visited lord Paisley again. And the old lord joyfully received him, and he abode at the "Place," as he had done on that earlier time when young queen Anne was with him. But the poverty-stricken town prayed him not to enter their gates, not to cross the river which bounded the orchard land.

The king had granted to the township the revenues of the altars and the chaplainries—the gifts of many old knights and barons for the health of their own and their kindred's souls. And the town with these revenues had endowed a school in its midst. Separated from its mother Abbey, it had no more wealth. James accepted the strange petition, and remained a guest at the *Place*.

So the house built for the king stood without its royal tenant. As some compensation, perhaps, to Sir James Semple and his dame Giles, a stately ceremonial was arranged in the great hall of lord Paisley. And the little son of the knight, "a prettie boy of nine yeeres," delivered a loving oration to the appreciative king. It is too curious to be left out. At the risk of discredit to Sir James's sense, and dame Giles's maternal carefulness, the curious adulatory, pedantic, allegorical document, shall be transcribed for who will.

Literature was in the family of Beltrees. Of Sir James— his biographer assures us "He was a great poet, as was his successors. He was the author of that epistle, well-known by the title of 'The Padler and the Priest.' He was succeeded by his son, Robert Semple, of Beltrees, who was the author of 'The Piper of Kilbarchan, or The Epitaph of Habbie Simpson;' whose son again was the author of two pieces, the first, entitled the 'Banishment of Poverty,' the second, 'She rose and let me in.'" Other poets are not named, but the family was doubtless poetical, which accepted fact may perhaps explain the wonderful prose here subjoined.

"A graver orator, Sir, would better become so great "an action, as to welcome our great and most gratious "sovereigne; and a bashful silence were a boye's best "eloquence. But seeing wee read that in the salutations "of that Roman Cæsar, a sillie sillie pye among the rest "cryed *Ave Cæsar* to; pardon mee, Sir, your Majestie's "owne old parret, to put furth a few wurdes, as witnesses "of the fervent affections of your most faithful subjects, in "these parts; who all by my tongue, as birds of one cage, "cry with me, Ave Cæsar, welcome most gratious king.

"Welcome then is the word, and welcome the work wee

"all aim at. A verball welcome were base, trivial, and for
"everie body; and a real or royal welcome, answering
"either our hart's desires, or your highness's deservings,
"*Ad hoec quis sufficiens?* Actions can never equall
"affections. Saying, then is nothing: shall I sweare your
"Majestie welcome? I dare; but it becometh not a boy
"to touch the Bible; and yet, because an oath taken by
"nothing, is but nothing, I sweare by the Black Book of
"Paisley, your Majesty is most dearly welcome.

"Thus have I said Sir, and thus have I sworne.

"Performance tak from noble Abercorne.

"Welcome then, Sir, every where; but welcomer here
"than any where. This seemeth a paradox, but if I prove
"it, your Majesty, I hope, will approve it. Three pillars
"of my proof I find in our old poet, Phœbus, his Clytia,
"and Lencothœ; whose fabulous allegorie, if I can apply to
"ourselves by true historie, all is well.

"Phœbus, Sir, you knowe, is knowen to all, because
"seene of all; that sunne, that eye, by which the world
"seeth, shining alike both on good and bad. And are not
"you, Sir, our royal Phœbus?—are not you as ane eye of
"the world, seeing upon you are the eyes of all the world,
"some for good, others for evill, according to their minds.
"And as that sunne in his course compasseth, and passeth
"by the whole world: so hath your Majestie, since you
"beganne to shine in your royal sphaere, inhanced a good
"part of the world; but passed by, and buried all the
"princes, as well of the Heathene as Christiane world. O
"shine then, our royall Phœbus!

"Now that your Majestie is the peculiar Phœbus of our

"westerne world, if any did doubt, *Ex ore duorum aut*
"*trium*, your three kingdoms are three witnesses. Still
"shine then, our royal Phœbus! Now, Sir, Clytia and
"Leucothœ were Phœbus' mistresses; Clytia, the daughter
"of the Ocen, Phœbus' first love. Hence did the poets
"faine, that the sunne, rising in the east, holdeth his course
"westward, for visiting his love, and, according to their
"long or short embracing, aryse our long or short days and
"nights. And are not wee then, Sir, of Scotland, your
"Majestie's owne old kindlie Clytia? Are not you, Sir,
"our Phœbus, coming from the east with glorious beames
"displayed, to embrace us in the mouth of the ocean?
"And is not this very place now, Sir, your westermost
"period? Ergo, Sir, your kindliest Clytia.

"Your Clytia, Sir, is of many goodlie members. Your
"Majestie hath past alreadie her head, neck, armes, your
"greater townes and cities; but till now came you never to
"her hart. Why? because in this verie parish is that
"auncient seat of William Wallas, that worthie warrior, to
"whomme (under God) wee owe that you are ours, and
"Britanne yours. In this verie parish is that noble house,
"of Dairnley-Lennox, whence sprung your Majestie's most
"famous progenitors. In the next you go to that noble
"race of Hamilton, wherein your highness's most royall
"stemme distilled some droppes of their dearest blood;
"and in this verie house is your Majestie's owne noble
"Abercorne, a chiefe sprigge of the same roote, removed
"only a little by tyme, but nothing by nature. And
"therefore are you in the verie hart of your Clytia, and so
"welcomer to her hart, than to any other part. And

"so I hope your Majestie's parret hath proved his
"paradox.

"Now, Sir, Leucothœ, that fairest ladye, Phœbus' second
"love, she is even your Majestie's own glorious England,
"most worthie of all love. When that Phœbus wowed
"that Leucothœ, hee was faine to transform him selfe in
"the shape of her mother, and so to shift her handmaids for
"a more secret visit. But when your Majestie went first
"to your English Leucothœ, you went lik your selfe,
"busked with your owne beams, and backed with the best
"of your Clytia: so were both you and wee welcomed and
"embraced of your Leucothœ. And returning now to your
"Clytia, you bring with you againe the verie lyfe (as it
"were) of your Leucothœ, these nobles and gentrie which
"accompany you; and should not both bee, nay, are not both
"most dearlie welcome to your Clytia.

"That Phœbus, in his love to his Leucothœ, forgot his
"Clytia; he came no more to her; her nightes grew long,
"her winters tedious, whereupon Clytia both revealed and
"reviled their loves; and so Leucothœ was buried quick of
"her owne furious father, and Clytia cast out for ever of
"Phœbus' favour. But your Majestie, in your most inward
"embracements of your Leucothœ, then were you most
"mindful of your old Clytia. Indeed, oure nights have
"beene long, a fourteen yeeres winter if wee weigh but
"your persone: but yet the beames of youre royall hart
"(the onlie lyfe of love) were ever awarming vs. The
"onely remedie were, that these two ladies, as their loves
"are both fixed on one, so themselves become both one;
"and what will not true love vnite? As they have alreddie

"taken on one name for their deare Phœbus' sake, let them
"put on also one nature for the same sake. So shall oure
"Phœbus shine alike on both; be still present with both;
"our nights shall be turned in day, and oure winter in
"ane endlesse sommer; and one beame shall launce
"alike on both sides of our bound-rod, and our Phœbus
"no more need to streatch out his armes on both
"sides of it, devyding as it were his royall person, for
"embracing at once two devided ladyes. He that
"conspireth not at this union, let never Phœbus shine on
"him more.

"Lastly, Sir, that poore Clytia, though shee lost her
"Phœbus favour, yet left shee never off to love him, but
"still whether his chariot went, thether followed her eyes,
"till in ende, by her endlesse observance, she was turned
"in that floure called *Heliotropion*, or *Solsequium*. And
"how much more, Sir, shuld wee who grow daylie in your
"grace and favour, bee all turned in a Βασιλειοτροπιον,
"with a faithfull *Obsequium*. Our eyes shall ever be
"fixed on your royall chariot; and our harts on your
"sacred person.

"O royall Phœbus, keepe this course for ever!
"And from thy deare Britannia never sever:
"But if the fates will rather frame it so,
"That Phœbus now must come and then must goe,
"Long may thyselfe, thy race, mot ever ring;
"Thus without end; wee end. God save oure king.
"Amen."

What effect this wonderful oration produced upon the learned king, no note has been left to tell us. But till within a few years the loyalty and disappointment of the old laird of Beltrees was commemorated by the *Black Land*, that tall house in the heart of the High street, built for, but never tenanted by James Sixth.

THE END.

---o---

DASHING soft from rocks around,
Bubbling runnels joined the sound;
Through glades and glooms the mingled measures stole,
Or o'er some haunted stream with fond delay,
Round a holy calm diffusing,
Love of peace, and lonely musing,
In hollow murmurs died away.
Collins.

NOT reaching down through the church, but through those warm human ties, which he gained by loss of his mitre, Lord Paisley's hand touches futurity. His eldest son was James, first earl of Abercorn, "a man of great parts, and highly esteemed by James Sixth." He was one of the king's privy councillors, and high-sheriff of Linlithgow. He gave him by another charter, in 1601, the lands and manour of Abercorn, Braidmeadow, etc. Likewise another charter to erect the lordship of Abercorn, the lands of Duddingstone, Newton, and Dunlarvie, into one free barony, dated 1603.

When James attained his larger kingdom, he still further enriched this son of the early abbot Claude, who had been so loyal to queen Mary. He created him lord Strabane. He granted him wide lands in Ireland, on which new estate the earl built "a strong and fair castle and church." Here he lived with his countess Marion. In 1618 he died; died on a March night, while his father, the old lord Paisley, lived on still at the "Place," with his burden of memories.

The son of lord Abercorn and Strabane married an English bride, the daughter of Gervase, lord Clifton. And this line of the abbot's family became extinct in their son George, "who died, unmarried, at Padua, on his journey to Rome." The estates passed by the line of the second son of the abbot, to another Claude Hamilton, as loyal as the last who bore the name. Claude was married to lady Jean Gordon, and the passionate love of both to the ill-fated Stewarts makes another page of romance. Claude, the abbot at Carlisle, waiting on captive Mary, and Claude, the earl at the French court, steadfast and faithful and fond to the exiled, throneless Charles, have the same pure traditions to keep, the same poetry of loyalty and love. It descends through three generations without stint or tarnish.

A pleasant link at this instant unites the Clugniac Abbey on the Cart, with far-famed, storied Port-Royal, so lit by genius and sanctity. The link is formed by a lady—not saintly, but a gay, court beauty—who was young in the cloisters of Port-Royal, and was taught by the abbess Angelique. This was Arabella Hamilton—*La Belle Hamilton*—the languid, blue-eyed beauty, whom Lely painted, and Charles Second loved, and from whose faultless classical head was modelled that of Britannia. *La Belle* was the great-great-grand-daughter of Claude, the last abbot, whose family still held the Abbey of Paisley in *commendam*. And if this link be remote between the ancestral monastery, and the famous French Cistertian convent, it, at least, is too pleasing to relinquish.

La Mère Angélique, like the great-great-grand-father of her pupil, the lady Arabella, at an age scarce beyond infancy, became supreme in her convent. She was but a child of eleven years when she was appointed abbess—like the abbot Claude at ten—because the Arnaulds, no more than the Hamiltons, could suffer such a dignity to pass from their family.

How the two lives developed, each claiming its own, making for themselves such different histories, suggests many things, as we pause on the juncture from which we look down both.

As for Arabella, she is not saintly, nor are her times so either. But the saintly group of Port-Royalists is touched with a light of its own. The silent, serene charm of these devoted lives, is a spell to be not analyzed, but yielded to with willing love. Separate groups of men they were, indeed, who made the French and Scottish centres of religion, with such typical contradictions as only one bond could unite. And the bond was unacknowledged. It lay deep in goodness and faith. But none could see it; nor willed to see it if they could.

Turning from the hot and eager contest of Scottish Theologians and Reformers; from that inborn mental

U

and moral activity, with its varied, not always happy out-come, its questioning, arguing, accusing; the sweet, devout passivity of these old French recluses, is as a white bloom of wild-flowers in the shadow of ragged oaks.

"This is all we have to do," said St. Cyran to his soldier-penitent, "we only need to come humbly before God, and think ourselves too happy in that He looks down upon us."

"Ask for nothing, desire nothing, refuse nothing," enjoined St. Francis de Sales, transfused with the same spirit of devout self-abnegation and humility.

And if the passive graces were perilously exalted here, and the joyous freedom of knowing and willing and asking was denied, yet to many weary moods of thought the gracious stillness of such comes back like a Sabbath on the soul, and in the deep content of that Sabbath, it feels itself nearest God.

This link between Port-Royal and Paisley, when it is named, all is told. "La Belle's" life is not said to have touched the ancestral "Place." Port-Royal was unconscious of Paisley. The history of Paisley was passed.

And now, too, are finished these fragmentary memorials of the Abbey. Fragments—no more—and fragments it must be confessed—much less of the monastic life, than of that stormy secular life which surrounded it, and at frequent intervals crossed it in violent abrupt lines, or found a refuge within it.

And so farewell, old Clugniacs, who have held so many threads of story; farewell the footprints of kings, and the shady walks of the abbots; farewell to the byeways of history, the shady places and quiet, where amid the fall of apple-blossom we hear the whisper of prayer, and learn what thoughts men had in that time so long ago, when they laid aside their armour after the heat of the day.

The nave of the Abbey of Paisley is now used as the Parish Church. On the beautiful chaste pillars no trace of violence is seen. The ruins of choir and chapel lie without the walls; within all is still completeness, the perfectness of beauty and peace. And the rude rich Scottish psalms rise now to the same echoes as the Latin chants of the Clugniac monks, who, so many centuries ago, worshipped here, in a different ritual, the same God and Christ.

The noble decendants of the last abbot still hold the Abbey lands. Fair lands no longer; the oak-forests are no more; the pearl fisheries are a tradition; the moss is only a sound. Under the low bridges the river makes mockery of its name; black, slimy, with poor old smoke-begrimmed houses coming down to its edge. And the Abbey, which queened them all once, is but hidden away among the rest; showing her stately features like a queen who cannot be disguised, but reverenced no longer by vassals crowding round her feet. The cloister-court is shady still, but with sickly, ghostly sort of trees, and rank little tufts of grass, and trodden brown patches of earth. And a weary old-world stillness falls upon one, as one softly wanders among the forgotten graves of the first royal Stewarts.

APPENDIX.

APPENDIX.

CARTA WALTERI FILII ALANI, FUNDATORIS, DE DIVERSIS TERRIS ET ECCLESIIS COLLATIS TAM CITRA MORAM QUAM ULTRA.

WALTERUS filius Alani, dapifer Regis Scotie universis sancte matris ecclesie filiis salutes tam presentibus quam futuris. Sciatis me dedisse et concessisse et hac carta mea confirmasse Deo et Sancte Marie et ecclesie Sancti Jacobi, et Sancti Mirini et Sancte Myldburge de Passelet et Priori ejusdem loci et monachis ibidem Deo servientibus secundem ordinem Cluniacensem, pro anima Henrici Regis Anglie, et pro anima David Regis, et Regis Malcolmi et comitis Henrici et antecessorum meorum defunctorum, et pro salute domini mei Wilelmi regis, et David Fratris ejus et mei et uxoris mee et heredum meorum, in perpetuam elemosinam et ab omni servitio temporali liberam et quietam, ecclesiam de Ennyrwic cum omnibus pertinentiis suis; Et molendinum de Ennyrwic totum preter unam marcam argenti quam dedi in eo Radulfo de Kent; Et ecclesiam de Ledgerdwode cum omnibus pertinentiis suis; Et unam carrucatam terre in Hastendene quam tenuit Walterus Capellanus per easdem divisas per quas eam tenuit; Et ecclesiam de Katkert cum omnibus pertinentiis suis; Et omnes ecclesias de Strathgrif cum omnibus pertinentiis suis, excepta ecclesia de Inchinan; Et illam carrucatam terre, quam Grimketel tenuit per easdem divisas per quas eam tenuit; Et le Drep cum omnibus pertinentiis suis in terris et in aquis per easdem divisas quibus Wilelmus illam tenuit; Et ecclesiam de Passelet cum omnibus pertinentiis suis; Et duas carrucatas terre mensuratas et perambulatas circa aquam Kert juxta ecclesiam; Et illam terram ultra Kert ex parte nemoris quam ego et Alanus filius meus eis perambulavimus per easdem divisas per quas eam cum probis hominibus perambulavimus; Et illam portionem terre que est sub dormitorio monachorum; Et totam terran quam tenuit Scerlo et per easdem divisas, cum illa maisura super rupem ubi aula mea erat fundata; Et totam insulam juxta oppidum meum de Renfru cum piscatura inter ipsam insulam et Perthec; Et unum toftum plenarium in Renfru et dimidiam marcam argenti de firma ipsius burgi ad luminare ecclesie; Et unum rete ad Salmonem; Et molendinum de Renfru; et terram ubi monachi prius habitaverunt; Et illam carrucatam terre que est inter Kert et Grif; Et ecclesiam de Prestwic, cum tota terra illa quam Dovenaldus filius Yweni eis perambulavit, inter terram Simonis Loccardi et terram de Prestwic usque Pulprestwic et secundum Pulprestwic usque in mare et a

mari secundum torrentem inter terram Arnaldi et terram de
Prestwic usque ad divisas Simonis Loccardi; Et illam
ecclesiam de burgo meo de Prestwick cum omnibus pertinentiis suis; Et totam salinam in Kalenter que fuit
Herberti camerarii. Dedi eis similiter et confirmavi
decimam plenariam de venatione mea cum corriis et preter
hec omnia corria cervarum quas cepero in Forineisun; Et
quatuor solidos ad luminare ecclesie de molendino de
Passelet; Et ut molant ibi absque multura proximi illi quem
molentem invenerint preter meipsum de bludo quod exierit
de proprio granario meo; moris meo; Et preter hec
plenariam decimam de ipso molendino de Passelet et de
omnibus molendinis que habeo vel habiturus sum. Dedi
eis insuper et concessi et hac mea carta confirmavi decimas
et cunctis vastis meis, et de omnibus terris que in forresto
meo edificate sunt vel edificabuntur; Et omnia aisiamenta
forreste mei de Passelet; Et pasturam in eo, domui sue et
animalibus suis et porcis suis propriis, sicut mihi, et suis
hominibus et meis. Si autem contigerit quod ego vel
aliquis heredum meorum peccora nostra infra forestum
habere voluerimus, providebitur eis una pars de foresto
que sibi et animalibus suis sufficere possit. Huic autem
predicte elemosine mee, cum ceteris dignitatibus suis, has
libertates concedo et confirmo, scilicet, sac et soke, tol et
them et infangentheof. Testibus Engelrano Glasguensi
episcopo, Ricardo Episcopo Sancti Andree, Johanne Abbate
de Kelcou, Osberto Abbate de Jedwrte, Magistro Marco
Salomone de cano, Elia Clerico, Magistro Johanne Alano
filio meo, Roberto de Mundegumbri, Baldwino de Bigres,
Roberto de Costentin, Gaufrido de Costentin, Roberto filio

Fulberti, Yweno filio Dovenaldi, Waltero de Costentin, Nigello de Costentin, Alexandro de Hesting, Hugone de Pad'inan, Ricardo Wal', Roberto Croc, Rogerio de Nes, Ricardo Clerico meo et multis aliis.

ORIGIN OF THE STEWARTS.

[Extract from "History of the Town and Castle of Arundel," by the Rev. M. A. Teirney, F.S.A., chaplain to his Grace the duke of Norfolk. Two vols. London: G. & W. Nicol, Pall Mall. 1834.]

CHAPTER ix. John Fitz-Alan, first earl of his family:— "The family of Fitz-Alan, like those of Montgomery and D'Albini, was of Norman origin. It derived its descent from Alan, the son of Fleald or Flealdus, who accompanied the conqueror to England in 1066; and received amongst other spoils of the vanquished natives, the castle of Madox ap Meredith, in Wales, with the lordship of Oswaldestre, in the county of Salop. His wife was a daughter of Warren, the bald sheriff of Shropshire, and consequently great-niece to Rodger Montgomery. By her he had two sons. William, who, adopting his patronymic, was called Fitz-Alan; and Walter, who pursued his fortunes in Scotland, and purchasing from king David the office of Grand Steward in that country, became the progenitor of the royal family of Stewart."

SUCCESSION OF THE ABBOTS OF PAISLEY.

ROGER, who, in the reign of king William, with consent of the convent, gives allowance to Robert de Croc, to build a Chapel-of-Ease.

William, who, in 1225, makes an agreement with Sir Hugh, the son of Reginald, ancestor of the Houstouns, about the lands of Auchincloss.

Andrew de Kelcou * was abbot of Paisley in the reign of king Robert the Bruce; and in 1318, his name is appended to an agreement with Sir Reginald Mure of Abercorn.

John, abbot of Paisley, who, in 1327, obtained a confirmation of the kirk of Kilkerran from the bishop of Argyle.

John, second abbot of the same name, succeeded to the abbacy in 1369.

John, third of the same name, was abbot in 1409.

William Chisholm.

John de Lithgow, † 1432 . . .

Thomas, abbot of Paisley, ‡ who appears in 1452 to have obtained from Robert, lord Lyle, the fishing of Crokatshot upon Clyde. ||

Henry, abbot of Paisley, who obtained, in 1466, from John Laumund of that ilk, a confirmation of the patronage of the kirk of Kilfinan.

Abbot George Schaw, of the family of Sauchie.

Abbot Robert Schaw, kinsman to the said George, promoted to the Episcopal See of Moray in 1509.

Abbot Robert Stewart, of the noble house of Lennox.

John Hamilton, natural son to James, earl of Arran.

Lord Claud Hamilton, third son of James, duke of Chatelherault. §

* *i.e.* Kelso. † *i.e.* Linlithgow. ‡ The same who is mentioned as having built a great portion of the Abbey Church. || Chartulary of Paisley.

§ Crawford's "History of Renfrewshire."

ORIGINAL CHARTER OF WALTER THE STEWARD TO THE MONKS OF DALMULIN.

WALTERUS, senescallus Scotiæ, salutem in domino. Sciatis me, divinæ charitatis intuitu, in honorem Dei et beatæ Mariæ, fundasse domum canonicorum et monachorum, ordinis de Simpringham, in loco qui dicitur Dalmulin super Air : Et dictis monachis concedo, et confirmo in perpetuum, stotam terram de Merns, cum omnibus infra istas divisa contentis, sicut rivulus descendit in Air, inter novam villam et fundum capellæ sanctæ Mariæ; et sic ascendendo per eundem rivulum usque ad divisas de Hauchincrew, usque ad terram Ricardi Wallensis de Hauchincrew, et sic per divisas ipsius Ricardi usque in Air, et præterea liberam et plenam communem, in turbariis de Prestvick, et medietatem omnium piscariorum meorum, quæ sunt inter castrum de Air et villam de Irvin ; in cujus rei testimonium, sigillum meum apposui. His testibus :—

WALTER, episcopo Glasguensi.
REGINALDO de Crawfurd, vicecomite de Air.
WALTERO OLIPHARD, justitiario Loudoniæ.
MALCOLMO LOCCARD, et
MALCOLMO LOCCARD, silio ejus.

HUGONE, silio Reginaldi.
RICARDO WALLENSI.
JOHANNE de Mungumri.
HECTORE de Currie.*

FROM A CHARTER, DATED AT BERWICK, GRANTED BY KING ROBERT BRUCE TO WALTER THE STEWARD.

ROBERTUS, Dei gratia rex Scotorum : Sciatis, me dedisse dilecto et fideli nostro Waltero, senescallo Scotiæ, in liberam

* Extracted by Crawford from the Chartulary of the Abbey of Paisley.

maritageam cum Marjoria filia nostra baroniam de Bathgeto, baroniam de Rathoe, cum terra de Riccartoun, et terras de Barns, juxta Linlithgow, et terra quæ vocatur le Brome, prope lacum ejusdem, et terras de Bonningtoun, Kingalach et Gallowhill juxta Linlithgow, et annuum reditum de Carse, Stirlyn, quas abbas et canonici monasterii sanctæ crucis de Edinburgh, tenent de nobis et annuum reditum centum solidorum percipiendi de terra de Kinpunt et terram de Edinam in vicecomitatu de Roxburgh tenend. idem Walt. et hæredibus suis inter ipsum et dictam Marjoriam filiam nostra procreandis, &c.*

ORIGINAL CHARTER BY JAMES FOURTH, YET EXTANT IN THE REGISTER OF THE MONASTERY OF PAISLEY.

"JACOBUS, D. G. rex Scotorum : Sciatis, quod, quod, ob singularem devotionem, quam habemus glorioso confessori asncto Mirino et monasterio nostro de Pasletto, per nostros nobilissimos progenitores fundato, ubi plurima progenitorum nostrorum corpora sepeliuntur et requiescunt, et ob singularem favorem et amorem quem gerimus venerabili in Christo patri, Georgio Shaw, moderno dicti monasterrii abbati, nostro consiliario apprime dilecto, ac pro fideli obsequio, per dictum venerabilem patrem nobis, temporibus retroactis, multipliciter præstito et præciquè ob virtuosam educationem et nutritionem charissimi fratris nostri, Jacobi ducis Rossens. in sua tenera ætate ; fecimus, infeodavimus, ereximus ; ac, tenore præsentis, chartæ nostræ, facimus,

* Extracted by Crawford in his history of the royal family of Stewart.

infeodamus erigimus et creamus villam de Pasletto, jacen. infra vicecomitatum de Renfrew, liberum burgum in baronia; concessimus etiam dictum burgum inhabitantibus et in posterum inhabitaturis, plenam et liberam potestatem emendi et vendendi, in ipso burgo, vinum, ceram, pannum laneum et lineam amplum seu arctum, et quæcunque aliá bona et mercimonia illuc advenientia; cum potestate et libertate habendi et tenendi ibidem pistores, brasiatores carnifices et tam carnium quam piscium macellarios, et artium quarumquunque operarios, ad libertatem burgi in baronia spectant. seu spectare valent. concessimus etiam burgensibus et inhabitantibus dictum burgum de Pasletto ut, in ipso burgo habeant et possideant crucem et forum pro perpetuo, singulis hebdomadis, die lunæ; et duas nundinas publicas quolibet anno in perpetuum; unam videlicet in die Sancti Mirini, et aliam in die Sancti Marnoci, cum tholoniis et aliis libertatibus, ad hujusmodi nundinas spectant. seu spectare valent. in futurum tenendi et habendi præfatam villam de Pasletto perpetuis futuris temporibus in merum et liberum burgum in baronia; cum prædictis privilegiis, libertatibus, concessionibus ac universis aliis libertatibus, adeo libere quiete, plenarie, integre, honorifice, bene et in pace in omnibus et per omnia sicut burgi de Dunfermling, Newburgh et Aberbrathick aut aliquis alius burgus in baronia, in regno nostro, quibuscunque temporibus retroactis liberius infeodatur seu tenetur. ac insuper concessimus, dicto venerabili patri et successoribus suis abbatibus de Pasletto, facultatem et potestatem eligendi annuatim præpositum, balivos et alios officiarios dicti burgi et eosdem toties quoties opus fuerit removendi et alios in corem locis de novo elegendi &c. In cujus rei testimonium, huic præsenti cartæ nostræ, magnum sigillum nostrum apponi præcepimus. Testibus reverendis in Christo patribus, Roberto, episcopo Glasguensi; Georgio, episcopo Dunkelden; delectis consanguineis nostris, Colino, comite de Argyle, domino Campbell, cancellario nostro; Arc. comite Angusiæ domino de Douglass; Patricio domino Halys, magistro hospitii nostri; Roberto domino de Lyle, justiciario nostro; Andrea domino le Gray; Laurentio domino Oliphant; Johanne domino Drummond; apud Stirling: Decimo nono die mensis Augusti, 1488, et regni nostri primo."

Churches under the Patronage of the Abbey of Paisley.

INNERWICK.	RUTHERGLEN.	CARMUNNOCK.
LEGERWOOD.	DALZIEL.	RICCARTOUN.
CRAIGIE.	DUNDONALD.	MONKTON.
St. EBOX.	PRESTWICK.	AUCHINLECK.
The Chapel of CORSBY.	ROSENEATH.	KILPATRICK in the
The Kirk of St. OSWALD.	KILCOLMENEL.	KILKERRAN. [Lennox.
EASTWOOD.	KILFINIAN.	CATHCART.
PAISLEY,	MEARNS,	NIELSTON.
INVERKIP.	KILBARCHAN.	LOCHWINIOCH.
KILLALLAN.	ERSKINE.	HOUSTON.

ALL THE CHURCHES IN BUTE.

www.ingramcontent.com/pod-product-compliance
Lightning Source LLC
Chambersburg PA
CBHW030747230426
43667CB00007B/875